WSQ

WOMEN'S STUDIES QUARTERLY

VOLUME 53   NUMBERS 3 & 4   FALL/WINTER 2025

An educational project of the Feminist Press at the City University of New York and York College, City University of New York, with support from the Center for the Study of Women and Society and the Center for the Humanities at the Graduate Center, City University of New York

EDITORS
Shereen Inayatulla, York College, City University of New York
Andie Silva, York College and The Graduate Center, City University of New York

EDITORIAL DIRECTORS
Dána-Ain Davis and Kendra Sullivan

POETRY EDITORS
JP Howard
Melissa Castillo Planas
Coco Sofia Fitterman
Kahina Meziant
Grisel Y. Acosta

CREATIVE PROSE EDITORS
Keisha-Gaye Anderson
Anna Joy Springer

VISUAL ARTS EDITORS
Maya von Ziegesar
jah elyse sayers
Crystal Z. Campbell
Shebani Rao

MANAGING EDITORS
jah elyse sayers
Maya von Ziegesar

**SOCIAL MEDIA &
EVENTS MANAGER**
Juwon Jun

INTERNS
Jennifer Bae Zorn
Abrelle Lawson
Isabella Pinkhasov
Hannah Salzer

EDITORS EMERITAE
Red Washburn 2020–2023 ▪ Brianne Waychoff 2020–2022 ▪ Natalie Havlin 2017–2020
Jillian M. Báez 2017–2020 ▪ Matt Brim 2014–2017 ▪ Cynthia Chris 2014–2017
Amy Herzog 2011–2014 ▪ Joe Rollins 2011–2014 ▪ Victoria Pitts-Taylor 2008–2011
Talia Schaffer 2008–2011 ▪ Cindi Katz 2004–2008 ▪ Nancy K. Miller 2004–2008
Diane Hope 2000–2004 ▪ Janet Zandy 1995–2000 ▪ Nancy Porter 1982–1992
Florence Howe 1972–1982; 1993–1994

The Feminist Press at the City University of New York

**ART
DIRECTOR**
Drew Stevens

**DEVELOPMENT COORDINATOR
& MANAGING EDITOR**
Rachel Page

WSQ: Women's Studies Quarterly, a peer-reviewed, theme-based journal, is published by the Feminist Press at the City University of New York.

COVER ART
Terra Pelada by Uýra Sodoma, photograph by Matheus Belém

WEBSITE
feministpress.org/wsq

EDITORIAL CORRESPONDENCE
WSQ: Women's Studies Quarterly, The Feminist Press at the City University of New York, The Graduate Center, 365 Fifth Avenue, Suite 6200, New York, NY 10016; wsqeditorial@gmail.com and wsqeditors@gmail.com.

PRINT SUBSCRIPTIONS
Subscribers in the United States: Individuals—$70 for 1 year; $175 for 3 years. Institutions—$99 for 1 year; $249 for 3 years. Subscribers outside the United States: Add $40 per year for delivery. To subscribe or change an address, contact *WSQ* Customer Service, The Feminist Press at the City University of New York, The Graduate Center, 365 Fifth Avenue, Suite 6200, New York, NY 10016; 212-817-7916; info@feministpress.org.

FORTHCOMING ISSUES
WSQ Chronic, Nancy K. Miller, The Graduate Center, City University of New York, Tahneer Oksman, Marymount Manhattan College
WSQ Portals, Desireé R. Melonas, University of California, Riverside, Zahra Ahmed, St. Mary's College of California, Tiffany Willoughby-Herard, University of California, Irvine, and University of South Africa

RIGHTS & PERMISSIONS
Fred Courtright, The Permissions Company, 570-839-7477; permdude@eclipse.net.

SUBMISSION INFORMATION
For the most up-to-date guidelines, calls for papers, and information concerning forthcoming issues, write to wsqeditors@gmail.com or visit feministpress.org/wsq or womensstudiesquarterly.com.

ADVERTISING
For information on display-ad sizes, rates, exchanges, and schedules, please write to *WSQ* Marketing, The Feminist Press at the City University of New York, The Graduate Center, 365 Fifth Avenue, Suite 6200, New York, NY 10016; 212-817-7916; sales@feministpress.org.

ELECTRONIC ACCESS AND SUBSCRIPTIONS
Access to electronic databases containing backlist issues of *WSQ* may be purchased through JSTOR at www.jstor.org. Access to electronic databases containing current issues of *WSQ* may be purchased through Project MUSE at muse.jhu.edu, muse@muse.jhu.edu; and ProQuest at www.il.proquest.com, info@il.proquest.com. Individual electronic subscriptions for *WSQ* may also be purchased through Project MUSE.

ISSN: 0732-1562   ISBN: 978-1-55861-349-2 $30.00

Contents

SECTION IV. **BOOK REVIEWS**

SECTION V. **PROSE**

Introduction and Editors' Note

Shereen Inayatulla and Andie Silva

To begin, we want to acknowledge the fraught and distressing sociopolitical conditions under which *WSQ* continues and this special issue has emerged. At present, it feels impossible to pretend at normalcy and trudge onward with a "business as usual" mindset. We are, in honest reflection, struggling to write this introduction—to put our minds to work, to be still enough to think and write amid the barrage of daily horrors designed to dizzy, exhaust, crush, and distract us. At the same time, navigating these horrors sharpens our resolve in the fight for justice, and the writing process reveals to us the way feminist research and creative work bolster and perform the action needed to survive and thrive amid rubble and ruin. Moreover, we are uplifted by a sprawling lineage of feminist writers, thinkers, activists, artists, and organizers on a local and global scale who show us that the struggle continues—that feminist labor cannot be extinguished in times of utter destruction. Along these very lines, we are overwhelmed with gratitude to each member of the *WSQ* editorial team who strives with us to sustain the work of this journal.

What follows below is a blended editors' note and introduction to this special issue, *Body Matters*, presented in a stylistically hybrid form. It is framed in part as a dialogue between the coeditors (Andie and Shereen). This dialogic approach is our preferred method of writing collaboratively, a style that has become somewhat of a tradition in the coauthored pieces we've published to date. We find this format both freeing and useful, as it offers a more transparent drafting process. Each segment responds to and builds upon the previous thought, mirroring how we riff on ideas in person, but granting us a measured and polished forum for this exchange. We view this dialogic method as a practice of feminist collaboration and knowledge

WSQ: Women's Studies Quarterly 53: 3 & 4 (Fall/Winter 2025) © 2025 by Shereen Inayatulla and Andie Silva.

construction, blending standard forms of academic writing with a structure that encourages the exploration of themes without removing improvisation, affect, and emotionality from the process. Readers might notice our insistence on maintaining the pronouns we/us/our in place of I/me/my within our individual entries, and this strategy contributes to our broader goals for collaborative writing.

Although our conversation focuses specifically on the production of this special issue, the format pays homage to iconic feminist dialogues/conversations/interviews that live in our imagination and shape how we engage a broader audience. We draw much inspiration from the conversation between Audre Lorde and Adrienne Rich (included in Lorde's *Sister Outsider*) for its expansive and textured insights on feminist activism and alliance-making; the dual-persona dialogue between bell hooks/Gloria Watkins (in a chapter of *Teaching to Transgress*) for its playful method of documenting a feminist pedagogical praxis; and the interview between Gloria Anzaldúa and Karin Ikas (in the final pages of Anzaldúa's *Borderlands/La Frontera*) for its reflection on the inseparability of identity, land, and writing. We view conversation as bodily practice that shapes the material conditions for feminist inquiry.

Through the dialogue that follows, we invite *WSQ* readers to explore the web of complex, furious, vexed, elated, hopeful emotions cycling through our present moment. We ask readers to join us, alongside the contributors to this volume, in envisioning and enacting spaces where all bodies are valued, valid, legal, protected, celebrated, and connected to the water and land shared with the nonhuman lives of this planet.

• • •

Andie: It's finally here! We proposed this issue back in the spring of last year, but it feels like a lifetime ago. *Roe v. Wade* had been overturned for two years already, yet we remained (indeed, remain) enraged, terrified, and filled with anxiety about the safety of our trans and nonbinary loved ones in particular. We decided we wanted our special issue to reflect on the nature of bodies—broadly defined, in all their constellation of meanings, but specifically attending to the ways regulations against body autonomy served, and continue to serve, as political battlegrounds. Inspired by Jules Gill-Peterson's *Sad Brown Girl* blog post "Toward a Trans History of Abortion" and Angela Y. Davis's legacy on race, class, and reproductive rights, we wanted to see an issue that "centralizes Black and Indigenous trans, queer, disabled, working poor, displaced, migrant experiences," as we wrote in the *Body Matters* call for papers. Of course, that was a year ago. And things are so much worse, scarier, and even more precarious now.

Shereen: And decrying these conditions does not reflect a desire to preserve the oppressive structures that were in operation! What we're experiencing is a collective rage that continues to snowball with each attack on health-care and bodily autonomy via bans on gender-affirming care, obstacles to disability justice (as coined by Stacey Park Milbern and discussed by Leah Lakshmi Piepzna-Samarasinha), and disappearance of reproductive rights. It's more than rage at this juncture—it's a colossal color wheel of emotions spinning rapidly, demanding strategic action. And never has it been so clear how the evisceration of healthcare and bodily autonomy is inextricable from desperate attempts to uphold the white supremacist, capitalist, cis hetero-patriarchal, settler-colonial paradigm that shapes our present-day reality. How it came to be that some bodies are deemed worthy, beautiful, power-ful, correct is a project no longer obfuscated among the Global Majority; the origin of this project has been traced, recorded, shared, and is being censored because the truth it exposes undermines the oppressive power held by the minority who govern. As the work of writers like Audre Lorde and Dorothy Allison reveals, storytelling is a bodily act of archiving. The work contained in this issue builds from the legacies of artists, activists, thinkers, writers, laborers, and revolutionaries who archived and shared knowledge using all available means.

Andie: Yes, precisely! And thinking about archiving knowledge is so urgent when so much work is being defunded and erased, whether by decree or by voluntary self-censorship. It's worth underscoring how much emotionality and embodiment are central to a pursuit for basic human rights. Affect and theory often go hand in hand for feminist thinkers, and locating the physi-cal presence of the body as the site for experiencing and exploring emotion has arguably become an imperative in the present moment, when govern-ments, unlawful judgments, and endless cycles of violence are taking place in rapid, dizzying succession. In our CFP, we invited contributors to think about what bodies might look like if free from surveillance, violence, and control. Although our issue is titled *Body Matters*, we also wanted to explore what it might look like to not *have* to matter—that is, what if we didn't have to assign value to human (and nonhuman) existence, and were therefore free from capitalist, neoliberal demands to be productive, to "contribute" to (white, Western, religio-political) society, where one has to "earn" (in more ways than one) being worthy of life, food, rights, or land?

These questions are laid bare in the everyday cognitive dissonance we experience as we manage a (so-called) work/life balance and join collective experiences through our engagement with social media. One moment we might be reading about the inhuman, unlawful treatment of those who were forcefully transported to El Salvador, feeling paralyzed by the ways human value can be so easily discarded or made "illegal" and thinking about our own positionalities as people whose presence, legality, validity in this world is often marked by the physical spaces our bodies are allowed to occupy. At the same instant, the next thing we read might be news of some overhyped celebrity function filled with lavishly dressed celebrities (and sometimes even lawmakers who are supposed to represent and protect us). How do we make sense of these juxtaposed images? How are these bodies—the celebrities and the incarcerated individuals—occupying the same reality? Indeed, where is the line drawn (and who gets to draw it) that determines whether one is granted personhood or whether one becomes relegated to being "just" a body?

Shereen: Absolutely. And we are not the first to draw attention to the range of ideas or definitions ascribed to the term "body." These varied applications should be tirelessly scrutinized. It is critical to observe how/when/where this term is deployed in ways that carry racist undertones and anti-Black, anti-Indigenous consequences. When using the term "body" to describe living human beings, the effect can be minimizing, dismissive, deadening. We notice and condemn how this discourse circulates in media reports about Black, Indigenous, Othered communities. "Body" can be weaponized—overtly and tacitly—to uphold dominant power structures and obfuscate the historical context that catalyzed the invention of race. As Dána-Ain Davis and Bisola Neil so precisely assert in their article "Black Anti-Bodies," included in this issue: "Whereas antibodies identify and neutralize threats, society translates Black bodies into 'Anti-Bodies,' institutionally marginalizing and suppressing them on a scale beyond the actions of individuals."

It follows that the broader discourse surrounding "bodies" can be used to advance a dangerous agenda. Just as corporations are granted the status and protections of individual humans, "body" can be used to animate what is unliving and inanimate. Again, it's worth observing how/when/where body discourse is used, emboldening arguments against reproductive choice—be that pregnancy prevention or birth control, abortion, stages of IVF procedures, or the like. Through these observations, we are compelled to ask: Who is granted literal subjectivity, who is the *subject* rather than the *object*, who is objectified, particularly in ways that reproduce anti-Indigenous and anti-Black racism? These questions must be centralized (to offer one specific direction) in every encounter with mainstream settler media reports on the ongoing struggle for justice surrounding Missing and Murdered Indigenous Women and Girls (MMIWG). Likewise, these questions should permeate the production and consumption of scholarship directed at Black women, for as Davis and Neil signal, "Black Anti-Bodies are captive bodies made porous on demand."

Andie: That is such poignant phrasing, and gets to the heart of the ways anti-Black racism—and misogynoir (see Moya Bailey) in particular—functions, whether it is manifested in violent attempts to write over the rights, bodies, and agency of Black women and people of color or in the ways racist constructs and settler-colonial paradigms make their way into laws, medical services, and even social interactions. Yet, as Davis and Neil also remind us, while bodies can be weaponized, they can also be leveraged as weapons of resistance. Or, to employ a metaphor that escapes vocabularies of war, bodies can be our grounding space for change. As many contributors in this issue explore, agency and autonomy can be productively expressed as an act of refusal. We don't have to accept our current reality as inevitable; indeed, fighting for change perhaps begins with a complete—and loudly articulated—rejection of the everyday horrors currently being glossed over, normalized, or made unspeakable. Dana M. Olwan addresses this in her Alerts and Provocations essay, underscoring the urgency of seeing bodies—particularly Palestinian bodies—within a feminist witnessing framework. By rejecting the death of Palestinians as unavoidable, unspeakable numbers, we can "create an alternative conception of the Palestinian body—not as a site of suffering that is inevitable but as a steward for an alternative future freed from the threat of war and the ravages of colonialism: A body whose truth will not be inscribed by violence." After all, what is a fight for justice that cannot be spoken out loud? That does not refuse colonial violence or take it for granted as a necessary first step to revolution?

Of course, that is not to say that we should not build on our embodied memories to shape a future free from suffering. In her piece for this issue, Niloofar Rasooli calls for an embodied praxis "of *writing fleshly*, as practiced by Black, Indigenous, and radical queer feminists of color . . . a practice of dreaming and dignity" (emphasis ours) that demands that we "name and own our wounds, to theorize from the collective body . . . to cause a radical rupture in the ways wounds are often disregarded." From here, with this notion of a collective body, we can draw a line directly to heidi andrea restrepo rhodes, who, in their piece, proposes that kinning pain can open up space for a "collective responsibility" that encompasses all living things on this planet. We see these two ideas as crucially interconnected; rejection is not (must not be) denial, because it is active, conscious, and begins with an acknowledgement of the body's validity, its basic rights to not just live/survive but to thrive. This line of thinking draws on a commitment to liberation and abolition that holds its roots in the body, grows through physicality and feeling, and refuses to be discounted.

Shereen: What a helpful reminder—the coupling of ideas and a commitment to liberation through bodily experiences have coalesced throughout this special issue. We want (and need more than ever!) to linger in this feeling of delighted, collective accomplishment. As coeditors of a feminist journal at this particular moment, it is easy to feel burdened and buried within a grim reality. But *Body Matters* has gifted us an opportunity to pause and marvel at the interactive energy each contributor brought to our call, and for that we are profoundly grateful. We hold this as a reminder that joy is itself a form of resistance, a refusal to be broken, a vehicle for collective struggle.

• • •

As we reread the articles included in this issue, we noticed stronger connections between the pieces than originally observed. Collectively, the articles offer an exploration of bodies not only as sites of resistance to colonial, cis, heteropatriarchal violences but also as vessels that transcend the present reality, refusing complacency around pain, suffering, and death or the viewpoint that these are inevitabilities. The authors in this issue envision a futuristic landscape where joy, life-affirming care, and respect are made possible through bodily autonomy and are expressed in deliberate engagement with pleasure, pain, motherhood, sex work, and/or advocacy.

We are heartened by the strategies the authors use to challenge and expand our initial conceptualization of "body matters," proposing bold new frameworks of critical thought around criminalization (Regan Moss and Teagan Langseth-DePaolis); paincraft (heidi andrea restrepo rhodes); fleshly narratives (Niloofar Rasooli); Black Anti-Bodies (Dána-Ain Davis and Bisola Neil); fermented subjects (Aimee N. Jurado); queer Tejano camp (Meagan Solomon); and the fat spectacular (Yessica Garcia Hernandez). We quote some of these contributions in our discussion above and encourage readers to explore the articles in this issue as a collective narrative, one that invites "radical reclamation of space, place, and culture" (Solomon) and fosters spaces "where the past is alive and fed by the present and by ongoing, dynamic interactions with other organisms, systems, pressures, and communities" (Jurado). Each article in this volume speaks to spaces where bodies demand to be visible, proposing strategies for activism, engagement, and change. We feel critically transformed by the vast and varied calls to action embedded within these articles, action designed to usher better, brighter, more sustainable worlds.

Our exquisitely brilliant cover art, created and very generously made available to us by Uýra Sodoma, exemplifies dimensions and possible futures of a material coalition of human/land. Uýra is an Indigenous Brazilian artist whose expansive vision and performance pieces are showcased in the documentary film titled *Uýra: The Rising Forest* (2022), directed by Juliana Curi. In the cover photo of *Body Matters*, Uýra lays on the ground next to a fallen tree trunk, touching her heart with one hand and the core of the trunk with another. Although this fallen tree could be seen as a symbol of devastation and deforestation, the inseparability of the human body and the tree also enacts a promise for a future of shared life (perhaps one devoid of destruction) and interdependence/mutual protection initiated by trans Indigenous people of color comprising and representing the Global Majority.

These connections are similarly explored in the visual art contributions to this special issue. We've chosen to feature artwork as the first section—a framing narrative for this issue. These images speak powerfully to intersections of physicality, materiality, and the human/nature kinship practices our planet so desperately needs in the present moment. Collectively, the artists invite us to confront racist, sexist, colonizing spaces and bring our bodies to bear (to witness as well as to withstand) when creating futures that center Black, disabled, Indigenous, aging, nonconforming bodies and experiences. They offer striking visual representations of the themes explored by the written texts in this volume, locating physical bodies in the often fraught spaces of art galleries (Jacqueline Hayden) and performance spaces (Jessica Mehta); celebrating body diversity (Emily Strong) and the blending of human and nonhuman identities (Jesse Harrod, Coralina Rodriguez Meyer); and also embracing body horror as a reclamation of the fractured self (Lohitha Kethu).

While keeping bodies at the center, our creative prose and poetry contributors invite us to explore forms of collective consciousness and witnessing that help us transcend individual experience. Physicality offers a through line to all living beings, inviting us to pursue mutual liberation, whether by resisting narratives and structures that impose normativity and constrain behavior (as explored by Gina Alexandra Srmabekian and María Mínguez Arias) or by finding resources and solace in the natural world, which allow bodies to trans-mutate beyond normativity. While Avery C. Castillo sees human, animal, and nature all as one body, Damien Kritzer invites us to embrace the so-called unnatural: "Let us all be monsters." Likewise, contributors explore the benefits of embracing alienation, disconnecting from our physical bodies or seeing them as ephemeral sites for potential transformation and becoming. As Aimee N. Jurado's article explores the power of the "fermented subject," in the poetry section, Megha Sood finds that "The Secret of Marination" is key to coping with resentment and generational trauma. Simultaneously, Lohitha Kethu argues that "we become archivists of the body by having bodies," and the act of critically examining the spaces where our bodies are selectively seen, erased, or judged can help us throw away encounters that no longer serve us and rebuild a new, gentler world (something Melissa Chadburn, Jia-Rui Cook, and Vanessa Chica Ferreira also explore in their pieces). We can embrace the body horror of being alive, preserve hope for going beyond survival and finding instead opportunities for remaking ourselves in our own image.

Throughout this special issue, contributors draw upon frameworks of racial, disability, gender, and ecological justice to construct possible and enduring futures. The scope of work comprising this volume galvanizes and broadens our aspirations articulated in the initial call for papers. This issue energetically follows a lineage of writers and activists that first inspired our theme. As mentioned above, this lineage is expansive, and a comprehensive bibliography would be a tome unto itself; however, we have the pleasure of including a few critical texts in the Classics Revisited and Book Reviews sections. We wish to express much gratitude to Aracely García-González,

Tèmítọ́pẹ́ (Temi) Fàmọdù, Raquel Coy, Ash M. Smith, Tuka Al-Sahlani, Katrina M. Phillips, Lava Schadde, jah elyse sayers, and Asma A. Neblett for honoring these works with their array of brilliant approaches.

We would also like to name and amplify the following texts that served as a curated reading list for *Body Matters* at its inception and at various points throughout the production process:

The Future Is Disabled: Prophecies, Love Notes and Mourning Songs
    Leah Lakshmi Piepzna-Samarasinha (Arsenal Pulp Press, 2022)
Fearing the Black Body: The Racial Origins of Fat Phobia
    Sabrina Strings (New York University Press, 2019)
Women, Race & Class (Chapter 12: "Racism, Birth Control,
    and Reproductive Rights")
    Angela Y. Davis (Vintage Books, 1983)
*Redefining Realness: My Path to Womanhood, Identity, Love
    & So Much More*
    Janet Mock (Atria Books, 2014)
The Cancer Journals
    Audre Lorde (Penguin Classics, 2020)
Becoming Human: Matter and Meaning in an Antiblack World
    Zakiyyah Iman Jackson (New York University Press, 2020)
*Native American DNA: Tribal Belonging and the False Promise
    of Genetic Science*
    Kim TallBear (University of Minnesota Press, 2013)
Keywords for Gender and Sexuality Studies
    Edited by The Keywords Feminist Editorial Collective
    (New York University Press, 2020)
Black Disability Politics
    Sami Schalk (Duke University Press, 2022)
The Routledge International Handbook of Fat Studies
    Edited by Cat Pausé and Sonya Renee Taylor (Routledge, 2021)
*Becoming Kin: An Indigenous Call to Unforgetting the Past
    and Reimagining Our Future*
    Patty Krawec (Broadleaf Books, 2022)
Sensual Excess: Queer Femininity and Brown Jouissance
    Amber Jamilla Musser (New York University Press, 2018)
Archive of Style: New and Selected Poems
    Cheryl Clarke (TriQuarterly, 2024)

*Care at the End of the World: Dreaming of Infrastructure
in Crip-of-Color Writing*
Jina B. Kim (Duke University Press, 2025)
Thick: And Other Essays
Tressie McMillan Cottom (The New Press, 2019)

At the local level, we are inspired by and indebted to the individuals making *Body Matters* and the day-to-day work of *WSQ* possible. Thank you to our exceptional managing editors, Maya von Ziegesar and jah elyse sayers, who oversee the *WSQ* production schedule with grace and sharp attention to detail. We are saddened that jah's term at *WSQ* is ending but wish them much success with their remaining doctoral work! Our team extends a warm welcome back to Googie Karrass, returning as managing editor in Fall 2025. We are grateful to Queens College and the Center for the Study of Women, Gender, and Society at the Graduate Center for their continued support in appointing interns to work on the journal. Many thanks to Abrelle Lawson, our Queens College intern, and Graduate Center interns Hannah Salzer, Maya Shabazz-Williams, and Jennifer Bae for their energy and labor in developing new ideas and spaces for *WSQ*. We are endlessly grateful to Rachel Page at the Feminist Press for her unwavering leadership and guidance, and to Jeanne Thornton and Lucia Brown for generous support with promotions. We extend much appreciation to Juwon Jun and Sampson Starkweather (Center for the Humanities) for spotlighting the work published in *WSQ*. As always, profound gratitude to editorial directors Kendra Sullivan (Center for the Humanities) and Dána-Ain Davis (Center for the Study of Women and Society) for their stalwart presence and insight, and to the *WSQ* editorial board as well as the poetry, creative prose, and visual arts editors for their tireless engagement and feedback on CFPs and submissions. A million thanks to this amazing *WSQ* team and our incredible readers for brightening the future of the journal.

We cede the remaining space in this introduction to a series of tributes to Nikki Giovanni and Dorothy Allison, whose influence and legacies have shaped so many of us at *WSQ* and, doubtlessly, *WSQ*'s readership as well.

Shereen Inayatulla
Professor of English
York College, CUNY

Andie Silva
Professor of English
York College, CUNY

Tributes to Nikki Giovanni and Dorothy Allison

TRIBUTES TO NIKKI GIOVANNI

It seems especially cruel to lose one of our warrior poets, Nikki Giovanni, at a time she would find all too familiar—that is, when a democracy begins to appear too close to achieving some of what it has long promised for those denied so much, and the backlash manifests with cruelty and blindness. Yet she has left us guidance, so to speak, on what it means to live in a moment forever on the precipice of change and destruction.

In *Black Feeling, Black Talk / Black Judgment* Nikki raps to us from the thick of it, making it seem easy to communicate such a whirlwind of thoughts, hopes, fears, suspicion, paranoia. This is no bird's-eye view, no clinical, bloodless analysis of a generation in the throes of transformation. It's not instruction, either, on how to be a revolutionary, no lofty heights towards which we are enjoined to soar.

There isn't a great deal of wisdom, and maybe there is a little foolishness, and this is the genius. Revolutions are visceral. More than anything else, we need blood, muscle, guts, tears, eyeballs, eardrums, toes ready to dance, fingers ready to grab.

Michelle M. Wright
Emory University

• • •

My first encounter with Nikki Giovanni's work happened when I was a child. The angelic face of a smiling Black infant beamed at me from a record cover. *Truth Is on Its Way*, the cover read. And indeed, truth was the voice of Nikki

WSQ: Women's Studies Quarterly 53: 3 & 4 (Fall/Winter 2025) © 2025 by WSQ Editorial Board.

TRIBUTES TO DOROTHY ALLISON

When I started identifying as nonbinary in 2019, I also took a new name—"Allison." Not because of my given middle name, which came with only one *l*, but because of Dorothy Allison. As a latecomer to academia, I looked to Allison for permission to embrace all of myself, especially those class-based, shameful parts I thought I had to hide. As a self-described "queer white trash" writer, "Zen redneck," "dyke mama," or even more colorfully, "a cross-eyed, working-class lesbian, addicted to violence, language and hope," Allison refused to conform to any rarefied literary identity. Reading her rough-edged short story collection *Trash*, I imagined nonbinary as a recognition of the fried and messy stew of my life, flavored by the white trash butchness and rage of my father, uncles, and aunts, the coworkers I met in the odd jobs I had worked since I was sixteen, and the scholars, artists, and lovers who gave me books and new language. Coming out as nonbinary didn't mean erasure of what came before, which has included at varying times "butch," "femme," and everything in between, but a turning toward something like Allison's multiple, seemingly contradictory process of naming—her refusal to make a choice.

K Allison Hammer
Southern Illinois University,
Carbondale

• • •

I can't remember who told me to read it. But then everyone was reading it, or had just read it. I was just out of college in 1992, when *Bastard Out of Carolina* came out. I had just graduated from Harvard, where I had developed a vaguely unhealthy relation to William Faulkner's character Quentin Compson—also a Southerner, also at Harvard, also out of place and depressed. Unlike Quentin, I had survived, but I was hanging around Boston in a fug of depression, working odd jobs. *Bastard*, clear as a bell, woke me up. I had come out in college, and had just made the decision (like Bone) not to see my stepfather again. Dorothy Allison showed me that there was not, on the one hand, a rarefied world of great literature and, on the other, grim reality. She had done it—made great literature out of the realities of class, abuse, and betrayal. *Bastard Out of Carolina* marked a watershed in my life: Its honesty and brilliance called me to reckon with what I had left behind.

Heather Love
University of Pennsylvania

• • •

I owe so much to Dorothy Allison. She is the writer who first taught me what it meant to think through my body, to see my own body as source of knowledge rather than as a distraction to be ignored or an obstacle to overcome. During the first year of my graduate studies in English, a professor I deeply respect gifted each member of our autobiography seminar a copy of Allison's memoir *Two or Three Things I Know for Sure*. I devoured the book in one sitting and spent much of the next few years thinking through and responding to its many insights. As a recently out, baby butch lesbian, I was just beginning to understand what it meant to occupy those identities publicly, and I was grappling with the body-shaming and cultural misogyny that most young women are forced to endure in one way or another. At that time, I had never encountered a writer who spoke frankly about living in a body she'd been conditioned to despise—"the story of the female body taught to hate itself." Nor had I read a writer who described the bodies of butch women with such love, tenderness, and shameless desire. Dorothy Allison's unflinching storytelling thus helped me to turn away from the scripts that had organized my life up to that point and begin to craft the stories, theories, pedagogies, and even friendships that have been at the center of my work ever since. Indeed, one of the greatest friendships of my life was solidified one night over cocktails in a Milwaukee bar when I read all of *Two or Three Things I Know for Sure* out loud to a PhD classmate whom I was just beginning to get to know. And now, more than twenty years later, she and I talk about how we teach this memoir to our own students and consider what it means to them in our current moment. Two or three things I know for sure, and one of them is that I will be forever grateful for the wit and wisdom of Dorothy Allison's writing and its ability to connect those who read it in a process of collaborative healing. Thank you, Dorothy.

Kate Haffey
University of Mary Washington

• • •

Dorothy Allison was made by a network of lesbian-feminists and the businesses and organizations they built. She became a best-selling novelist alongside poet, sex radical, lover, mother, and teacher. If Dorothy Allison were a young writer today, she would be engaged in the vibrant lesbian and feminist activities happening now. I can see her as a young woman working on the feminist socialist magazine *Lux*, named after Rosa Luxemburg; contributing work to *WMN*, a publication of lesbian poetry and art, and *Foglifter*, a LGBTQ+ journal and press. (Recently, she contributed an essay to *Sinister Wisdom*, a lesbian-feminist journal I edit.) She would be buying all the books published by Stephanie Andrea Allen at BLF Press and Aunt Lute Books. Young Dorothy Allisons, and there are many out there, are finding a vibrant literary world to make them, to challenge them, to nurture them, to thwart them, to vex them, just like Allison did. Imagine the lesbian, queer, feminist, nonbinary, trans writers being nurtured today in gatherings at Burdock Books in Alabama and Violet Valley Books in Water Valley, Mississippi; in the pages of radical periodicals; and in books published by independent presses. The worlds that made Dorothy Allison continue making new writers, activists, radicals, and lovers.

Julie R. Enszer
Editor, Sinister Wisdom

SECTION I. VISUAL ART

Coralina Rodriguez Meyer, *Abuela, Ija Desnuda Surgio del Sacrificio Triangulo Bermuda*, 2022–23. Installation at the Colonial Florida Cultural Heritage Museum in Miami as part of the Virgen Gruta, Mother Mold series. Mixed materials including human hair, vintage serape textile, coral, sponges, spirit bottles, seeds, foxtail palm stamens, used medical gloves, construction gloves, condoms, wood stud, neon lace window curtain, sand and building debris from the Surfside building collapse, nail salon glitter, spray paint, exterior house paint, building insulation foam, gypsum plaster, metal lathe, and industrial floor resin, 64 × 40 × 24 in.

Abuela, Ija Desnuda Surgio del Sacrificio Triangulo Bermuda and Camino Umbligo (Coralina Triptych)

Coralina Rodriguez Meyer

A photograph from the Virgen Gruta series, *Abuela, Ija Desnuda Surgio del Sacrificio Triangulo Bermuda* (Museo de la Cultura Colonial de Florida), depicts a figure, extant and resting in a verdant retablo nested within the sanctuary garden at the Colonial Florida Cultural Heritage Center in the redlined Allapattah, Miami, neighborhood hovering above tide lines. Situated within the Catholic archdiocese's collection of artifacts conquered from the Americas and Caribbean, the *Mother Mold* monument, a fertility effigy, is a site-specific installation for the AIM Biennial Miami 2023–2024, offering material refuse as maternal refuge. A coral cast figure composed of four years of collecting seashore debris along Miami Beach, intimate waste, and environmental ephemera from the artist's neighborhood rests in repose within the fishtail palm tree fronds to welcome viewers. The fertility effigy restores dignity and divinity to the refuse materials. Upcycled memories are formed in the shape of a pregnant body whose resting pose and sea-sponge texture is wafted by flittering fishtail light. A wet resin surface bonds restored coral onto a pregnant body in recline. Departing from the stiffened dolphin dorado taxidermied bodies popular in commercial fishing piers or tourist shops in the Caribbean, the figure's pose and marine layer are cradled by the rustling frond frame. A blinding sky beyond serves as a pillow for the exhausted effigy figure.

WSQ: Women's Studies Quarterly **53: 3 & 4 (Fall/Winter 2025)** © 2025 by Coralina Rodriguez Meyer.
All rights reserved.

Abuela, Ila Desnuda Surgia del Sacrificio

Coralina Rodriguez Meyer, *Camino Umbligo (Coralina Triptych)*, 2022. Site-specific installation at Colonial Florida Cultural Heritage Museum in Miami as part of the Virgen Gruta, Mother Mold series. Mixed materials including coral, sponges, chancletas, palm husks, palm stamens, shells, condoms, straws, and spirit bottles, 76 × 36 × 28 in.

Camino Umbligo conjures the intersecting forces of global South liberation mythologies and American colonial legacies with the "Chancletazo," the legend of El Dorado (Lost City of Gold), and shrunken-head mummification techniques of the Andean Americas. Woven Old Man palm and coconut fronds archive the funerary and domestic architecture traditions of island nations ranging from the South Pacific to the Caribbean, where the artist first learned roof-thatch membrane weaving techniques that were also used in life-cycle rituals as headstones to commemorate the transition of equatorial ancestors. The artist's head appears twice in this work—one crowning through the figure's threshold and the other at its feet, where coral grows forth from its veins.

Born in a car in an Everglades swamp, raised Ital and Tinkuy (queer) between Homestead, Florida, and the Caribbean, **Coralina Rodriguez Meyer** is a mixed-race Indigenous Andean American (Muisca/Inca) Brooklyn- and Miami-based Quipucamayoc artist working across documentary sculpture, photography, installation, archives, and advocacy. MamaSpaBotanica (2007–present) is a full-spectrum cultural medicine workshop restoring dignity and divinity to vulnerable, unvanquished people, plants, and hybrid habitats. Collaboratively created by, of, and for LGBTQIA+ melanated kin, the works are moving monuments to survivors of conflicting climate and reproductive health crisis to transgress structural violence in American mythology. Documentary sculpture, photography, and agency-building workshops illuminate plantology wisdom vibrating in our neon narratives. Transforming sterile, institutional walls into vibrant, multisensory sanctuaries, the habitats resist assimilation with retablo installation. Meyer can be reached at coralinameyer@gmail.com.

Because I Am Flesh

Emily Strong

My figurative landscapes invite contemplation of physicality through meticulously painted fleshy compositions. I create raw, intimate spaces that explore the many complexities of physical relationships, with the self and with others. This series is a celebration of humanity and form.

The tangled limbs and corpulent hills create a bewildering landscape, challenging the viewer to decipher how many figures are present, what parts of the figures they are seeing, and what genders may be represented. This ambiguity allows my work to question: What stereotypes and biases do we, consciously or subconsciously, bring to viewing a figurative work of art?

By not including other objects, an environment, or personal identifiers, these works invite the viewer to consider the form exclusively within its own context, freeing the subjects from roles they may be given based on perceived traits or identities.

This series evolved to include another layer of connection between viewer and subject: each painting is accompanied by a transcript of an interview conducted with the model(s). The interviews give the models a voice in the process and the platform to express their own experiences with their body and identity and how they are challenged or supported in the way they physically exist in the world.

WSQ: Women's Studies Quarterly 53: 3 & 4 (Fall/Winter 2025) © 2025 by Emily Strong. All rights reserved.

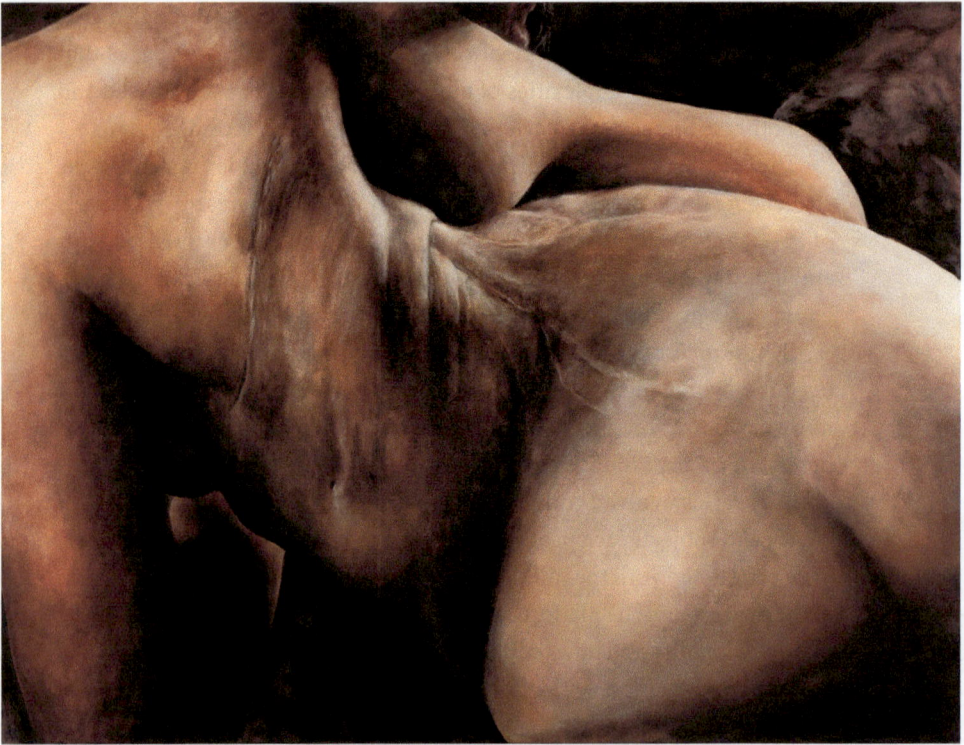

Emily Strong, *Reflection*, 2021. Oil on canvas, 30 × 40 in.

Reflection

Age 28
Assigned Sex woman
Pronouns she/her
Gender Identity woman
Race white

Do you mind saying what disability you have?
There's one that's basically an umbrella term for any birth defects that usually happen in one, which is called VATER, but I usually don't mention that because it's so vague and irrelevant. But, scoliosis and a radial club hand [and] arm.

It looked like you have some scarring; have you had surgeries?
I've had about a dozen surgeries, some on my arm and some on my back. Also, because of my scoliosis, I also have a smaller lung capacity. In college was the fourth or fifth time that I got hospitalized for pneumonia, so I have too much scar tissue and have to have oxygen full-time now.

How have your family and close friends been supportive of your appearance and self-perception?
If I'm having an illogical thought, they squash it. We are "tough love" people. Growing up—I realized later, when I was in college and stuff—that me and my family don't really talk about appearance. It's just not a thing. We don't care—like, we've never talked about it. In some cases, yeah, especially if we're just being bullies to each other as siblings.

With my mom, it's just never even been a topic, because it was irrelevant. I think that helped a lot with—if somebody would bring something up or mention something that had to do with looks, my reactions would always just be like, "Why are we talking about this?" So, that helped a lot with formative years anyway. And now, at this point, I feel like people— my close friends and family and stuff—just supporting my vulnerable work really helps, because as I do more and more things on the public internet, I'm working through those things on my own, but support to keep doing that is really helpful.

Has the response online been mostly positive?
It helps to hear that the things that I do—the representation—has helped some people or it's kind of held a mirror up to some people about their ableist mindsets or something. So, that also makes any thoughts about appearance kind of irrelevant. Which is also the goal.

Has there been negative feedback or rude comments, or have people mostly been supportive?
Mostly really supportive. Every now and then there's some trolls, which is why I ended up making merch anyway. Somebody was like, "You're just ridiculous and skanky." Like, that's not the insult you think it is. I'm gonna make merch for it!

Someone else was like, "You're just half naked on the internet for attention!" and I asked, "Have you even read any of my posts? Do you know what I'm doing at all, or the fact that I didn't even want to do this to begin with?" But here I am and now I don't care. There were some other similar responses like that.

I was just thinking, "Who do you think you are? What are you trying to do? I don't care what any stranger has to say (that isn't constructive), so what's your goal here?"

And eventually, I finally put it in my bio that "I'm not your inspiration," because I've gotten so many of those comments. It's not exactly always negative, but it is if you know why it's an "inspiration porn" thing. So, I've tried to have many conversations about it to explain to people that you need to figure out what the difference is. Is it because I'm disabled? Or because I've actually inspired you to do something different? That upsets people, because I'm implying or straight up saying people have bad intentions when they don't even know they do, so there's backlash from that. If you would just give it some thought, though, you'll find out I'm right. If you REALLY really mean it in the right way, awesome. But 90 percent of people don't.

Or I'll get creepy comments or people in my DMs, but that's just a swift hit of the "delete" button.

You said you didn't want to do this in the beginning, so what led you to doing this very vulnerable exploration of intimacy and the self online?
I guess it wasn't fair to word it that way, because I did want to do it. Otherwise I wouldn't have done it, but sometimes it feels like an obligation. If I post something and I get a lot of support, I have mixed feelings because I'm like, there shouldn't be such a reaction to this 'cause it shouldn't be an issue. But it is, so it's a big reaction from people—whether it's good or bad—it just shows me that there's so much work to be done. It's exhausting being vulnerable all the time and it can make you feel gross. But then it's great, so the benefits and the impact are well worth feeling gross or the exhaustion from it. The fact is, if anybody has been helped by it, which they have been, I'm gonna keep doing it.

It does feel a little bit like an obligation, just because I feel like I am willing to do it, where some people can't, or they would never feel comfortable. I am apathetic about being naked on the internet. Well, not naked, but you know what I mean. So, if I don't have social anxiety, and I have the tools, and I know marketing or the platform well, then I should do it. Where some people don't know social media, or have social anxiety, or aren't photographers, or aren't good at networking. I do things that are easily digestible, like photography, modeling, and writing, so I have these skills and tools to give messages and representation. So, if I can do all this and I'm just annoyed sometimes because I feel like I shouldn't have to do it, because it shouldn't be an issue, then that's just a privilege.

I'm always going to do it, but there are bubbles of weird feelings. I think the reasons I started were more about pushing boundaries and being more vulnerable. I was focusing most on vulnerability and that's why it started. I was just doing a trade with another photographer. They photographed me and that's when I started modeling. I was more so just showing up in an unapologetic way, just being like, "This is what I look like, I'm giving you permission to look."

That's one of my main things: If I'm posting a photo of it, you can be curious, and it is an attempt to remove the side-eye stares. Online, I'm just letting you fully stare at me. You do it on your screen, you're good; you get that out of your system and then we can talk about it. I'd rather have it all out in the open together to destigmatize than have whispers in the grocery lines or kids staring across the street. If we had more representation, it wouldn't be so weird when you see people that look different. I started because of those types of things, and after that I kept doing more and more with that and disability representation, and I decided I should just keep doing more with this then.

One of the biggest issues was I kept pushing my boundaries and vulnerable things and I realized, okay, well, I've gotta start going after the big boss, I guess. It feels really vulnerable for me to do the disability and sexuality series, but it's something that's never talked about. It was more of a proclamation of sexuality. I'm like, "Surprise! Disabled people have sexualities. No matter what type it is, it's there, because we're humans," and that's when it kinda all blew up.

Were people taken aback by it?

No, the first time there was a lot of the weird feeling of, "This shouldn't be so inspirational to people." That was the first one that I was like, everybody is so glad that I posted it, everybody thinks it's so beautiful, they had no idea that these were issues. It's the first time it's on their radar or they've ever thought of these things. None of it is on anyone's radar. They felt like I was airing out this big issue, when it's always been there, and I was left to sit with the discomfort while everybody was just so excited about the project. That's just what happens with social issues, though. The people who are doing the work get the weird feelings about it and everyone else gets to learn. But it was good, there were overwhelmingly good responses, which was awesome. It was more than I thought it would be. So that day, it was great, then the next day was the slight emotional hangover.

What makes you feel beautiful? What makes you feel empowered?

When I feel very comfortable doing whatever I'm doing, looking however I look; not thinking about how any of us look feels awesome. Like, laughing or dancing and only being concerned with how it feels. If you don't have to think about it, you're just having a good time AND you feel like you look good—that's the goal.

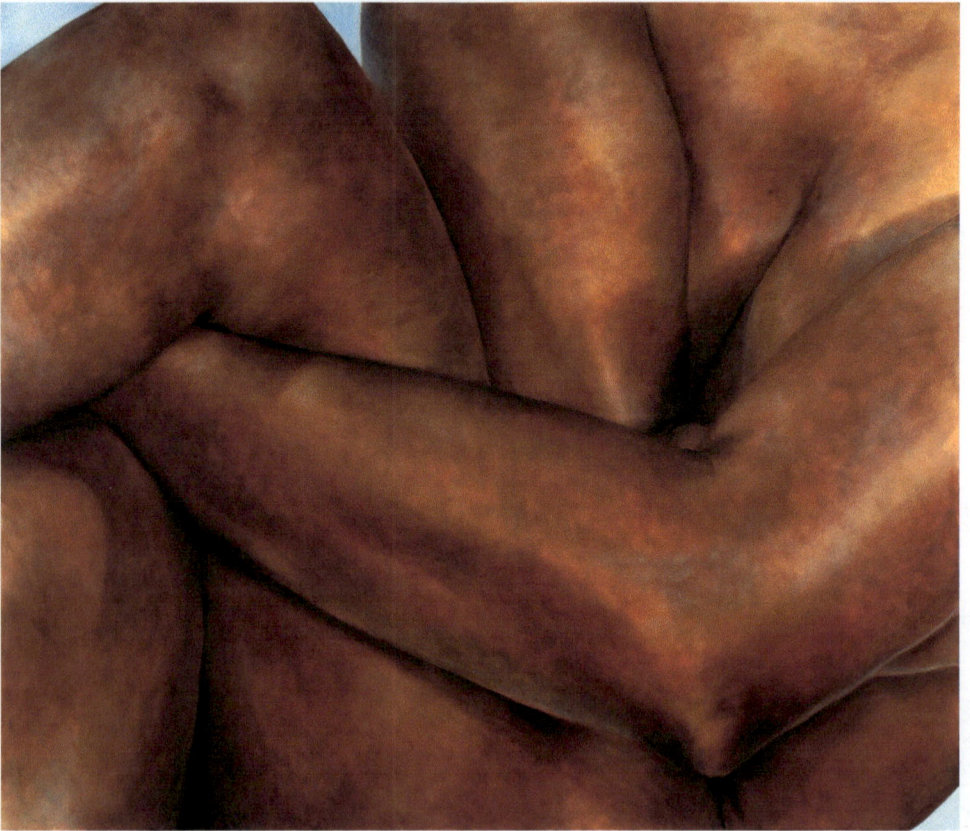

Emily Strong, *Essential*, 2021. Oil on canvas, 5 × 6 ft.

Essential
Age 32
Assigned Sex female
Pronouns she/her
Gender Identity female
Race African American

What is your gender identity? Please describe.
Female. Tomboy, if that is still an accepted term. I love aspects about all genders.

What does femininity mean to you? Masculinity? How do you relate to these terms?
Fem was forced upon me since I was little, and for multiple traumatizing reasons. I rebelled as much as possible, except for the aspects that I liked and chose to express for myself. Masculinity was also both a positive and negative influence in my life. From being a Black tomboy in a predominantly White community that only saw Black people one way, from what was perceived on news channels, to being pursued in a threatening manner, or for sexual purposes from multiple races but mainly from the White and Black community.

I was targeted multiple times and am also a victim of rape. But sadly, it was because of the way society taught little Black boys how to act, both by themselves and around others. This was an issue that was a taboo topic within the Black community. The fascination of educated Black girls, especially ones who are "nerds" or "geeks," or "plain" . . . anything that was labeled as "for White people only." I felt sorry for him. He never found someone of his race that loved anime, wasn't a forced stereotype, and could "hang with the boys" without jealousy or other issues.

I hated gender roles and norms, but also never knew how to accept myself. My narcissistic mother wanted me to be the perfect, obedient fem slave, and my father never got the son he always wanted, so I was the replacement and became the outlet for his failings in life.

I became both [feminine and masculine], and I loved it. I wanted to express myself in multiple ways and not just the stereotypical way that was associated with my assigned sex at birth and ethnicity. I was tired of being ridiculed for basic uncontrollable bodily functions such as burping or passing gas. I would always be ridiculed for whistling, which was labeled as a "masculine" trait.

Have there been times in your life when your race has influenced how others have treated you?

Multiple times, for the good and bad depending on the situation. One aspect from these situations is code-switching. I cannot vouch for other ethnicities, but as Afro-Americans, we are taught this indirectly. When in the presence of anyone outside of your home, you are to act as if perfectly educated, well put-together, blend in as well as you can in hopes of succeeding in life. Basically, a survival tactic.

And sort of along the lines of the same old-school tactics used in earlier times. For example, the type of thinking that was forced upon females, to make their homes look as perfect as the first day they bought it and to hide all of their belongings as to look like no one lives in this house.

But as an example, in my case, if I act younger, less knowledgeable, and cute, then I will most likely get a positive motherly [or] fatherly reaction or one less harsh than what was going to be dealt to me. Same goes with the tone in my voice. If I speak in a softer, bubbly voice, I receive a more laid-back and accepting reaction, versus using my actual lower tone of voice, where the person on the receiving end has to go through a series of reactions within their mind to give an "acceptable and hopefully not overly judgmental" tone.

Even to this day, I use my actual tone to signify my age and experience nonverbally, compared to my much higher, younger-sounding tone, where even though I would get a more favorable response, it comes with the possibility of being perceived that I am too young to have experienced anything in life and need unwarranted advice and direction. And it also comes with unfavorable ignorant responses that are taught to be "less racist, ignorant, et cetera," such as "Oh, you're so nice for what or who you are or your kind! You're so well spoken! I didn't know your kind liked animals, different kinds of food, shows, music, or anything that was not labeled a Black trait." I have even lost jobs because of this. Where I simply and calmly questioned their supposed "compliment" and I received an extremely harsh reaction such as, "I don't know! Why do you people have to question everything we say?! This is why our races can't get along: because you can't take a simple compliment!" Even though it wasn't a compliment at all and it showed your ignorance and bias, plain and simple. "Black people only listen to one type of music: rap. I didn't think you knew Lady Gaga or Katy Perry was, or even Queen?!"

Have you felt pressured to change your appearance by close family and friends?
Friends never, but family yes. My family had always had a hold on how I was supposed to present myself and my gender. I was a "girl" but also Black, so I must wear these specific things. I hated dresses and skirts for the longest time. I was a tomboy and I wanted to wear jeans, especially bell-bottoms. Going to Catholic school was the bane of my existence. Every time I had to buy a uniform, they would barely fit and it lowered my self-esteem every time. My friends always supported me no matter what I wanted to be. My family, unfortunately, had another agenda—the community norms they wanted to stick to out of fear.

Have you felt pressured to change your appearance by people you know only casually or by business associates?
Both, especially random strangers. I've had peers, teachers, and random people in a store or on the street treat me like a pet that needed to wear clothes to suit their needs. I've had my hair extensions pulled out of my head in the hallway at school just so everyone, including teachers, could laugh at me because it was something they had never experienced. They were afraid of asking, afraid of change within their community. I had my hair chemically straightened so I would look more acceptable to my peers and employers. That was still never enough. I would get fired from a job over "not meeting the criteria of being more white and less Black, for it was too intimidating and seems too 'thug.'"

Have you felt pressured to change your appearance by the media? What aspects of the media have impacted your self-perception the most? Commercial? Social? Other?

I wasn't allowed to watch certain types of media or listen to much music besides Oldies 99.9. I was only influenced by what my mother would force me to wear or buy me with minimal intervention. The most influence that came to me was when my mother started forcing me to attend talent groups in hopes I would become a star and get rich enough to care for her for the rest of my life.

I always had a deep-rooted hatred for being as dark as I am, and even more so toward anyone darker than me. The typical beauty standard was what got attention and I felt that I would never succeed because of that, or anyone in my community. It wasn't until college that I tried to change my image to what would be best accepted in the media, or at least the modeling and acting community. But with age and some extra traumatic experiences and burnout, I slowly began to give that up to try to find what I wanted to be.

Do you do anything to alter your natural appearance (tattoos, piercings, hair dyeing, makeup, etc.)? If so, why?

I've always had an attraction to tattoos, mainly, and then secondly to piercings—but unfortunately this is some sort of coping mechanism and excuse to not self-harm because of depression, anxiety, and burnout. Hair dyeing was particularly scary for me, especially since curly [and] nappy hair care was not a thing until later. I always had the fear of my hair falling out, and being perceived as an example of how ugly Black people are when bald.

What makes you feel beautiful? What makes you feel empowered?

I feel beautiful and my best when I'm naked. No makeup. No jewelry. Hair out. In a quiet room or greenhouse, surrounded by the sounds of mother nature.

Emily Strong is a figurative oil painter based in Easton, Pennsylvania. Strong was born in Allentown, Pennsylvania, in 1992 and received her undergraduate degrees in studio art and psychology with a minor in sociology from Moravian University in 2015. Strong works primarily in oil on canvas, creating realistic, intimate depictions of figures and spaces that explore the many complexities of relationships with self, other, and environment, as well as existence, isolation, and identity. In addition to her studio practice, Strong is currently the exhibitions and collections coordinator at the Baum School of Art in Allentown, Pennsylvania. She can be reached via email at emilystrongfineart@gmail.com.

Ancient Statuary Series and Figure Model Series

Jacqueline Hayden

From 1991 to 1996, Hayden photographed nude older figure models, sixty to eighty-four years old, in a studio, creating the *Figure Model Series*. The models were professionals actively working in art schools in New York City, Boston, Chicago, and western Massachusetts.

From antiquity to the present, through artistic representation, we have amassed an image of our ideal selves. Hayden's intention was to challenge these culturally sanctioned ideals of beauty and youth as well as image. As professional image-makers, the models and Hayden actively created an "image." Informed by their own histories as image-makers and the immediacy of impending mortalities, they constructed a projection of the idealized pose altered by reality.

The *Ancient Statuary Series* (1996–2000) are platinum and palladium prints derived from digitally generated halftone negatives. Hayden created digital composites of her photographs of older figure models (*Figure Model Series*) and photographs she made of ancient statuary in situ using Photoshop 3.0 when layers were available for the first time. Grafting older bodies onto ancient statuary forms gave her the means to critically engage the visual history of aging as one of invisibility.

Making platinum and palladium prints, a nineteenth-century printing method, was used to question the limitations of visual representations in art history.

WSQ: Women's Studies Quarterly 53: 3 & 4 (Fall/Winter 2025) © 2025 by Jacqueline Hayden. All rights reserved.

Jacqueline Hayden, *XIV Rodin*, 1999/2000.
Platinum palladium print, 10.5 × 15 in.

Jacqueline Hayden, *XVI Leda and the Swan*, 2000.
Platinum palladium print, 10.5 × 15.5 in.

Jacqueline Hayden was professor emerita of film and photography at Hampshire College, Amherst, Massachusetts, from 1990 to 2016, and founding faculty member at the study abroad program in Havana, Cuba, from 2001 to 2017. Hayden was project director of the Havana Archive Project from 2012 to 2020 at the Office of the Historian in Havana, a digital archive in Spanish and English of the 1,055 significant buildings chosen to be renovated in Old Havana. See more at https://compass.fivecolleges.edu/collections/digital-photographic-archive-historic-havana. Hayden started photographing older nude bodies in 1991 to critically engage the invisibility of aging in Western art history and media culture. Women, fat bodies, transgendered bodies, and dying and effluvial bodies have been Hayden's subject for thirty-four years.

See more at https://jacquelinehaydenphotographs.com. Hayden can be reached at senorajh@gmail.com.

500 years AGO

Jessica Mehta

As an Aniyunwiya (citizen of the Cherokee Nation) artist, my practice bridges the past and present to confront and reimagine colonial narratives. My work is rooted in decolonization, utilizing archival materials, reclaimed objects, and experimental forms to provoke dialogue around identity, history, and collective memory. Whether transforming treaties into erasure poetry or embedding Cherokee heirloom seeds into installations, I explore the intersections of trauma, resilience, and reclamation.

My process is guided by Indigenous methodologies, emphasizing reciprocity and interconnectedness. I seek to disrupt Western linear frameworks, instead creating immersive works that invite viewers to engage holistically—with mind, body, and spirit. Each piece is a conversation with ancestry and a call to action for cultural sovereignty and ecological balance.

My recent projects, such as "Deep Seeded" and "Red/Act," explore themes of assimilation, identity, and reclamation, often engaging with archival and material remnants of Indigenous histories. Through avant-garde conceptualism, I aim to honor the untold stories of my community while cultivating spaces for healing and resistance.

My work serves as both a testament and a tool—bridging generations and envisioning a future rooted in justice, creativity, and reclamation.

WSQ: Women's Studies Quarterly 53: 3 & 4 (Fall/Winter 2025) © 2025 by Jessica Mehta. All rights reserved.

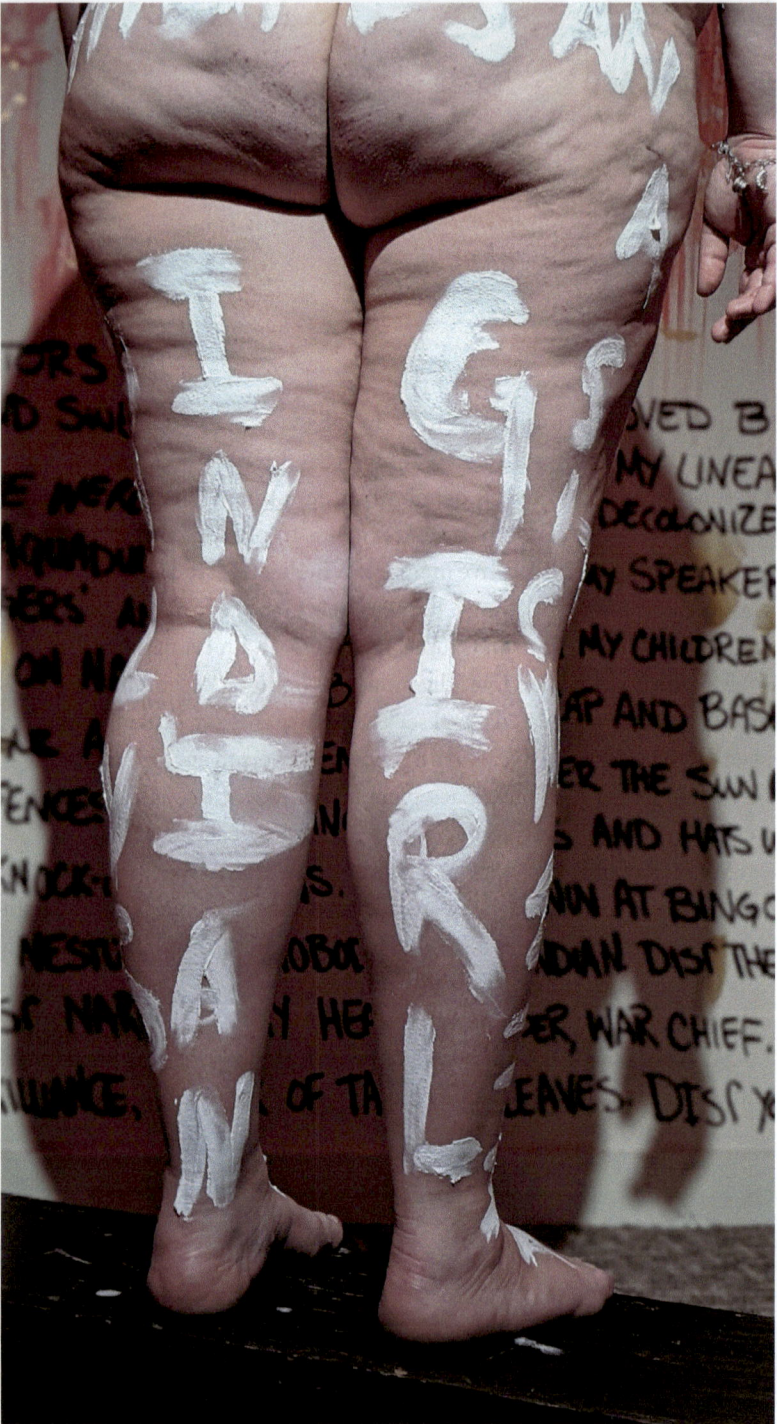

Jessica Doe, *500 years AGO*, 2024. Mixed materials.

There's so much trauma we hold in our bodies,
there's so much trauma in the land.
                                        —Klee Benally

the Indigenous Land/s of Turtle Island—which can encompass so-called canada, mexico, the united states, all of north america, and/or all Land on Earth, depending on which Native person, elder, or tribal community you ask—has been fractured, pillaged, used, exploited, desecrated, & raped relentlessly by explorerssettlerscolonizers beginning circa 500 years ago. so much has been taken, stolen & abused of this Sacredness, much more than can be represented here tonight: Uranium, Copper, Lithium, Water, Forests & their Timber, so many of our four-legged, winged & scaled Relatives, to name just a few. in this spirit, of this Spirit, of this reality, I have chosen just three key "resources" (a colonial word that suggests "to be used") to highlight: Assimilation, Gold, & Oil. A.G.O. 500 years of Assimilation, Gold (-mining), & Oil (-drilling).

my children (Oglala Lakota) chose to participate tonight, offering temporary visual access to their bodies to nourish discourse & un-erasure. to correct colonial lies & buried truths. they are our burgeoning future, our only hopeful route to decolonization & Indigenization. my youngest child represents Gold, brandishing the glittering hue across her brown body that echoes the color of Earth. my eldest exemplifies oil ripped from the land, the prophesied black snake of their tribe, slicks of black tarnishing her skin as it does this now-shared World. the Indigenous adult poet (Eyak) represents assimilation, the twin of erasure, white paint indicating the attempted & successful whitewashing via colonization at so-called "Indian residential schools" ("residential"), the 1960s scoop, the disproportionate number of

Indigenous children still in foster care today, the wrong & missing history books in our schools. our Languages, histories, spiritual practices, lineages, ancestries, & ties to the Land that were attempted to be stripped from us. but we are still here & not in pieces. we remain, sustain, stitched & plaited together. whole.

the poems painted on these NDN bodies, **bodies** that have been hyper-sexualized, fetishized, and/or under- & mis-represented since contact, speak to where we are today. to what we have lost, what we have kept, & all that we stand to (re)gain. the models here are blinded, gagged, & bound in succession by maga, as many people are—& not just due to colonial politics, conservative politics, but to ignorant, scared, & hateful "politics." here we are again. we can choose. again. so, let us choose to see, to speak, & to act Indigenously. if you are not, cannot, be Indigenous, then be an accomplice. let us turn, transform, maga to MANA.

each model also wears a mitre made of muslin burial shroud, splattered with the Blood of my youngest, golden child, printed with text from inter caetera, the papal bull which drove the doctrine of discovery. the doctoring of "**discovery**." this makeshift pope's headdress points to & inverts not just to the catholic church's vast role in colonization & residential institutions, but to the summer 2022 instance of the pope wearing of a Cree warbonnet in so-called canada during a trip to apologize for the church's role across this Land's bloody, violent history & genocide attempts. attempts that continue today.

i invite you to become not just witness, not a passive ally, but an active participant in decolonization. we are all of the Sky & will end this body's journey in & of the Land. it is not too late. 500 years is not even a blink in the life of the World, the Universe. may we move forward, together, in Healing, in Ceremony, in Peace.

Jessica Mehta (Doe) is an Aniyunwiya (Cherokee Nation) artist, writer, and scholar. She is the author of several books, including *When We Talk of Stolen Sisters*, *Savagery*, and the forthcoming *The Fig Years: Sivvy, Frybread (Lack Thereof), and Me.* Learn more at www.thischerokeerose.com. She can be reached at jmehta@centrocultural.org.

Crossed Legs and Nothing Is Dead Down Here

Jesse Harrod

Jesse Harrod's work spans sculpture, painting, stop-motion animation, and other media, reimagining forms of gendered, sexual, and disabled embodiment. Their practice engages the intertwined histories of abstraction, sculpture, and fiber art, drawing from craft traditions like macramé, weaving, basketry, ceramics, and stained glass. Harrod's work investigates how texture, color, and materiality can evoke intangible modes of identity and experience.

Central to Harrod's practice is a broader effort to explore abstraction and queer aesthetics. Known for their embrace of macramé, Harrod creates tactile, voluminous, and colorful works that function as both wall-based art and freestanding sculptures. Recent sculptures experiment with furniture-like forms, engaging architecture, gravity, light, and negative space to shape their design. By combining welded steel, crafted wood, and woven fibers, Harrod's work invites viewers to experience the body in new ways, using variations in scale, color, and texture to disorient and reorient perceptions.

Harrod's work is informed by feminist and queer artistic traditions, punk material culture, and rich histories of craft, textile, and tapestry design. By questioning conventions of form, medium, and taste, Harrod creates art that occupies the space between sculpture, dimensional tapestry, and abstract painting, imbuing materials with personality and offering new ways to understand and experience identity.

WSQ: Women's Studies Quarterly 53: 3 & 4 (Fall/Winter 2025) © 2025 by Jesse Harrod. All rights reserved.

Jesse Harrod, *Crossed Legs*, 2023.
Paracord and brass, 37 × 24¾ × 2¾ in.

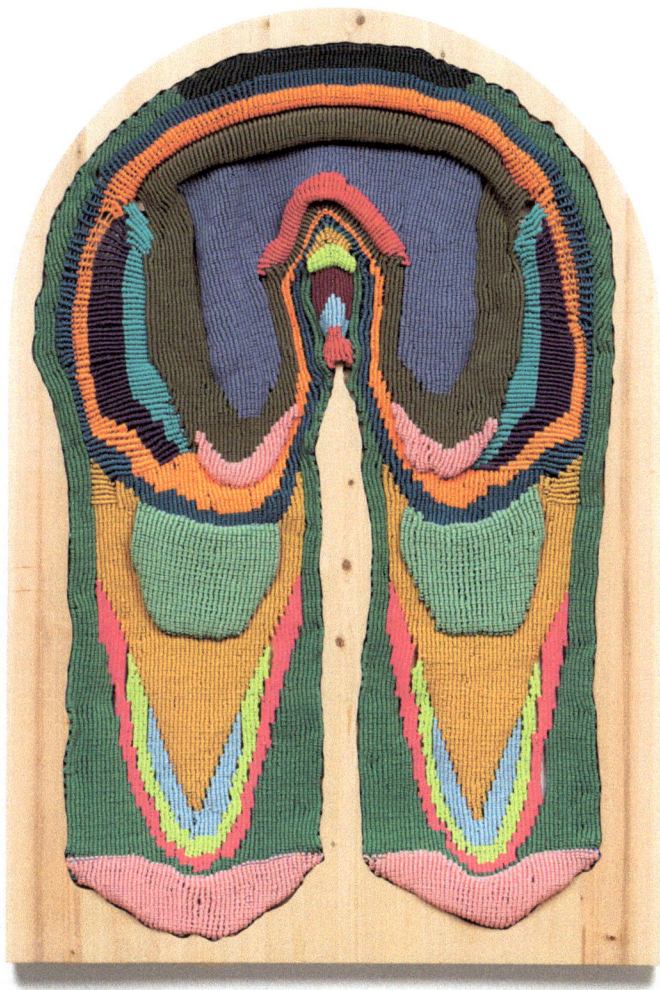

Jesse Harrod, *Nothing Is Dead Down Here*, 2023.
Paracord and wood, 67 × 47½ × 4 in.

Jesse Harrod is a multidisciplinary artist based between Philadelphia and New York. Their work spans sculpture, painting, stop-motion animation, and more, exploring gendered, sexual, and disabled embodiment. Harrod's solo exhibitions include *Tough Nut* (2023), *Hatch* (Los Angeles), and *Rope* (Seoul). They have received numerous accolades, including a Pew Center Visual Arts Fellowship (2020) and residencies at the John Michael Kohler Arts Center, Fire Island Artist Residency, and Banff Centre. Harrod earned an MFA from the School of the Art Institute of Chicago and is head of Fibers and Material Studies at Tyler School of Art and Architecture at Temple University. They can be reached at jesseharrod@temple.edu.

body, haunting

Lohitha Kethu

Informed by their medical art training, Lohitha's personal work explores the body, disability, rage, spirituality, gender, sexuality, and all of the mess in between. While illness has impacted their life in irreparable ways, they are learning to relate to the body, not its ability to produce but as a collection of fluid desires, obscenities, offerings, and connections. Truly achieving peace with one's body or ability is ongoing and complex; what happens when one stops fighting their own bodymind? Does your body become a part of mine, and mine a part of yours?

WSQ: Women's Studies Quarterly **53: 3 & 4 (Fall/Winter 2025)** © 2025 by Lohitha Kethu. All rights reserved.

Lohitha Kethu, *body, haunting*, 2023. Digital painting.

Lohitha Kethu (they/them) is an award-winning South Asian, queer, disabled medical illustrator, artist, and writer based on the east coast of the United States. They have illustrated books on health literacy and have been published in a number of independent journals and zines. Their research and artistic interests include the roles of technology and spirituality in experience of sexuality, gender, illness, and grief. Their work can be found at lohithakethu.com. They can be reached at lohitha.kethu@gmail.com.

SECTION II. **ARTICLES**

"Where Did Your Revolution Go?":
A Fleshly Narrative of Enghelab-e Jina

Niloofar Rasooli

Abstract: This paper narrates Enghelab-e Jina through the lens of embodied knowledge, reading the revolution as lived, felt, known, desired, and dreamed by the collective body. It challenges linear frameworks for interpreting revolution, proposing instead the wound as a site of remembrance and resistance, and as an epistemological ground for understanding and narrating revolutionary dreams and desires, continuities, and connections. Drawing on Black, Indigenous, queer, and other liberatory traditions, it theoretically and methodologically shifts writing about revolution in Iran by centering anonymously authored feminist texts. Ultimately, the paper proposes writing revolution from the flesh as a practice of accounting for the intertwined and interconnected revolutionary dreams and desires that help us insist on livability in the face of negation. **Keywords:** Enghelab-e Jina, body, wounds, writing from the flesh, revolution

See this body, and observe the entirety of the history.

—L

This text emerges from a question that has never left me: "Where did your revolution go?" Nearly two years have passed since the state murder of Kurdish Jina Amini in Tehran, Iran, in 2022, which ignited widespread unrest. Some called it the "Woman, Life, Freedom" movement, stripping it of its Kurdish revolutionary roots. Others saw it as a transnational "unifying axis for grassroot resistances" (Kermanian 2024, 797). Some named it "Ghiyam-e Jina" (Jina's Uprising). Many embraced "Enghelab-e Jina" (Jina's Revolution), reclaiming the term *enghelab* (revolution), which had long been monopolized and capitalized by the Iranian state to be used in a new way: a feminist one. Yet many hesitated to call it a revolution, arguing

WSQ: Women's Studies Quarterly 53: 3 & 4 (Fall/Winter 2025) © 2025 by Niloofar Rasooli. All rights reserved.

that given the absence of clear political change, no revolution had occurred. This lack of resolution granted them permission to ask: "Where did your revolution go?"

Those days, when I received this question and when so many people suddenly became interested in Iran, are long gone. At this moment, as I write this essay, their focus has shifted elsewhere: to the humiliating suffering of massacred Palestinian bodies and to the suppression of any revolutionary voice attempting to forge a coalition to stop the genocide. Yet here I am, thinking, remembering, re-feeling, and writing *Enghelab-e Jina* in these very moments, trembling, terrified. I rarely hear the question "Where did your revolution go?" anymore, and this is precisely why I feel compelled to write now, knowing that, except for the wounded, no one else expects this text— perhaps for the better.

What becomes of Enghelab-e Jina? What happens to any feminist revolution? How do we read, embrace, feel, and theorize revolution when the bodies of our sisters bear its scars? When violence is inscribed on our flesh, where do we seek refuge? Whose revolutionary theory holds our wounds of revolution close? I write this text not to provide precise answers to these questions but to narrate a feminist revolution founded on the collective body and its wounds, sprouting the lexicon of insisting and resisting.

To write *Enghelab-e Jina* from the flesh, I do not wish to bring yet another fleshless theory of a revolution but to carve it from the collective body, its many wounds, desires, and dreams. In my desire to keep conclusions and gods outside the lines of this text, I intimately follow the tradition of fleshly writing, as practiced by Black, Indigenous, and radical queer feminists of color. It is in following this path that I hear Gloria Anzaldúa calling me to write with the "tongues of fire"—to open our wounds, but never in recon- ciliation with "the oppressors who whet their howl on our grief" (Anzaldúa 2021, 161, 171). I hear Dionne Brand and think of the wish to write the fleshly revolution as a way of "moving the pen in scars" (Brand 2023, 59). I think with Jennifer C. Nash and wonder how the very practice of fleshly writing must "stay close to the bone" (Nash 2024, 4, 25–47). I let this text dream of revolution in the manner of Dian Million's "intense dreaming" (Million 2011, 2014). And above all, I keep Linda Tuhiwai Smith's words close and dear, that we must "tell our own stories, write our own versions, in our own ways, for our own purposes" (Smith 2022, 31).

Black and Indigenous feminisms, alongside many other liberatory tradi- tions, teach us that writing about our lingering flesh wounds must be a practice of dreaming and dignity—of weaving liberatory stories that help us in insisting on livability in the face of negation. To write from the flesh is to uphold our own ways of knowing, our own life-affirming practices of revolt, and, to think with Christina Sharpe, embracing our own sensibilities of "defending the dead" (Sharpe 2016, 10). To write revolution from the flesh is to set aside justification and argumentation, gods and conclusions, and instead let it be a reckoning—a refusal of words that reek of victimizing rhetoric, as well as a re-creation of a tapestry of imaginaries. Writing fleshly is what Fargo Tbakhi calls as to "write with sharper teeth" (Tbakhi 2023). It must cut, unsettle, and lay bare the raw nerve of resistance. The reason for writing in this fleshly way is simple, and Katherine McKittrick reminds us why: "We know more than the abjectness that is projected upon us. We are not obsequious. We are not abject. We know more. We know. We know ourselves" (McKittrick 2020, 46).

This text is built upon the vast and diverse writings of the anonymous fighters of Enghelab-e Jina—those who return from the streets, bleeding yet unbroken, writing, inscribing, and insisting on narrating from and for the flesh. It is my intention to cite and center anonymously written pieces as the heart of theory. Citation can be an act of liberation, particularly when writing revolution from the flesh. McKittrick reminds us that citation, beyond the referential politics of calculating names, can rearrange voices, unsettle power over the voice, and thus, offer "a suggestion for living differently" (McKittrick 2020, 19). My citational practice here is one of weaving—stories into theories and theories into stories. With this, I wish to liberate "revolution" from the constraints of rigid theorization and destiny-driven narratives, envisioning it instead as a tapestry filled with many life-forms—born and raised between its warp and woof, in its torn pieces, its worn edges, and in the many definitions and stories of flesh.

The voices I gather here hum and echo through every line and word, shaping the contours of this text into what Sara Salem calls "a felt-archive" of a revolution (Salem 2021). Perhaps, in some way, this text dreams of being June Jordan's "living room" for those anonymous writers and fighters—a space "where the land is not reduced to a tombstone" (Jordan 2021, 94) but remains alive, giving life to the bruised living and the beaten dead alike. Echoing these voices in my heart, thoughts, flesh, and words, I see this text as my love letter to those who hold and uphold their wounds, teaching us many revolutionary dreams and strategies, showing that there is still light left for those of us who demand a world beyond the rhetoric of dehumanization and destruction. I write this text from my flesh and for the fleshly lives and afterlives of any feminist revolution—past, present, or future.

Where Can a Revolution Go?

"Where did your revolution go?" folks in Zurich's left circles often asked me. Whether on podiums, panels, or stages; during solidarity parties or radio interviews; on May 1, at Das Andere Davos,[1] on March 8, or at FLINTA* meetings[2]—it mattered little which collective, group, or media outlet invited me to speak. The last question was always the same: "Where did your revolution go?"

The very first time I heard this question was in November 2022. In Iran, the streets were still busy, bloody, and boiling, with the first wave of executions looming on the horizon. Nothing had been concluded. Yet, for many comrades in Zurich, I was invited to their panels to be the mouth that announced an early failure. Their Swiss politeness kept them from delivering the verdict themselves. I never did. It was never over.

They had their reasons: Without a head and a tail, a defined path, and an even more defined destination, without a father holding his book of revolution in hand, there could be no revolution. To them, "the thing happening in Iran" was significant. It could portray many radical things; it could be a revolt, a resistance, a reclamation, an uprising, or an unrest. It could be many things and anything, but not *enghelab*, not revolution. To some, the political core of the unrest in Iran was more about "liberal rights," perhaps a delayed echo of "my body, my choice."

"What do you think of women burning their veils?" This more "polite" question surfaced in conversations, layered with suspicion. What mattered more to them than the burning bodies were the burning veils. It made them uncomfortable—ignorant. They struggled to hear the "compulsory" *before* "veiling." They held more opinions than inquiries. They showed little interest in understanding how "compulsory veiling" in Iran carries vastly different connotations than it does in the West. To them, the West's political context had to define the lived realities of the rest. The issue of veiling had to fit perfectly within their framework, with its politics and arguments rooted in the fascist implications and agendas prevalent in the West. "Contextualization" was as irrelevant a word as "compulsory" with respect to veiling in Iran. Anything beyond, or not directly tied to, Western political context was seen as either suspicious or of little internationalist value—too complicated to bother with.

Understanding the complexities of weaponizing the veil—not as a religious symbol or personal choice but as an authoritarian political tool in Iran—was utterly irrelevant to those in Zurich. Meanwhile, the fascist media eagerly rode its Islamophobic and xenophobic horse, taking delight in labeling "the thing happening in Iran" as "anti-hijab" protests. It mattered little how many times one had to explain that things are not about (the Western understanding of) hijab in Iran. The Left in Zurich mostly preferred to leave things unaddressed because, as they put it, "it is not politically correct for us to enter the subject." Who asked them to enter the subject? Their lingering fear was being labeled "Islamophobes"—not by us, the Muslim women, but by their other white leftist queer friends. If the language of "civilizational feminism," as Françoise Vergès shows, is "You don't have freedom. You don't know your rights. We will help you reach the right level of development" (Vergès 2021, 14), then "You don't have theory. You don't know your correct terms. We will help you reach the right level of correctness" is that of the Western left's intellectual saviorism.

"But really, where did your revolution go?" Hearing their question, Sara Hegazi's voice would echo in my head: "Those who make a half-revolution dig their own graves" (Hegazi 2020).[3] So, where did it go? "Half of it is happening, and the other half is digging itself into the grave." This was my reply—not to them, but to myself, in my head.

Revolting under the Western left's gaze: They were eager to hear us but had little interest in listening. Our stories had to align with their theories. Everything had to be clear-cut, either/or, with the center of evaluation being how things were perceived within their own contexts, and what they considered to be knowledge. Their aim was not to learn revolutionary lessons, let alone dare to shatter their assumptions about us, but mostly to know precisely how to politically position themselves in relation to Iran—so as not to be criticized or called out (again, not by us, but by their own comrades, for we were not their comrades).

It took some digging for me to realize that the issue was not just a matter of disagreement about the means and meanings of revolution but rather about their already shaped ideas on anti-imperialism and the geopolitics of contemporary Iran. Some implied their mistrust, questioning how one could be sure that the movement was not merely Western propaganda aimed at undermining the so-called anti-imperial politics of the current Iranian state. In general, the question of contemporary Iran, when presented to the Western world, is largely required to fit within two frames: It must either satisfy liberal feminist or homonationalist views by depicting Iran as a hell for women and queer people, or as Ghoncheh Ghavami and Bahar Noorizadeh point out, it must present the country as either "a case of failed or triumphant antagonism against American imperialism" (Ghavami and Noorizadeh 2024, 2). Responding to the same concern, Aytak Dibavar beautifully says: "To hell with liberal feminist agendas and white savourism, to hell with neoconservative propaganda." Instead of being trapped in the colonial and imperial dualistic modes of argumentation, Dibavar writes, "we need a space to think for ourselves, to imagine for ourselves, to talk to each other, and to DESIRE" (Dibavar 2023, 183).

Surely, the way our realities are deemed irrelevant by both liberal feminists and the Western left means that their reductive theories and analyses of us remain equally irrelevant to us. We know that, for the most part, we have only ourselves in our fights. And what a privilege it would be to revolt hidden from the Western gaze. This, however, never means political loneliness. We have each other. Enghelab-e Jina is the explosion of many already existing tongues speaking on their own behalf—loud, sharp, unapologetic. We are fighters, sisters, mothers, and lovers, doing the collective labor of dadkhi (justice-seeking) from this vast, unmourned corpse of pain and loss. We are not sudden existences, even though the world is just discovering our presence. We have long been here: "We have long been the dreamers of Azadi" (Bahar 2023, 12:26–29).

The Left in Zurich was not the only group of impatient seekers of gods and destinations—there were others. Many male Iranian intellectuals, if not all, invoked the gods of the Western Left, lamenting the absence of deities in revolts born from wounds. Hegel, Marcuse, Adorno, Arendt, Habermas— all were summoned from their other lives to serve as judges, evaluating the "worth" of our struggles, debating whether it was a revolution, a revolt, or an uprising, and questioning whether it would lead to something—or if it was anything at all. At best, the conclusion referred to Asef Bayat's view: a "non-movement." A negation, "the revolution of the hopeless"—a nonentity—was all such theorizing could offer.[4]

Understandably, the weight of countless unrealized dreams of freedom has long burdened those who carry such demands in their hearts and pens.

People, including male intellectuals, are exhausted, paying a high price, and enduring the daily grind of hopelessness. This is further compounded by the ever-growing fascist rhetoric against the Iranian left in general.[5] Certainly, our male comrades suffer no less under the sharp claws of fascism. They are our comrades, but that does not exempt them from criticism, nor should it prevent us from imagining revolution differently from them.

Revolution is more than just a slogan; it is a collective labor over time. As Pat Parker reminds us, *"it's not neat or pretty or quick"* but, rather, *"a long dirty process,"* a difficult work of willing and wishing to make things happen and keeping the flame burning still, all against what time dictates (Parker 2021, 241, emphasis in original). Only those who have labored and seen their efforts turned against them can tell us how this continuous state of nonhappening feels—and the harm it inflicts on our critical imaginations, our words, and our very dreams of freedom. But we are not lacking in words. We are more than bodies thrown onto the streets—beaten, shaken, taken away, stolen, imprisoned, tortured, executed. We have words, many of them. Living through counterrevolutions does not equate to rejecting the very idea of revolution. We continue making feminist revolutions—on the terms of our wounded bodies, for ourselves.

What sums up many writings of Iranian leftist male intellectuals? Assigning patriarchy solely to the state—leaving the evil to the evil. Easy. And yes, there is anger boiling between these sentences. And yes, many of us still hold angry questions, refusing to shy away from asking them: How could they so easily absolve themselves of our wounds? They should have known better, that we, the writers and bodies they never read, let alone cited, carried the bruises of patriarchy and gendered violence, of homophobia, class oppression, and ethnic erasure, inflicted both by the state and by our dear male comrades. Was Adorno dearer to them than our wounds? We had to defend our throats and flesh while also harshly rejecting any narrative of "saving brown women from brown men," against any genocidal claims of making brown and Muslim men into angry, homophobic, violent savages—"big bad wolves with furrowed eyebrows, sharp fangs, and terrifying political incorrectness" (El-Kurd 2023). While we were—and still are—rightfully and unconditionally defending them against racist, colonial, and imperial theories of supremacy, they were—and still are—citing those same theories to analyze the "success" and "values" of revolts that emerged largely from the wounds of our bodies. They had little interest in holding up a mirror to see their own reflection—to consider how, in the face of "what was happening," they, too, could engage in self-reflection and ask themselves about their contribution to our wounds. They could "reach down into that deep place of knowledge inside themselves and touch the terror and loathing of any difference that lives there." They could "see whose face it wears" (Lorde 2017, 113). But most of them never did.

Those rushing to their high-theoretical tool kits to debate an unrest branding itself under the slogan of Jin, Jiyan, Azadi, had little interest in engaging with the theories or writings of jins, zanan, or women. Saba Memar (2025), in her profound response and critique of the structural erasure of non–cis men in leftist intellectual arenas in Iran, particularly after Enghelab-e Jina, coins a term: *andishmardan*—"menthinkers." As Memar argues, "If in the past men commanded us *what to be*, the intellectuals of our time are constantly striving to tell us *how to be* and *how to think*" (Memar 2025). To andishmardan, white left theory is god, and before this god, the writings of women and queer, trans, Kurdish, Baluchi, Arab, Afghan, and Azeri people, as well as many other "wretched" voices, are unworthy of the divine: raw, unshaped, weak, too angry; not discursive, dialectical, Marxist enough; and lacking the "academic rigor" required to theorize a sacred keyword like *revolution*.

At best, they adopt a Western understanding of "inclusivity," inviting women and gender-nonconforming people primarily to serve as moderators for their discussions: "They say they need a woman and a queer person; you are both, even better. This way, we don't have to bring two of you."

A friend reads these words: "Dari ba dom-e shir bazi mikoni" (You are playing with the lion's tail). Am I? Are we? She laughs. We both know we aren't just poking the lion's tail but its head. Still, the lion's preference is to ignore or dismiss us—*because we write emotionally*—see us as nonexistent—*because what we say comes from anger, not theory*—some flies who will soon disappear—*better to be quiet, listen to their heated political conversations and prepare the tea while they are debating, put it on the table, and then disappear*—into the kitchen or depression—*see, we are overtaken by our sentiments*. Don't disturb the lion, he is busy tweeting about revolution, theoretically.

If "Where did your revolution go?" was the oft-asked question of the Western Left, then "Is it a revolution or what?" was that of Iranian male intellectuals. What united both lines of questioning was an anxiety over the shortcomings of the gods when faced with a revolution born from the collective, nonmale wounded body—its knowledge of flesh, its generationally inherited pain, and the anger lodged in its throat. But the wounded ones already knew: "All the gods are dead." As Mina Jafarisabet says, "Even if the gods themselves are unaware of their own death, many of us have already witnessed the castration of all the gods of history" (Jafarisabet 2022).

Let us remember what bell hooks taught us, that "theory is not inherently healing, liberatory, or revolutionary. It fulfills this function only when we ask that it do so and direct our theorizing towards this end" (hooks 2014, 61). Let us hold Barbara Christian's fear deeply and dearly: "My fear is that when Theory is not rooted in practice, it becomes prescriptive, exclusive, elitist" (Christian 1987, 58). Let us hear the words of Dian Million, that "theory may also colonize" (Million 2014, 37). Surely, a feminist revolution must first and foremost cause a crisis with gods and their fixed and fixating tool boxes of theory, challenging the very way the notion of revolution has been frozen, trapped, singularized, and made elite.

It is not we who will deal with how the revolution is theorized. The revolution needs to deal with us.

The Wounded Knees

For me, the idea of writing revolution through collective wounds comes from a conversation with a dear friend in Iran, from which I will mostly share a fragment: "They can't take them out. Eighteen pellets. I bend my knees, and I remember everything. The pain isn't like when I was shot, but sometimes, when it's too cold or too hot, the pellets burn deeply. Then I remember everything—every moment of it. So, NO! DO NOT WISH ME TO HEAL."

Almost two years have passed. I have exhibited these eighteen pellets, which inhabit nowhere in my body, in the vitrines of my writings and readings. I have spoken about these wounds as if they were mine. They are not. I pay no price for them. While the pain has caused another body to suffer, I have suffocated myself in the effort to theorize and historicize these wounds, to extract meaning from something that needs no meaning, no analytical framework, no theory, no story from me. Who am I to do so? Many times, I ask myself: Where does this entitlement come from? Am I, too, turning into a Theoretician? These wounds do not leave me alone. They hurt in my body. Perhaps, by now, a thick layer of fat has encircled each of them—the body giving shelter to its invaders. Am I, too, an invader? Is this my presence?

"My knee is wounded / see How I Am Still Walking" (Chrystos 2021, 53). I read and reread Menominee poet Chrystos's "I Walk in the History of My People." Is history a wounded walking thing, limping, dragging itself across stones, asphalt, tombstones? In "Tarikh-e ma ra Kasi Minevisad dar Ruzegar-e Tigh?" (Will Anyone Write our History in the Era of Razor?; Karan 2024), Karan's question urges us to insist on telling our stories, holding "the razor" against time, and writing our futures from those limping knees, embodying the lingering pasts. Can the knee be an archive? If so, what do we wish to archive in and with these wounds? What exactly do we wish to remember? Let me re-pose what Saidiya Hartman asks: "How might one write the disaster, the terrible history carried in our gestures, residing in our bodies, marked on our flesh, etched onto our retinas?" (Hartman 2023, 226). The voice echoes again, dignified and resolute: "DO NOT WISH ME TO HEAL."

Among the many critical and collective tools that wounds offer us, one is their role as repositories, holding our otherwise unarchivable fleshly moments of rebellion. In this context, the wound becomes part of a collective political project, the one that defies the dictates of time and space, their forces, and their limits. In thinking about wounds as "felt-archives" (Salem 2021), I draw on the writing of Elahe, a feminist activist and researcher from Iran, who addresses the challenge of preserving personal memories of a movement under conditions of fear, terror, and scrutiny (Elahe 2024, 27–31). Elahe asks: Where can such moments be kept when a line, a word, a phone call, or a thought—whether written or unwritten, existent or nonexistent—can be used as evidence against the person involved and their intimate circles? The answer is simple: nowhere.

If one fights with love in Iran, they must know to set their chat histories with friends, lovers, and family members to self-destruct or avoid as few social media traces as possible. If one lives with love in Iran, they already know how to exist and archive the traces of life across many nowheres, through countless ruptures in memory. But where do these memories go if they are shaped by the awareness of their inevitable loss? What is the geography of this nowhere? Elahe offers us a concept to consider: "memory-archive." This is the nowhere of collectively remembered moments with little evidence, a space that lives in many "holes born of erased personal memories" (Elahe 2024, 31). Thinking alongside Elahe, we see that wounds can be one of many nowheres of revolution: the temporal geographies of the collective memory. One's wound becomes another's history. Another's wounds become one's memory. And willing the wound not to heal ensures that something remains deep within, in flesh. "So, NO! DO NOT WISH ME TO HEAL."

Seeing wounds this way, as the storage of revolutionary and freedom dreams, helps us better understand the meaning of *badan-e jamie* (the collective body), its knowledge of the flesh, its spontaneity, and its affinity to other wounded bodies. In this sense, the wound becomes a source of knowledge, the place from which the collective body takes action, where it remembers itself, and where it organizes and mobilizes its desires and dreams. It is no wonder, then, that badan-e jamie is central to the writings of many rebel bodies of Enghelab-e Jina, and that it is this felt, collective wound, rather than a clear-cut organizational structure, that transforms many anonymous bodies into figures of resistance.

"What desires were released from the prison of our bodies during these days!" These are the words of L (2022), an anonymous writer, whose text "Figuring a Women's Revolution: Bodies Interacting with their Images" was published less than a month after the unrest began, and remains one of the defining framings of Enghelab-e Jina as a feminist revolution told through wounded and resisting bodies. Among the many moments that L brings from the street to the text, one of the most striking is how the resisting body relates to its wounds: "The body is 'warm' when it is being beaten, and we don't experience pain in the way we might expect" (L 2022). And the cooling, L explains, is when "the memory reaches the body." Seeing bruises, for L, is the body remembering. And what does L remember in that moment? "I had not simply been beaten; I had also resisted and threw a few punches and kicks. My body had unconsciously performed those things I had seen other protestors do" (L 2022). What stands out in narrating revolution through the collective wounded body, as L demonstrates, is a complete departure from understanding the body as a commodity—something static, defined, regulated, binary, or passive. Instead, L allows the body to teach us about its own authority, will, and desires. It guides us to places our minds might not think to go, revealing its revolutionary capacities—capacities we never knew existed.

L teaches us that a body, once committed to rebellion with its bare flesh, can never return to being the same body as before. The revolution might not end as intended. The dream might bring more death than freedom.[6] And yet, something has radically shifted: the body, growing new wounds over the old ones. Time ruptures. The body now knows too much about itself—a dangerous kind of knowledge. Its skin has developed a radically different affection for and dedication to the resistance. It has tasted liberation, if only for seconds. This skin now produces knowledge of pain and weaves it into the skin of others in pain, for the sake of collective dignity. This skin remembers, insists, and holds each of its wounds. It resists healing.

To feel and know revolution is to learn, unlearn, and relearn the body. It is a collective return to the body—to be surprised by the wounded knees still running, to witness the mouth unlocking itself, unleashing screams from an unknown depth, not from the throat but from the belly. It is to begin learning each muscle one by one: to understand which muscle can hide, which one hold, which can pull, which can shake, which can shoot.

I write these sentences, and in between the words, I hear screams, explosions, sirens, blood, sweat, tears. I remember those few seconds when I felt liberation; it is still here, in the flesh of these fingers typing.

"Memory serves. We re-member hundreds of thousands of relationships—to wind, to flora, to fauna, to humans, to the dead, the star world, sky world, sea world," writes Lee Maracle, offering us the keyword of "re-membering" to grasp the many ways in which the wounded body upholds its collective memory (Maracle 2016, 27). Memory serves in the wounds, and as Niharika Pandit states, re-membering can function as "an embodied presencing" (Pandit 2023, 102–22).

To name and own our wounds, to theorize from the collective body, is to cause a radical rupture in the ways wounds are often disregarded. As . . . , the anonymous writer from Iran, states: "All over, our bodies are full of wounds and injuries that [we] have never talked about, because [if we do so,] we ourselves will be blamed for our wounds" (. . . 2022). Seeing our wounds as radical sources of dismantling intersecting structures of oppression, as . . . writes, means coming to understand them as revolutionary resources, of weaving many bodies in pain together, and remembering that "we draw our courage from our wounds" (. . . 2022).

But do all wounds lead to such radical responsibility? The answer is simply no. Like revolution, wounds can rot, turn inward, leave worms, and their stench may be tolerated only by themselves. Revolution and wounds are not inherently liberating. If not kept fresh, woven beyond their borders, wounds can become the source of exceptionalist supremacy, even to the point of humiliating others' wounds in pursuit of purity in one's own. See how the wounds of Palestinians and Arabs have been demonized and dehumanized by those self-proclaimed Iranian feminist "leaders." See how the ongoing fascism against Afghan people in Iran is ignored by them. See how those who brand themselves under the Persian-only flag of "Woman, Life, Freedom" react when an Afghan, Kurd, Baluch, Azeri, Arab, or any other ethnic, rural, poor, or working-class person criticizes Iranian feminism from any perspective other than the center. See what happens if we point to the capital they have gained in our name. See what happens if we disrupt their capital, if we strike, if we speak in our own wounded tongues, if we write from our working hands, if we make coalition with Palestine. Wounds are not inherently liberating.

Wounds, in their flesh, are fabric. They are woven materials. If we fail to see them as inherently part of a weaving practice, as transborder and transnational matters, if we do not constantly refresh our wounds through each other's pains, if we singularize and freeze them, we risk distorting them with supremacism. Wounds can be co-opted as excuses for murder and oppression. After all, wounds are bloody being.

Wounds are liberatory when they are put into relation with our collective liberations. Hear Dasgoharan, a collective of Baluch women, when, in solidarity with Palestine and against any co-optation of the Baluch struggle to fuel anti-Palestinian rhetoric, it unapologetically says: "From Baluchistan to Palestine, Jin Jiyan Azadi" (Jina Collective 2024).

> Whoever I am
> I must believe
> I am not
> and will never be
> the only
> one who suffers (Moraga 2023, 86–87)

Everywhere as Weeds

A feminist revolution is a matter of "everywhereism": a way of stretching everywhere like weeds, growing here and there, upholding collective roots dearly, persisting in growth though constantly cut, expanding, and becoming those "space invaders" (Puwar 2004). Let me explain what I mean by "weeds" and why I think of the feminist revolution in these terms.

"Hiz toei, Harzeh toei, Zan-e Azadeh Manam" (You are the pervert, you are the ruined, I am the free woman). Among the many slogans that emerged during Enghelab-e Jina, this one stuck with me, mainly because of the word "Harzeh." *Harzeh* is an insult derived from *harz*, meaning wasted, ruined, pointless, or wrong, often with a sexual implication. Like many sexualized insults, *harzeh* defines a body within a structure of time and space. *Harjaei-budan* (being of everywhere) is also an insult, implying the same constraints as *harzeh*, of a woman who goes everywhere and does everything. This makes me think of "everywhereism" as a way to reclaim sexualized insults by distorting the temporal and spatial constraints they impose. This is why I think of a feminist revolution through alaf-e harz, the weeds. Zan-e harzeh (ruined woman) and alaf-e harz share much in common: both are harjaei, of everywhere. They are the wronged ones, whether bodies or plants, not knowing their spatial and temporal limits, going and growing where they should not, and always, moving, appearing, growing. Zan-e harzeh and alaf-e harz are both disruptive and disturbing by their very existence— they refuse to disappear. They resist being defined by a single root, cause, or end—they are unpredictable, uncontrollable, undefinable. Above all, they seem harmless, understated, weedy, erasable, bodies coming out of nowhere and disappearing into nowhere, lacking god, father, map, road, or destination. This is where the power of weeds lies. They are "nobodies," the wrong, the ruined, the out-of-place ones. They do not seek recognition, neither visibility nor legibility. There is no desire for that, only for disturbing, disrupting, dismantling.

"Freedom is inextricably bound and attached to the concept of space, and is realized or not realized depending upon the access or restriction placed on individuals and their communities within the space they are entitled to occupy and utilize," Lee Maracle writes (2016, 125). Enghelab-e Jina echoes Maracle's words, reflecting how what was—and still is—disturbed and distorted is the linearity of space and time: how the wounded body, again and again, self-determines its own geography and temporality, owing no explanation to anyone but its growing roots.

There is much freedom dreaming embedded in the shape of each and every weed.

Parva, a feminist and social researcher from Iran, views Enghelab-e Jina as a pluralistic feminist revolution with no singular, predetermined goal, god, or end. In "Inflection Points of a Pluralist Feminist Revolution," Parva (2024) teaches us that theorizing a feminist revolution requires dismantling the linearity of time and its promises of the future. She writes, "the time for this revolution is not the future" but, rather, "akin to a future in the past, a time that has begun but has not concluded, and is now 'picked back up' somewhere in the past" (Parva 2024, 58). Parva reminds us that a feminist revolution "springs from many places and seeks diverse ends. It does not uphold one kind of life as the best, right kind of life. No 'one' bears responsibility for its future, nor is it meant to reach 'one' ideal destination" (57). So, where does a revolution go? Parva answers, it goes into "many revolutionary ends," all of which share one thing in common: "ingraining the habit of resistance" (59).

"Where did your revolution go?"

I was asked this question so many times that I started to take it very literally: Where can a revolution go when it is no longer walking in the streets, when it is no longer camping in Maidan, the square? Is revolution a moving being? Does it walk? I sat and envisioned it. I made a list: It can run, it might hide, it must pause, look back, take the hand of the one fallen on the ground, and then run like hell. It can go to read a poem, to a grave, to prison, to exile. It can reside in the throat, in the fists, in the jaw hurting from holding in anger and grinding its teeth. It can go to draft itself in revolutionary statements, many of which are left unfinished, or turn itself into an unwritten poem with just a title. It can emerge as the weeds emerge from our wounds, from us, growing, to us.

A feminist revolution is weeds growing from our many wounded knees. We "sprout from the wound"[7] on our collective bodies. We are weeds. Growing. Intertwining. Spreading. Disturbing. Dismantling.

Niloofar Rasooli is a writer and dreamer from Iran with a radical passion about the intersection of anti-colonial queer feminisms, erased memories and archives, resistance, rebellion, revolution, and the reclamations of the built and lived environment. Previously, Niloofar has worked as a journalist in Iran, and is currently busy writing their doctoral thesis at the Department for History and Theory of Architecture at ETH Zürich. They can be reached at rasooli@arch.ethz.ch.

Notes

1. Das Andere Davos is a yearly counter-gathering organized by Die Bewegung für den Sozialismus (BFS) in response to the World Economic Forum (WEF) annual meeting in Davos, Switzerland.
2. FLINTA* is an acronym, mostly used in German for female, lesbian, intersex, trans, and agender, referring to spaces where cisgender men are not permitted entry. Despite its popularity, especially among white Swiss and German queer groups, for those of us who are not white or see our

3. cisgender men as comrades, this acronym represents a white understanding of feminism and queerness.

3. Sara Hegazi did cite this quote, but I prefer to hear it as if remembering her voice.

4. Asef Bayat's book *Revolution Without Revolutionaries: Making Sense of the Arab Spring*, particularly after the 2019 Bloody November in Iran, has gained popularity specifically among Iranian male left intellectuals. It offers them the term "a non-movement," which they rush to theorize and use to label the worth and degree of people's bloody battles as a negation. Simply put, this term implies a lack of organization and agenda, god and father, road and destination—things desired by the male theorists of revolution. A simple search of "Jina uprising" and "non-movement" will bring you a series of such articulations. Enjoy reading them.

5. One quietly striking recent example is a post published by Abdolreza Davari, a former politician who has served as the chief leader of many official media agencies in Iran, on September 14, 2024, on X. The horrifying post reads: "Since the filthy and traitorous leftists are the greatest enemies of Iran, 'leftist extermination' is the greatest service to Iran and Iranians." The post has not been removed yet. I am grateful to Mahtab Mahboub for her critique of the same quote in an unpublished piece, where she rightly calls on all of us to uphold love in a world that seeks to kill each different part of us in different ways.

6. Think of Palestine! (My thanks to the anonymous reviewer!)

7. The quote comes from an Iranian feminist song titled "Soroud-e barabari" (The Equality Song) or "Javaneh Mizanam" (I Sprout).

Works Cited

... 2022. "Ma Shoja'at-e Khod ra az Zakhm-hayeman Migirim" (We Draw Our Courage from Our Wounds). harasswatch, November 4. https://t.ly/6zqKV.

Anzaldúa, Gloria. 2021. "Speaking in Tongues: A Letter to Third World Women Writers." In *This Bridge Called My Back*, edited by Cherríe Moraga and Gloria Anzaldúa, 163–71. 4th ed. Albany: State University of New York Press.

Bahar. 2023. "Ba'ad az Jina" (After Jina). *Radio Marz*, season 1, episode 58, September 9. https://pod.link/1412116121/episode/73de92bdb9b178a55083dc5eda9c4a1f.

Brand, Dionne. 2023. *A Map to the Door of No Return: Notes to Belonging*. Toronto: Vintage Canada.

Christian, Barbara. 1987. "The Race for Theory." *Cultural Critique*, no. 6, 51–63.

Chrystos. 2021. "I Walk in the History of My People." In *This Bridge Called My Back*, edited by Cherríe Moraga and Gloria Anzaldúa. 4th ed. Albany: State University of New York Press.

Dibavar, Aytak. 2023. "A Short Reflection on the 'Woman, Life, Freedom' Movement." *Kohl: A Journal for Body and Gender Research* 9 (1): 181–83. https://kohljournal.press/woman-life-freedom.

Elahe. 2024. "Cleansing Personal Archives and the Birth of the Black Hole of Collective Memory." Translated by ZQ. *e-flux Journal*, no. 145 (May): 27–31.

El-Kurd, Mohammed. 2023. "The Right to Speak for Ourselves." *The Nation,* November 27. https://www.thenation.com/article/world/palestinians -claim-the-right-to-narrate/.

Ghavami, Ghoncheh, and Bahar Noorizadeh. 2024. "Editorial." *e-flux Journal*, no. 145 (May): 1–6.

Hartman, Saidiya. 2023. "Afterwards: A Room with History." In *A Map to the Door of No Return: Notes to Belonging*, by Dionne Brand, 225–34. Toronto: Vintage Canada.

Hegazi, Sarah. 2020. "The Egyptian Revolution: Nine Years Later." *Springmag,* January 24. https://springmag.ca/the-egyptian-revolution-nine-years-later.

hooks, bell. 2014. *Teaching to Transgress*. London: Routledge.

Jafarisabet, Mina. 2022. "Enghelab-e Jina, Tekrar-e Mokarrar-e Esm-e Khas va Ghofteman-e Tahlili" (Jina's Revolution: The Frequent Repetition of a Specific Name and Analytical Discourse). *harasswatch*, November 3. https://t.ly/e5ALC.

Jina Collective (@jina_collective). 2024. "The Voices of Baluch Women, Dasgoharan." Instagram, June 5. https://www.instagram.com/p /C72BNv1N2K9/?img_index=1.

Jordan, June. 2021. *The Essential June Jordan.* Edited by Jan Haller Levi and Christoph Keller. London: Penguin Random House.

Karan. 2024. "Tarikh-e ma ra Kasi Minevisad dar Ruzegar-e Tigh?" [Will Anyone Write Our History in the Era of Razor?]. *harasswatch*, May 24. https://t.ly/Ekb-q.

Kermanian, Sara. 2024. "Geopolitics of Inter-Subaltern Colonialism and Gender: Challenging Methodological Dualism Through the 'Woman, Life, Freedom' Journey from Kurdistan to Iran." *South Atlantic Quarterly* 123 (4): 779–802.

L. 2022. "Figuring a Women's Revolution: Bodies Interacting with Their Images." Translated by Alireza Doostdar. *Jadaliyya*, October 5. https://www.jadaliyya.com/Details/44479.

Lorde, Audre. 2007. *Sister Outsider*. New York: Ten Speed Press.

Maracle, Lee. 2016. *Memory Serves: Oratories*. Edmonton: NeWest Press.

McKittrick, Katherine. 2020. *Dear Science and Other Stories*. Durham: Duke University Press.

Memar, Saba. 2025. "Zanan va Meydan-e Andishmardan" [Women and the Arena of Menthinkers]. *harasswatch*, February 6. https://harasswatch.com/news.

Million, Dian. 2011. "Intense Dreaming: Theories, Narratives, and Our Search for Home." *American Indian Quarterly* 35 (3): 313–33.

Million, Dian. 2014. "There Is a River in Me: Theory from Life." In *Theorizing Native Studies*, edited by Audra Simpson and Andrea Smith, 31–42. Durham: Duke University Press.

Moraga, Cherríe. 2023. *Loving in the War Years and Other Writings, 1979–1999*. Chicago: Haymarket Books.

Nash, Jennifer C. 2024. *How We Write Now: Living with Black Feminist Theory*. Durham: Duke University Press.

Pandit, Niharika. 2023. "Re-Membering: Tracing Epistemic Implications of Feminist and Gendered Politics Under Military Occupation." *Feminist Theory* 24 (1): 102–22.

Parker, Pat. 2021. "Revolution: It's Not Neat or Pretty or Quick." In *This Bridge Called My Back*, edited by Cherríe Moraga and Gloria Anzaldúa, 238–42. 4th ed. Albany: SUNY Press.

Parva. 2024. "Inflection Points of a Pluralist Feminist Revolution." Translated by ZQ. *e-flux Journal*, no. 145 (May): 55–61.

Puwar, Nirmal. 2004. *Space Invaders: Race, Gender and Bodies Out of Place*. Oxford: Berg.

Salem, Sara. 2021. "(Anticolonial) Revolution as a Felt Archive." *Egypt / Arab World*, no. 23, 123–34.

Sharpe, Christina. 2016. *In the Wake: On Blackness and Being*. Durham: Duke University Press.

Smith, Linda Tuhiwai. 2022. *Decolonizing Methodologies: Research and Indigenous Peoples*. London: Bloomsbury Publishing.

Tbakhi, Fargo. 2023. "Notes on Craft: Writing in the Hour of Genocide." *Protean*, December 8. https://proteanmag.com/2023/12/08/notes-on-craft-writing-in-the-hour-of-genocide/.

Vergès, Françoise. 2021. *A Decolonial Feminism*. London: Pluto Press.

The Body in Paincraft: Queer, Crip Notes on Hurting

heidi andrea restrepo rhodes

Abstract: This essay combines scholarship with personal essay to consider a politics and poetics of pain and what pain can be and do. Drawing primarily on queer, crip, and feminist of color writing as well as my own experiences of chronic illness and its attendant pain, I propose the idea of "paincraft" as a mode of tending our somatic archive and caring for pain's bodily, historical, political, and affective intersections, opening space for new ecologies of being and relation. I suggest that through insisting on pain's very shareability, as well as cultivating practices of kinning with pain, we might divert from assumptions of pain's effects as being only that of suffering and obliteration and cultivate generative possibilities for liberatory worldmaking with and through our individual and collective pain. Ultimately, I ask, "What is a relationship to pain that frees us all?" **Keywords:** becoming, body, crip, ecology, pain, queer

I have always been too sensitive, a weeper
  from a long line of weepers.

I am the hurting kind.
            —Ada Limón, "The Hurting Kind"

We need new, different languages, for what hurts.
            —Mimi Khúc, *Dear Elia: Letters from the Asian American Abyss*

The etymology of the English word *pain* traces back to meanings associated with *penal*—pain's early conceptualizations were inseparable from ideas of punishment. In Christian thought, pain and suffering were seen as payment

WSQ: Women's Studies Quarterly 53: 3 & 4 (Fall/Winter 2025) © 2025 by heidi andrea restrepo rhodes.

to God, punishment for disobeying his authority, the most extreme form of which was hell in the afterlife, the burn of eternal fire. In the biblical story of Adam and Eve partaking of the forbidden fruit of knowledge in the Garden of Eden, God's punishment is doled out through the pain of childbearing and work. The Protestant work ethic took this notion and made work and pain-bearing virtuous endeavors that would be blessed by God with wealth.

Dominant culture in the United States has internalized this ethic and transposes it onto sick and disabled bodies, so that those who are healthy are deemed to be good workers and therefore good citizens of the nation, and those who are disabled, chronically sick, or suffer chronic pain represent the failed work ethic. In Eli Clare's critique of the medical industrial complex, he suggests that the ideology of cure as it has emerged in a context of capitalism makes imperative the overcoming of disability, illness, and pain backed by "the belief that we can defeat or transcend body-mind conditions through individual hard work" (Clare 2017, 10). When we fail to transcend, we are subject to social punishment, along with economic, political, and environmental punishment, as the penal repercussions of our crip "failure" beget further physical, emotional, and spiritual pain.

If the Adam and Eve story is a founding mythology about pain that infuses in the collective imagination a painless, Edenic Human past, we must acknowledge how this informs the ideology of cure and the fantasy of wholly painless futures. This is part of the genealogy of a secularized moralism that blames individuals for their own pain—a pattern only exacerbated by living under a neoliberal order oriented not toward transforming the conditions of possibility for our pain but that responsibilizes us to individually manage our pain in order to maintain our place in the workforce. Western paradigms have inherited from this biblical mythos of original sin and subsequent punishment by way of the pained body. Our subjection to any pain is often understood within an order of behavior, discipline, and meritocracy, leaving us to question, "What did I do to deserve this?"

As Alison Kafer has noted, the focus on the social model of disability, which emphasizes the disabling effects of society and its architectures, "overlooks the often-disabling effects of our bodies" and "renders pain and fatigue irrelevant to the project of disability politics" (Kafer 2013, 7). Consequently, for those of us committed to critiquing and refusing the ideology of cure, it becomes easy, as Kafer suggests, to deny our own pain, as any potential desire to cure our pain is easily interpreted as internalized ableism and submission to, or compliance with, the ideology of cure. For Margaret

Price, the understanding of pain as "bad" threatens a politics that hinges on the insistence of disability's desirability (Price 2015). But, according to Liz Crow, as a result of denying our pain, "our collective ability to conceive of, and achieve, a world which does not disable is diminished" (quoted in Kafer 2013, 8).

It feels important, then, that crip and disabled thought not only stop denying pain or moralizing our desires to be in less pain but also that we must continue to think and feel pain beyond a primarily individualistic framework, toward a generative and liberatory collective politics. In exploring the multiverse of pain, its phenomenological and political-material effects, its practices, I want to ask how crip thought can reimagine our relationships to pain, inviting us to queer, and kin with, pain. That is, how can we tend pain's meaning-making and materializations by refusing to settle into society's too-easy narratives about who is destined for and deserving of pain? What would it look like to kin with pain if kinship were not conceptualized via hetero-nuclear family formations, nor, as Nathan Snaza writes, as something to be claimed "at the level of shared ontologies or ritual practices," but instead as a desired possibility conducive to decolonial tending of worlds that "could be articulated at the level of political orientation and haptic entanglements (that is, relations of care)" (Snaza 2024, 75)?

Additionally, if pain is variably intrinsic to the condition of being alive—however painfully unjust its distribution—I want to consider how we can both diminish pain's suffering *and* cultivate pain's generative qualities. I want to do so by reconsidering what pain *is* and *does,* through a politics and poetics of pain as well as by asking how we might be less victim to pain and in an active praxis of what I am here calling "paincraft." If pain has for many of us been a source of suicidal ideation, paincraft might be those moments when we hack our relationship to pain and divert from suffering's oft-perceived endgame of obliteration. We make ourselves and our world anew not *in spite* of pain and its "kinfolk," as Audre Lorde names pain's accompanying sensations, but harnessing pain and its kinfolk as a potent modality for transforming life (Lorde 1980, 38).

Ultimately, I am interested in how pain's circulations can shift our ontological assumptions about our very being and therefore play a role in transforming our everyday practices of relation toward possibilities for worldbuilding. As Mimi Khúc suggests, "It is okay to hurt. We must allow ourselves to hurt, to trace the losses, the heartbreak, the death. . . . I tell you this to free you, but also to show you how to allow others to be free" (Khúc

2024, 14). The permission Khúc seeks to give us encircles the vortex of the ideology of cure, its mandate to eliminate pain altogether. It asks us to contend with the world that hurts, and our place in it. To spin off Kai Cheng Thom's writing on mental illness, what if instead of "clinging to the fantasy" of a painless existence "in order to deny our suffering, we asked our suffering what it is trying to say" (Thom 2019, 9)? What if turning toward our pain can be an open door to getting freer? In other words, what if we are not seeking the *abolition of pain* exactly (which I believe is an impossible task), but an *abolitionist relationship with pain*?

Languages of Pain

I am in pain almost every day. I wake into the morning hours stiff and aching. I eat the wrong thing, and my gut twists in spasm for hours. The weather changes, and my body is a pressure chamber of screaming bones. I flare from psychological or chemical stress; my limbs swell and hurt. Migraines pierce my skull, transfiguring light and sound into daggers. I get chilled and my immunity dips, the viruses housed in my throat and upper spine tingle in soreness beneath my flesh, at times ravage my face with prickle and sting. I walk too much, and my hips burn, my femoral joint and its benign tumor twinge, my calves tighten, a fire tears through my lower half. In the throes of my moon and the heightened pain signaling of prostaglandins, the dull lightning in my lower back nags; my breasts, their own tender misery. Sharp pains shooting down my thighs weaken my ability to walk. My uterus throbbing can leave me curled up a weight of lead and tears on the floor. The lingering tendernesses of sexual trauma and fibromyalgia threaten vaginal pain in the wake of too-quick moves to penetration. Pain—my own and that of others—asks me to be slow, slow. To listen, attune, and accommodate bodily and psychic needs.

With trauma and grief come pain. The system we live in is painstakingly painful. Those of us who feel everything feel the world. Transduction of history into inflammation, ancestral and collective feeling-with, violence's signal transmission through our ascending and descending pathways. Routes of knowing we cannot continue in this manner of the world, exploited and estranged. Systems of oppression, noxious stimuli. My body-and-psyche a fever of dance between neurons and axons, electrical pulses reaching for relief.

In contrast to biomedicine's claims on pain as private, individualized, tragic, and always to be avoided, crip thought insists on pain's politicization, its place in the public sphere, and the necessity of our relating to it and through it, to bearing it collectively. In speaking of their chronic illness and pain, Johanna Hedva (2022) speculates: "Perhaps the more accurate way to account for myself is to say that I am alive on this planet and imbricated into its social, political, economic, and historical systems." More than biochemical imbalance, depression "could be traced to histories of colonialism, genocide, slavery, legal exclusion, and everyday segregation and isolation that haunt all of our lives" (Cvetkovich, cited in Hedva 2022). A wider network of crip writers and artists extend this proposition to all chronic illness and pain.

As a "hyper-empath," I also absorb the pain of others. My pain reminds me I am ontologically, as Erin Manning (2012) writes, "always more-than-one," spilling beyond the fiction of singularity on which Western individualism hinges. I am body. Virus. Tumor. Lingering sting of venom. Chemical trace. Ancestral memory and epigenetic carriage. As Sara Ahmed suggests, "pain does not produce a homogeneous group of bodies who are together in their pain" (Ahmed [2004] 2014, 31). To assume I fully understand another's pain is to appropriate, reduce, and contain that which is otherwise irreducible and uncontainable, forcing its legibility. This is different than the possibility that pain *does* produce a *heterogeneous* group of bodies who are *together* in their pain.

When I say I share the pain of others, I mean I deeply feel the field of affective intensities ever circulating in the world and its beyond. I mean that my bodymind and its experience is never separable from the bodymind experience of others. I mean we are all made of electricity, accumulations of voltage, all contact points for the jump of a charge, the synaptic arc of pain and pleasure. There is always a bleeding-over, a feeling-with that is a critical element of my being in the world. As a body living a queercrip existence, the binary between pained and non-pained bodies allowing the fiction of pain's unshareability, does not resonate for me. Pain's interdependences mirror the entanglements of our lives in planetary living.

For Alyson Patsavas, "when cultural discourses construct pain as the cause of feelings of devastation, they oversimplify complex cultural, historical, and political phenomena . . . [and] prevent us from examining the structural conditions that *make* experiences of chronic pain tragic" (Patsavas

2014, 204). As much as I have been told by doctors that my pain is the cause of my perpetual sadness, I have also been told many times that my feelings of overwhelming devastation, my depression, are the cause of my pain. (Over and over, I am offered high-dose painkillers and antidepressants as a fix to this cycle in which psychic and physical pain blur.) This, too, oversimplifies complex cultural, historical, and political phenomena, preventing us from examining the structural conditions that leave us in devastated states. It is a great fuckery of capitalism, its making us feel wrong for feeling the world and for not being able to *keep calm and carry on*. To blame us for the weight this gives to our limbs, the flare-up of our nervous systems firing in dismay at the state of the planetary everyday.

If the nervous system is an antenna that exceeds beyond the soma, we are receiving a whole array of sensory and ecosomatic inputs perpetually, inseparable from the pain of the earth and its devastated ecosystems, inseparable from human and more-than-human suffering and life being lived at our doorsteps, as much as half a world away. Yet, we have a limited vocabulary for pain in the Western imaginary. To return to Khúc, "We need new, different languages for what hurts" (Khúc 2024, 13).

Kinning Pain

In "The Pain Scale," Eula Biss writes, "'I breathe, I have a heartbeat, I have pain . . .' I repeat to myself as I lie in bed at night. I am striving to adopt the pain as a vital sensation" (Biss 2007, 82). Can pain also nourish us? In the depths of pain and its isolations, I repeat to myself my own spells: I am alive I am alive I am alive. Through tears, my body curled, crumbled, crumpled: I am alive I am alive I am alive. The pain is both a hell and a vital sensation. Both a foil and a lens onto beauty. As Ashna Ali writes in their Substack, *Pain Baby*: "There are so many routes to God, and my relationship to pain will always be one of them" (Ali 2024).

In his essay "Pain, My Kin" (2020), Travis Chi Wing Lau writes of developing kinship with his pain, refusing resignation to it, and finding ways to live in sustainable relationship with it: a "process that does not shy away from pain's presence but is in fact constituted by pain and its vagaries." What Lau invites us to consider is what happens if we do not disavow our pain, nor force it into performing an aesthetic, nor submit it to the logics of cause and effect or the parameters of Western metaphysics, allowing it instead "no singular origin or conclusion, but a living spectrum beautiful in its fullness, in its shifting forms and intensities" (Lau 2020). The urge to expel pain completely from the body and the body politic belies pain's inevitability.

It is important to acknowledge that pain's distributions across the social field are inequitable and deeply tied to other distributions—of life chances, racial and gendered violence, economic wealth, access to life-giving and life-saving resources, including time off for the body's recovery, et cetera. Escaping pain's grip, or staving it off entirely, tends to come with a certain degree of privilege given the modalities gathered and made available under the Western medical system for contending with pain. But kinning pain isn't about progress narratives that ultimately take us to a linear end of pain's overcoming—a curative model society deploys to blame the individual for *moral* failure. Kinning pain isn't, either, about finding the silver lining, but about cultivating an otherwise of relating to pain. Relating to pain differently means gathering and making available new modalities not beholden to institutional knowledge and intervention. It means that building "a practice of painful kinship feels that much more urgent if only to enable reckonings with our own painful histories and institutions, our own respective relationships with our pain, and with each other as painful kin" (Lau 2020). Can kinning with our pain lead us into new rituals and routes, new ecologies of relation, and tending, caring for, each other's bodies and histories? Can this mean the histories in our bodies, as much as our bodies in time and materiality shaped by the political?

Body-Mind-World: Pain Is Political

Neoliberalism treats chronic pain as a thing to be managed—to be pain-free, we should simply adjust our attitudes, "think positively." But Saraswati reminds us, "pain is never only personal. It is also social, structural, political" (Saraswati 2023, 3). Government policies affect how we carry pain. Racism and patriarchal violence affect how we carry pain. It is a widely known fact that women, queers, trans and nonbinary people, and people of color are not only subjected to greater pain by systems of oppression but are taken less seriously about our pain. We are viewed as having higher capacity to endure pain, for the assumed fact of feeling pain less—a holdover from early scientific models that positioned these groups closer to animality than white, able-bodied, heterosexual, cisgender men. We have also historically been subjected to greater levels of violent experimentation as the medical establishments of both authoritarian and democratic states have sought to understand pain and invent its remedies. Pain is deeply political.

Audre Lorde, in her *Cancer Journals*, reflects: "There is no room around me in which to be still, to examine and explore what pain is mine alone—no device to separate my struggle within from my fury at the outside world's viciousness, the stupid brutal lack of consciousness or concern that passes for the way things are" (Lorde 1980, 12). Is any pain mine alone? Is there any separation to be had between our struggles within and our fury at the outside world's brutal and banal viciousness-made-normal? For Saraswati, pain also "refers to an ecology (which includes human and non-human, and material and non-material) that causes the very pain to begin with" (Saraswati 2022, 11). Is this inseparability between individual and collective pain of the world not pain's trenchant and entrenched ecology? Pain's "materiality of power" (Saraswati 2022, 15), as part and parcel of a larger system of power at work, directly constitutes the whole of our individual and collective experience. But it is also an ecology within which we find power to resist the conditions of possibility for the production of our pain. As Gloria Anzaldúa offers, pain is also "the creation of new forms of being" (Anzaldúa, cited in Saraswati 2023, 4). My pain has led me to people, places, and encounters with art and literature, that I might never otherwise have known. On the other side of every pain flare, I am other than what I was before it began. What is "I" and "mine" has been placed entirely up for question.

We are taught that pain is a feeling, or material effect, of damage done to the body. When in heightened trauma states, pain is increased. In prolonged trauma states, we may feel as though we are always on the edge, barely living, barely holding on. Pain can begin to feel like a meaningless Sisyphean sentence. But pain can be generative and *re*generative, particularly from the liminal spaces those of us in chronic illness know all too well, as we are not dying of our dis-ease, nor are we headed toward cure. Chronic illness is another borderland, and "though it is a source of intense pain, its energy comes from continual creative motion that keeps breaking down the unitary aspect of each new paradigm" (Anzaldúa 1987, 80). In other words, this irresolution, this perpetuity, this pain, in undoing us and bringing us to our knees, might also be a prayer, music, an opening, a way out of modernity's alienated paradigms and the rigid fixity of colonial differentiations.

Further, what if pain is itself many things, does many things? What if it is a field of experience through which we move or curl, immobile, with others? What if it is also an actant within a constellation of actants that include vast and diverse forms of human and more-than-human existence? What if pain does not move through us, but we move through the topography of pain, through its environs? What if we move with and in pain as companion, however imposing and unwelcome at times? Might pain also be the uninvited stranger we open toward?

When Ada Limón writes, "I have always been too sensitive, a weeper / from a long line of weepers. / I am the hurting kind," she names being-in-pain as a genre of existence, an inheritance of sensitivities and pain's expressibility (Limón 2021). She entangles, across space and time, the experience of hurting with the experience of others hurting. In this, pain is deindividuated, disalienated from its relegation to the singularity of body-selves alone in their pain. Etymologically, *hurt* refers to injury and wound but also bears meaning rooted in the Old French *hurter*, meaning "to stumble (into), bump into; charge against, rush, crash into; knock (things) together."[1] I wonder at how this incites us to think about hurting, to think about pain, as always emergent from, and requiring attention to, our contact with others. What formations and practices of care—attunements to each other's pain and tending of collective pain—unfold in the haptic propinquity between bodies, histories, selves? What does that change about collective social orientations to pain as an ethics of relation? And how might tending hurt as stumbling, crashing, knocking encounters, contacts, and intimacies of the historical present allow us to hurt less?

Paincraft

While receiving my first tattoo on a wintery afternoon in Brooklyn—a two-hour-long herbal-medicine-artwork-as-ritual-and-protection-spell undertaking—I experienced a very wide range of kinds of pain within a rather short time. Burning pain. Searing pain. Soft pain. Drilling pain. Sweet pain that sent pleasure through my whole body. Numbing pain. Pain that made my bones scream beneath my skin. Pain that awakened me, sharpened my vision. Pain so polyvalent it actively confounded any placement or measure on a scale. Sensory voices moving between harmony and dissonance in complex arrangement of song, my pain, a chorus of many.

Through it, I found myself reflecting on my relationship to my chronic pain and illness, how much time I spend avoiding that pain or preempting it. How I hadn't gotten a piercing in years and had avoided even the needles of acupuncture for over a decade. A small voice in my head asked me, "After years and years of the pain you endure, why seek this out? Is this not entirely counterintuitive? Knowing the correlation between stress and flares of pain, why put your body through this stress?" Reminding myself to breathe, in response, I kept thinking repeatedly, "This is pain I accept. Pain I kin. Pain that weaves me into sustained relation with ancestors. Pain that gifts me."

Hannah Turner (2023) writes about tattoos as a reclamation of chronic pain into evidence, a therapeutic relief brought on through the power of a pain aroused toward beauty. Similarly, I am alchemizing my pain, willing its transfiguration from something that only happens *to* me, to something with which I more deeply kin with others in the world. I open to it, it opens me, drawing deep into my body-psyche, its visual and somatic archive.

It is also a practice in trauma healing. Early in 2023, after over fifteen years of medical appointments and experiments in remedy, trying to figure out the source of my chronic illness, and after many appointments with a new doctor, he told me he believed, through all the tests and clinical history we'd completed, that my chronic illness and pain were ultimately rooted in my complex trauma, my CPTSD. "Western doctors know trauma can flip a switch in the body that seriously impacts the functioning of the nervous and immune systems, among other things, and makes them go haywire. And I'm sorry to say, we don't know how to unflip that switch," he told me. "The best I can offer you is support in pain management such as medication and physical therapy, but I encourage you to seek out other modalities for addressing the trauma at the root of your pain and illness."

This wasn't another in a long line of years of doctors gaslighting me by saying that my illness and pain were in my head, "mere" depression, or simply nonexistent. It was a humble admission of the limits of Western medicine in contending with the body-mind-world connection, a naming of a source of my experience, and an acceptance that the Western episteme is poorly equipped to connect with that source. As for Ahmed, "pain is not simply an effect of a history of harm; it is the bodily life of that history" (Ahmed 2014, 34). My chronic pain and illness are not, of course, imagined but, rather, the bodily life of the history of harms woven through psyche and soma: Generational inheritances of alcoholism, domestic violence, poverty, traumatic family deaths, colonization, war. Childhood and family trauma. Religious trauma. Racial trauma. Financial stress. Homophobic death threats from neo-Nazis and other angry men. Intimate partner violence. Sexual assault. All living an accumulated bodily life in me. I felt both relief and grief in hearing the doctor's conclusion. It was validation of my body-mind-world experience that most doctors had never given me. To accept this premise for my chronic illness gave me a point of departure from which to more intentionally explore healing work beyond the decades of somatic and trauma therapy I'd undertaken, rather than bumping around in the dark as I look for the light. What we inherit of trauma epigenetically, politically, and spiritually is accompanied, too, by what we inherit of resilience, and what we then make of that pain in moving forward, how we transmute it into possibility.

After decades of living in variously fluxing states of hypervigilance and fight, flight, ease, or appease, I began the healing work of trying to teach my bodymind and being that we are safe and do not need to exist in those trauma states perpetually. Tattooing became one experiment among many in this reconfiguring of my body-mind-world and its knowing. If pain is, in part, a message from the bodymind that we are in danger, trauma sets us up to always, on some level, feel as if we are in danger, even when we are not. By telling my body over and over that we were safe while reclined on the table with the artist's needle buzzing, that we were safe within this pain, the experience of the tattoo became a container within which I could help my system in its slow learning that not all situations in which it feels unsafe actually are. This was a clear situation in which the signal of pain did not equate to unsafety or real harm, and in acknowledging that, I was able to both enjoy the pain and feel the pain of that moment lessen. The haptic noise of the pain spreading across my body, from the epicenter of my biceps, quietened. This is, I think, a kind of paincraft.

In the center of the main room of a play party hosted by a QTBIPOC kink community organization, I'm bent over a table being dominated and spanked by P., whose joy in their role in giving me pain is an exuberant and expressive one. They press my face into the vinyl tabletop, tug a fistful of hair at the base of my skull, and with each firm landing of their hand on my ass, a bright and shiny pain shimmers across my skin, up to my skull and down my legs, shivering in my spine. There is an intensity in palm to skin, but I've got nothing but love for this public handling and pain. The pain I feel is not merely in the impact but—differently than kink play with lovers in private spaces—is also a kind of psychic and neurodivergent pain of being exhibited, of feeling the synesthetic piercing of my flesh and being by the onlooking of the crowd, the taste of purple in my want. More a voyeur than an exhibitionist, I do not usually seek to be on display. But this I choose, I invite. It worlds me into a queer public intimacy of eyes that open me, expanding me further into the constellated intersubjective sensations that are the pride and pulse of this party. P. and I share in the joy of this pleasure-pain. It is not joy *in spite of* pain but joy in the making of it. It is a pain of electricity humming through the entire space—a space shaped by a politics of care and queer and trans crip joy, centering COVID safety through mask mandate, centering the pleasure of black and brown bodies—we are in an ambience and social architecture of collective paincraft. Making pain liberatory.

I am alchemized into a flying vapor of flesh and adrenaline, transfigured, a body of bird, my skin sings. When I leave the party, I am a different creature than I was when I arrived. The next morning, I wake up smiling and curled in my sheets, feeling the tenderness of pink—the endurance of the pleasure-pain on and in my body is its own archive of my becoming something otherwise. Pain to which I say yes, pain that gifts me, pain with which I circumvent the being-victim that pain's chronicity can evoke, pain that is instead invocation of my own power to submit. The thing is, our bodies in pain are deemed dangerous, and this is a danger with which I want to kin. Pain I kin and pain with which I kin with others.

As Ahmed writes, pain is "bound up with how we inhabit the world, how we live in relationship to the surfaces, bodies and objects that make up our dwelling places. Our question becomes not so much what is pain, but what does pain do?" (Ahmed 2014, 27). What does pain do, both in the materiality of our lives and in the meaning we make of them? As I write in this moment, I am in another flare of pain and fatigue, bedbound, tender in my belly and my shins, swollen in my joints, unable to eat. As I write this paragraph in this moment, in early December 2023, Palestine is under an ongoing genocidal siege and bombardment by the state of Israel, since October 7, 2023, and over twenty thousand have been killed in less than two months. My beloveds and I weep and speak of this political moment as the most horrific thing we've witnessed in our lives. For, however much we join protests, make art, call Congress, organize mutual aid benefits and poetry readings and teach-ins, Palestinians are still being brutally maimed and killed, bombed and raped and starved, and the United States government continues to fund it. We are watching a genocide livestreamed, unfolding in real time. I do not believe that these two things—this pain flare I am in and this genocide, the pain of Palestinians—are disjointed, but rather, that they are thoroughly entangled. It is nowhere near being an equivalent pain, but they are connected. It is always this way for me, and not isolated to this political moment or geography. My soma reaches and extends through global intimacies of pain across space and time, geographies scattered with pain in what Petra Kuppers calls "pain patterns" (Kuppers 2022, 109). The agonizing paincraft of state violence is a horror regime we also inherit. A machine of pain-making.

To return to Ahmed's questions, what does this pain do? And in what ways is it bound up with how we inhabit the world, how we live in relationship to other bodies, for example, from the center of empire here in these United States? What is the shape of a collective, liberatory paincraft we are called toward, through the modalities and tenets of disability justice? Lilla Watson's famous declaration that "your liberation is bound up with mine" is subtended by the notion that your pain is bound up with mine. Another way to put it: In living in what Denise Ferreira da Silva and Arjuna Neuman name as "deep implicancy," we are bound up with each other not only in these present iterations of body-mind-world but in the primordial process of our mattering (The Showroom 2019). In opening to pain as portal, allowing pain's sharedness to flow through the vast matrix of its topographies, we might further open to an embodied sense of how we are implicated in all other human and more-than-human life, instilling a sense of collective responsibility, calling us to respond.

The Crips for eSims for Gaza mutual aid effort, helmed by a network of crip and disabled activists in the U.S. and Canada, is one example. When the Israeli Occupation Forces cut off Palestinians' Wi-Fi and cellular service, the resources offered by Crips for eSims for Gaza allowed Palestinians in Gaza to access "information, be in touch with their families to let them know they're alive, and . . . to get the word out about bombings and conditions in Gaza" (Shi et al. 2023). The documented activation of over 14,000 of the 18,000 eSims sent to Gaza suggests that while this effort could not end the genocide, it perhaps aided in survival and resistance for thousands living and dying in the disabling environs of the ongoing occupation and its onslaught of atrocities. This disability justice activism also constitutes crip paincraft—the tending to planetary and historical entanglements and deep implicancies of our bodies, lives, and futures, in the attempt to divert from genocide's endgame of obliteration, to make something else possible.

The labor of paincraft as a collective endeavor must also attend to pain's social meanings and mechanisms for its production and mediation, as they have varied across history and geography. Capitalism's upkeep requires regulatory mechanisms for surveilling and controlling our pain. Writing about the opioid crisis in "The Body in Painlessness," Niko Maragos (2018) returns us to the fact that capitalism is a system "that essentially was created to ensure a certain kind of white body relief from pain." In the U.S., that relief has inversely relied on the production, neglect, and denial of Black pain and the pain of migrant workers and disabled people—a fact that has only become clearer since the beginning of the COVID-19 pandemic and Black Lives Matter protests in 2020 (Altschuler and Constantinesco 2024).

Further, the medicalization and subsequent criminalization of pain, manifest in various institutions, according to Michelle Smirnova, "extend and intensify a carceral net that surveilles, controls, and punishes" (Smirnova 2023, 24) groups of people already marginalized and subject to the painful impacts of structural violence lived under a regime of racial capitalism. Pain's shifting definition, within institutions with regulatory power over how pain is addressed, serves this politics of pain deployed in service of maintaining the governability of the population. Summarizing Keith Wailoo's *Pain: A Political History*, Maragos (2018) explains how definitions of pain have "mutated as the courts, the medical establishment, and public opinion reinterpreted it to fit the changing cultural landscape." Shifting criteria for pain's "facticity" were "vital to protecting the nation from the socialist 'Trojan horse' of pain. The body in pain, conservatives would repeatedly (and still) argue, could always be lying."

The system we live under thus operates on the necessity of both meanings rendered in the *minimization* of pain—its pharmaceutical relief enough to keep workers working, as well as the diminution of individual experience as produced within a system. Pain utilized as a mechanism of social regulation means that pain must be seen as individual failure. This is a tactic of capital, to bar pain's articulation in the collective imagination as a political effect in need of addressal. The individualization of pain as an ontological and phenomenological fact keeps us isolated from contending with it politically, collectively.

But, for Claudia Leeb, pain is, under capitalism, "what makes us rebel" (Leeb 2017, 109–40). I have at times wondered if my body in pain is rebelling against capitalism in protest of the fact that the conditions of our existence currently do not allow us to sustain life in these United States without participating in capitalism's physical, spiritual, and relational death march. What, then, is asked of us in cultivating an anti-capitalist, abolitionist relation to pain? What will our pain make us rebel against? What world-building does our chronic pain, as a symptom of a larger ecology of relations, conjure us toward?

Arguing for abolition medicine (which we should distinguish from the abolition of medicine), Yoshiko Iwai, Zahra H. Khan, and Sayantani DasGupta write that police violence is the cause of pain, death, and disproportionate suffering: "Police brutality is a public health emergency" (Iwai et al. 2024, 159). As we work to abolish the police and the carceral systems they serve—these afterlives of slavery that cause disproportionate, massive suffering for specific racialized communities and truly cause harm to all—what is an abolitionist tending of pain? One not contingent on liberal valuations of individualist agency and *choice* as freedom (i.e., "I choose my pain and I am free from all involuntary pain, and therefore am free")? One that nonetheless values the complexities of and call for self-determination that bear upon our political and ethical relations in the search for collective well-being of human and more-than-human life?

In "The Politics of Care," Christopher Paul Harris turns to Afro-pessimism's call to the project of "materially, discursively, and ideationally" undoing the world, as one historically contingent on Black pain as a form of abjection required by white supremacy "for its coherence and preservation," organizing all forms of othering (Woodly et al. 2021, 906). This call to unmake and remake the world is an abolitionist one that is, importantly, oriented toward transforming collective approaches to addressing harm, and therefore, also, pain. As Shatema Threadcraft reminds us in the same article, abolitionism summons us to attend to pain by prioritizing care as a radical praxis rather than resourcing punishment, which only serves to further entrench us in the larger carceral-racial capitalist system, as well as, I would add, the Christian moral narrative of pain's deservedness (Woodly et al. 2021, 901).

The critiques offered by abolitionist thought—of punishment (such as mass incarceration) as a means by which to contend with harm—align with my critique at the beginning of this writing, of pain's genealogical roots in narratives about Christian punishment for transgression of God's authority. In fact, these two formations of punishment are themselves connected as the state assumes a kind of divine-secular authority over the law and its implementation. Common between them is the individualization of responsibility for harm, for pain. Shatema Threadcraft proposes we instead take "collective responsibility to change the social contexts in which (dispro-portionately racist, sexist, homophobic and transphobic [and I would add, ableist] harm takes place" (Woodly et al. 2021, 900–901).

Abolition's worldbuilding endeavor requires this collective responsibil-ity for pain as well. It seeks to honor our haptic entanglements, such that we cannot turn away from the pain of any other, whether our closest and more extended communities or strangers, from those in the prisons stippling the U.S. American landscape to those suffering the more acute genocides of global militarisms. From the river to the sea, the decolonial work of tending the field of pain becomes not a *should* but a *will-have-had-to-have-been* as our tomorrows depend on each other's in a pained futuring for the always-now and not-yet. To echo slant the words of Ashna Ali: There are many routes to liberation, and pain, its metamorphosis by way of collective paincraft, could be one of them. This project demands we see pain not as something that ends us, and, rather, as a potential beginning, an entry point into undoing the world as it is, undoing the occupations at pain's root and rot, becoming otherwise for what might be—a becoming through pain—yours and mine and theirs and those now gone and those to come, at the center of which is the question: What is a relationship to pain that frees us all?

Acknowledgments

Thank you to Adele Failes-Carpenter and MK Thekkumkattil for your care through different stages of this writing, and to the anonymous peer review-ers for your feedback, which helped develop this work further.

heidi andrea restrepo rhodes (they/them) is a queer, crip/disabled, brown/Colombian writer, scholar, cultural worker, and professor of feminist, queer, and disability studies, currently at Pomona College. They are author of *The Inheritance of Haunting* (University of Notre Dame Press, 2019), *Afterlives of Discovery: Speculative Geographies in the Settler Colonial Imaginary* (Duke University Press, 2025), and *Wayward Creatures* (Host Publications, 2025). Their more recent scholarship focuses on queer-crip, abolitionist, and anti-colonial thought and can be found in *Disability Studies Quarterly*, *Feminist Studies*, and *Frontiers Journal*. They can be reached at heidiarhodes@gmail.com.

Note

1. "Hurt," *Etymonline*, accessed April 25, 2025, https://www.etymonline.com/word/hurt.

Works Cited

Ahmed, Sara. (2004) 2014. *The Cultural Politics of Emotion*. Edinburgh: Edinburgh University Press.

Ali, Ashna. 2024. "Priyo@Parlay Returns! Happy Pride! Free Palestine!" *Pain Baby* (blog), June 9. https://painbaby.substack.com/p/priyoparlay -returns-happy-pride-free.

Altschuler, Sari, and Thomas Constantinesco. 2024. "Pain After 2020: An Introduction." *American Literature* 96 (2): 141–62. https://doi.org/10.1215 /00029831-11218858.

Anzaldúa, Gloria. 1987. *Borderlands / La Frontera: The New Mestiza*. San Francisco: Aunt Lute Press.

Biss, Eula. 2007. "The Pain Scale." *Creative Nonfiction*, no. 32, 65–84. http://www.jstor.org/stable/44363570.

Clare, Eli. 2017. *Brilliant Imperfection: Grappling with Cure*. Durham: Duke University Press.

Hedva, Johanna. 2022. "Sick Woman Theory." *Topical Cream*, March 12. https://topicalcream.org/features/sick-woman-theory/.

Iwai, Yoshiko, Zahra H. Khan, and Sayantani DasGupta. 2020. "Abolition Medicine." *The Lancet* 396 (10245):158–59. https://doi.org/10.1016 /S0140-6736(20)31566-X.

Kafer, Alison. 2013. *Feminist Queer Crip*. Bloomington: Indiana University Press.

Khúc, Mimi. 2024. *Dear Elia: Letters from the Asian American Abyss*. Durham: Duke University Press.

Kuppers, Petra. 2022. *Eco-Soma: Pain and Joy in Speculative Performance Encounters*. Minneapolis: University of Minnesota Press.

Lau, Travis Chi Wing. 2020. "Pain, My Kin." *Brevity* (blog), September 21. https://brevity.wordpress.com/2020/09/21/pain-my-kin/.

Leeb, Claudia. 2017. *Power and Feminist Agency in Capitalism: Toward a New Theory of the Political Subject*. New York: Oxford University Press.

Limón, Ada. 2021. "The Hurting Kind." *The Rumpus*, May 6. https://therumpus. net/2021/05/06/rumpus-original-poetry-the-hurting-kind-by-ada-limon/.

Lorde, Audre. 1980. *The Cancer Journals*. San Francisco: Spinsters / Aunt Lute Press.

Manning, Erin. 2012. *Always More-Than-One: Individuation's Dance*. Durham: Duke University Press.

Maragos, Niko. 2018. "The Body in Painlessness." *New Inquiry*, March 28. https://thenewinquiry.com/the-body-in-painlessness/.

Patsavas, Alyson. 2014. "Recovering a Cripistemology of Pain: Leaky Bodies, Connective Tissue, and Feeling Discourse." *Journal of Literary and Cultural Disability Studies* 8 (2): 203–18. https://doi.org/10.3828/jlcds.2014.16.

Price, Margaret. 2015. "The Bodymind Problem and the Possibilities of Pain." In "New Conversations in Feminist Disability Studies," special issue, *Hypatia* 30 (1): 268–84.

Saraswati, L. Ayu. 2023. *Scarred: A Feminist Journey Through Pain.* New York: New York University Press.

Shi, Jane, Leah Lakshmi Piepzna-Samarasinha, and Alice Wong. 2023. "Crips for eSims for Gaza." *Disability Visibility Project*, December 25. https://disabilityvisibilityproject.com/2023/12/25/crips-for-esims-for -gaza/.

The Showroom. 2019. "Denise Ferreira da Silva and Arjuna Neuman: *4 Waters: Deep Implicancy.*" *e-flux*, March 26. https://www.e-flux.com /announcements/251881/denise-ferreira-da-silva-and-arjuna-neuman 4-waters-deep-implicancy/.

Smirnova, Michelle. 2023. *The Prescription-to-Prison Pipeline: The Medicalization and Criminalization of Pain.* Durham: Duke University Press.

Snaza, Nathan. 2024. *Tendings: Feminist Esoterisms and the Abolition of Man.* Durham: Duke University Press.

Thom, Kai Cheng. 2019. "The Myth of Mental Illness." In "Open in Emergency," edited by Mimi Khúc, special issue, *Asian American Literary Review*, 2–10.

Turner, Hannah. 2023. "My 27 Tattoos Have Helped Me Reclaim My Chronic Pain." *Refinery29*, November 28. https://www.refinery29.com/en-us /disabled-chronic-pain-tattoo-therapy.

Woodly, Deva, Rachel Brown, Mara Marin, et al. 2021. "The Politics of Care." *Contemporary Political Theory*, no. 20, 890–925. https://doi.org/10.1057 /s41296-021-00515-8.

"Fat Women Can Be, and Are, Sexy": The DIY Fat Spectacular Aesthetic of April Flores and Carlos Batts's Porn Work

Yessica Garcia Hernandez

Abstract: This article analyzes the porn work of the Latina adult performer April Flores to explore not only how Latina fat sexual futures are represented on-screen but also how they are lived, transmitted, and felt in the body. I focus on the porn work collaboration between Flores and her late husband, Carlos Batts, which featured what they defined as a "DIY spectacular aesthetic"—a cinematographic gaze that captures the futurity of the fat body through a valuation system in which the fat body desires and is desired. Drawing on the notion of the spectacular, I argue that Flores's early porn work created a fat feminist avant-garde aesthetic that mixed art with porn and centered a participatory engagement with fans that used her fat body and her cyborg plastic body as a canvas for the imagination. **Keywords:** Latinx studies, fat studies, porn studies, cultural studies, performance studies

The book *Fat Girl* (2013) captures the life story and artistic journey of Mexidorian performer April Flores.[1] Through seven short chapters and visual storytelling, Flores gives her testimonio of what it was like to grow up as a "chunky" Latina kid in Los Angeles, California, and shows how sex work, particularly the photographing of the fat body, helped her gain a sexual confidence that she is now transferring to her fans. The 127-page volume includes images from Flores's early modeling career taken by her late husband, Carlos Batts, who met Flores and photographed her for the first time in 2000. The book project was first conceptualized in 2005, when Flores and Batts were inspired by the book *Porn Art 2* (Dahmane and des Lysses 1998), a couple's journey of documenting their intimate lives. Flores's

WSQ: Women's Studies Quarterly 53: 3 & 4 (Fall/Winter 2025) © 2025 by Yessica Garcia Hernandez.
All rights reserved.

collaboration with Batts eventually brought her to the adult industry, and she became a pioneer of fat feminist pornography.

When describing her sex work career, Flores acknowledges that her entry into porn was unique, slow, and nontraditional. Batts was her photographer, director, and producer. When she started shooting with Batts, Flores had a full-time job that gave her the opportunity to be selective about whom she worked with. She describes her work relationship with her husband as a form of privilege because few adult performers have the cultural capital to work with their partners and to work at a slow pace. This collaboration allowed Flores to be intentional about her impact and long-standing legacy in the industry. By the time she shot her second film, Flores had proclaimed her purpose in the adult industry: she wanted to use her body and sex work as a vehicle for fat activism, particularly in the realm of representation, but also in teaching other fat girls that their bodies are desirable.

After the publication of *Fat Girl*, Flores went on to receive the first *Adult Video News* award in 2014 for plus-size winner of the year; she received it again in 2015. She was the first Big Beautiful Woman (BBW) to shoot with Kink.com and KinkUniversity.com. She hosted Vivid Radio's show titled *Voluptuous Life* and has made movies in almost every genre of pornography, including hardcore and queer. In 2008, Flores collaborated with Topco Sales, an adult toy manufacturer, to produce the first plus-size sex toy, which was molded from her fat body. Although anti-porn critics (Dworkin 1998; Long 2021) have expressed skepticism about the BBW genre because they perceive it as offensive and humiliating to fat women, Flores's feminist, queer, transgressive fat porn performs the ongoing work of creating a sexual future for fat Latinas: It challenges the assumption that fat Latina sexuality is asexual, and offers confidence as a new structure of feeling for fat Latinas. As Flores states, "This book is an *exhibition of my confidence* and happiness as a plus sized woman" (Batts and Flores 2013, italics added).

I read *Fat Girl* as an artifact that illustrates how Flores utilizes her fat body as a means of performing and crafting a poetic future for herself, a future in which she is also a mediator of other fat Latina sexual futures. Fat studies scholars have noted that "fat bodies of today are commonly assumed to have no future at all," and this perception of fat flesh as failure trains society to not recognize fatness, to ignore it, or merely to look at it with disgust (Tidgwell et al. 2022). I use the book as an archive that directed me to her earlier film work, where Flores and Batts coproduced this Latina sexual

future via Flores's exhibition of her fat body and Batts's cinematic care—
that is, his intentional moving of the camera and his use of lighting and
sound. I argue that Flores and Batts's porn work displays a future-oriented
aesthetic mobilized by Batts's spectacular cinematography and by Flores's
mission to promote a new system of valuation for fat bodies. Flores's navi-
gation of the art world and the adult industry allows me to read her porn
work as a crucial part of the fat feminist porn avant-garde, particularly in
the 2000s, at a time when exposing the fat body in erotic ways was not yet
normalized. Predating the mainstream fat-positive movement, Flores's porn
is a case study of how feminist pornography aims to create a two-way recognition of fat belonging, validation, and aspirational confidence for fans.

The Politics of the BBW Genre

Pornography exists in a dialectical relationship with mainstream culture,
frequently challenging or contradicting societal norms and conventional
views on sex. According to Laura Kipnis, the defining feature of all pornography is transgression. While it also excites, shocks, and titillates, Kipnis
asserts that one of its greatest pleasures is "to locate each and every one of
society's taboos, prohibitions, and proprieties and systematically transgress
them, one by one" (Kipnis 1999, 164). Kipnis explains that these transgressions are largely aesthetic in nature, as pornography often presents bodies
that may repulse, such as larger bodies, or disrupt gender norms in ways that
are jarring (165). In this sense, pornography creates "a counter-aesthetic to
dominant norms for bodies, sexualities, and desire itself" (121). Within the
category of pornography as a whole, the BBW genre, which is the subcategory of pornography that features fat bodies, creates a counter-aesthetic
of fat representation that stands in contrast to mainstream visual culture,
where the fat sexual body is invisible. And over the past twenty years, the
BBW genre has developed a new aesthetic vision that has transformed its
cinematic rules and conventions.

Clint Woods, one of the leading BBW producers in the industry today,
stated that in the early 2000s—when Flores entered the adult film industry—the BBW genre was largely overlooked, with production companies
unwilling to invest in makeup, hair, or sets for plus-size models (Garcia
Hernandez 2024). Companies recording fat porn viewed fatness as a fetish
and did not invest much time, money, or effort in their shooting philosophy.

Michael Goddard (2007) reminds us that the BBW phenomenon began mainly as an internet culture, "and that it is the distinct properties of the net itself that have enabled its emergence and continue to provide an ideal space for the valorization of an excessive corporality that would normatively be seen as monstrous" (188). Gonzo, a style that places the viewer into the scene, has been the main style of shooting in the BBW porn genre. Goddard (2007), for instance, argues that in BBW porn, the emphasis is usually on breast and oral sex rather than vaginal penetration. Goddard found that BBW sites invest in a rhetoric that affirms BBW subjectivities (190). Moreover, Helen Hester (2016) argues that BBW pornography circumvents the "male genital paradigm" by "displacing the model of seminal emission." Focusing primarily on photorealistic heterosexual hardcore, Hester argues that the technique of juggling is unique to the genre of BBW porn. However, Hester has expressed skepticism "about the subversive possibilities of much BBW pornography, and urges against any reading of this material that positions it as inherently radical, disruptive, or queer" (945). Despite this skepticism, Hester contends that this genre creates "a different visual vocabulary of sexual experience" (951).

Today, contemporary BBW adult performers are finding that fans have become so demanding about the quality of the porn that companies have to invest more money in its production (Garcia Hernandez 2024). In previous research, I argued that Shape of Beauty, a fat-positive adult series produced by the Adult Time platform, deliberately disrupts mainstream pornographic aesthetics by centering "hot curvy girls and plump models as muses of adoration and lust" (Garcia Hernandez 2024). Shape of Beauty is directed by Bree Mills, a multi-award-winning director who is revolutionizing lesbian and fat pornography with her porn theater approach that focuses on improvised character development and chemistry between performers. In 2020, Shape of Beauty had already shot with the top three BBW Latina stars in the industry: Flores, Karla Lane, and Sofia Rose. According to Breana Kahlo (Garcia Hernandez 2024), one of the nominees for that category, Shape of Beauty is the future of fat pornography: "I believe that Shape of Beauty is how porn is actually leaning towards; it is more like storytelling and a lot more sophisticated scene. People are getting more demanding on the quality and I feel like that's what they are doing" (102). In the sections that follow, I show how the collaboration between Flores and Batts served as a crucial precedent for the transformative aesthetic of Shape of Beauty.

The DIY Fat Spectacular Aesthetic

As a filmmaker and director, Batts was very intentional about having a diverse cast, and he used film contracts with mainstream companies like Adam and Eve, Heart Core, and Bad Seed to give diverse artists an opportunity to create. This was the case when he produced some of Flores's documentary series: he used a five-picture deal with Adam and Eve to hire Flores and other "Black, Latin, and Fat people" (UCTV 2013). Batts's strategy of using mainstream money to create a counter-aesthetic to mainstream ideas about beauty and sexiness gave him and Flores the opportunity to explore their style and persona on camera. Eventually, with the creation of a production company called C. Batts Fly Productions, he mastered the fat feminist avant-garde aesthetic. Batts (UCTV 2013) has described his style as a "DIY spectacular aesthetic," a phrase that conveys his choice to be authentic, thoughtful, fun, and in sync with the soundtrack for a scene, and to prioritize the process with the artist over the product. In the films he made with Flores, the spectacle is divided into several vignettes, each with its own storyline. Each vignette attempts to break "all the taboos" and eliminate the category guidelines of the adult industry that dictate that different fetishes do not cross over (e.g., BBW, boy/girl, fetish, gonzo, BDSM; Isthisnormalshow 2011). The spectacular aesthetic was therefore intended to push back on the way mainstream companies create fat porn. For Batts, the spectacular included giving the actress sufficient freedom and good lighting to make her the star.

Batts's reference to the spectacular conjures up a particular politics of looking at the fat body and capturing and reading it in a spectacular way. He shot fatness with a spectacular lens that created a track toward futurity. To theorize Batts's cinematography and porn work, I borrow from Ann Millett-Gallant's (2010) use of the word *spectacular* to describe bodies that perform agency through the spectacle of self-exhibition. Millett-Gallant draws on the gaze-stare dynamic of the spectacle and spectacular, paying attention to the co-making and co-performance process between seeing and wanting to be seen. When something—be it a body, image, or object—is described as a spectacle, the term suggests that it is being purposefully presented for an audience. When someone "makes a spectacle of themselves," they are deliberately, though often irrationally or emotionally, breaking social norms concerning behavior and appearance, with the awareness that they are being closely observed by others. The spectacular is "being sensational, dramatic, and visually awe-inspiring" (Millett-Gallant 2010, 15). Millett-Gallant uses the term "spectacular spectacles" to describe what individuals do when they control their self-representation and strategically navigate visibility, or invisibility, through performance. These acts are often bold, playful, confrontational, and aimed at challenging established norms, and the artists skillfully manipulate the visual domain to their fullest advantage. They also solicit and reverse the gaze or stare, in a conscious decision to display the body and to defy social norms (Millett-Gallant 2010).

The films that Batts and Flores made together were spectacular spectacles in this sense because they enacted fat desire not just as a counter-aesthetic but as spectacularly artistic. The films powerfully showcase Flores's ability to long for her own fat body and stare at it with power. Flores displays her spectacular fat body in ways that transgress the role of the fat body in society—her performance insists that her body is a sexually appealing work of art. The goal is to use the camera to capture this autoerotic experience that is often unimaginable for fat femmes. Flores stares at the camera in a way that gives her power and subverts the gaze-stare dynamic between the filmed subject and the audience. Flores has written about the sense of power she derives from self-exhibition: the idea of having viewers see her body on display for the camera excites her. When she looks at the camera, we feel that her gaze is strategic and intentional. In interviews, Flores has stated that she imagines fat women as spectators: she recognizes that porn is typically made for men, but when she makes films, she imagines the other fat women she wants to inspire and transform with her confidence.

We can see the spectacular aesthetic play out in the documentary series that consists of *Alter EGO* (2006), *Voluptuous Life* (2007), *Glamazons* (2009), and *Artcore* (2011). Several of the photographs that appear in *Fat Girl* come from these early docu-porn films. The spectacular aesthetic is evident in the way Flores's body is captured by the camera. Batts makes deft use of lighting, blur, glass-reflection effects, and color to convey that the fat body is beautiful, sexy, erotic, and artistic. His nonlinear storytelling and attention to mood and tone via the soundtracks that he selects also contribute to making these films experimental and futuristic. These films rarely have any dialogue, moaning, or additional narrative.[2] The focus instead is on the visual textures that capture Flores's fat femme body and her confidence in it. One important technique that Batts uses is what I call the "mirror and glass effect," which captures Flores's pleasure in self-exhibition. The glass

FIGURE 1. April Flores in *Alter Ego* (2006), produced by C. Batts Fly Productions, in opening scene with makeup and mirror. Reprinted by permission of the rights holder.

effect adds a layer of voyeuristic desire that interpellates not only the viewer but also Flores herself, particularly since she engages in many solo acts. Flores's reflection through the glass, her gaze toward the camera, and her ability to look at herself through the reflection and seduce herself are what is being eroticized in these moments. In the spectacular vignettes, Flores is communicating with us that the future of fat femmes is in their ability to be seduced by their own fat bodies. It is in this self-indulgence—the desire for one's own fat body—that fat futures live.

Alter Ego opens with a shot of Flores looking at herself in the mirror, putting on eyelashes while a voice-over of her speaking plays (see figure 1). We are immediately taken to a place of reflection, beauty, pleasure, and enjoyment in looking at the self. In the next shot, she is nude and applying lotion to her legs. She caresses her legs slowly, and when she is done, she walks over to the restroom mirror to finish applying the lotion to her belly and back. She walks back to the main bedroom and puts on a pair of pink underwear, and the screen fades to black. But the vignette is not yet over. To convey a voyeuristic feel, the next scene resumes with the panning of the camera behind a curtain. It captures the silhouette of Flores's body, and once the curtain is drawn back, we see her dancing while looking at herself in the mirror. Her seductive gaze is aimed at both herself and the camera. Less than two minutes into the first vignette, we already know that the mirror plays an important symbolic role in the film: it speaks to the pleasure that Flores takes in viewing her body. According to Gillian Perry (2007), the spectacular on the stage involves a "flirtatious appeal" between the actress and the theatre. Like other instances of the spectacular, this film has a teasing relationship with seeing and being seen.

In the next vignette, Flores is wearing a long-sleeved black shirt with black panties and fishnet stockings. A close-up shot of Flores's face opens this vignette as well, and the camera follows her as she walks into someone's house and searches their kitchen. When Flores goes back outdoors, she is captured through many low-angle shots on a staircase, shots that make her body look powerful and strong. This vignette has two songs. When the music transitions from suspenseful high-beat music to a slow, dreamy song, Flores sits on a brick bar and urinates (see figure 2). This scene is not unique in her oeuvre; she has another urination scenario in a different vignette as well. As a filmmaker and artist, Batts was inspired by artists who rebelled against social norms. In high school, for instance, he was inspired by the 1990s sex art world of Robert Mapplethorpe, Andy Warhol, and Andres Serrano, all of whom incorporate urination in their art work.[3] In Batts's work, urination becomes a sign of vitality, as well as the ultimate sign of Flores's exhibitionism, since she looks straight at the camera while she holds her panties to the side with both hands. The way she holds her panties, and the way her exposed lower belly reaches her hands, captures Flores's body "in the act of becoming" spectacular (Bakhtin 1984).

Flores stares at her urine and back at the camera; with her lower belly exposed, she is queering the display of urination. If we apply a Freudian psychoanalytical reading of urination that interprets urination as displaying the temptation of one's own desire, we can read this moment as a request to gaze in a different way at the fat body. Instead of merely focusing on the fat belly, we are invited to gaze at the entire body, including her eyes and lips, which in that moment become an extension of Flores's fat pussy. Similar to Warhol's *Blow Job* (1964), where there is no actual fellatio taking place but only the face of a man who we speculate has just finished, Flores's face conveys the erotic knowledge of her enjoyment, not of climax per se but of her exploration of her body. In fact, throughout her oeuvre, Flores does not just eroticize her genitals and belly; she also devotes time to nongenital parts of her body like her head, face, eyes, lips, feet, and nails, a choice that emphasizes the sensuality and eroticism of her entire body.

In *Alter Ego*, the urination scene is an example of intimacy and the documentation of quotidian life, and at the same time an expression of growth,

FIGURE 2. April Flores in *Alter Ego*. Reprinted by permission of the rights holder.

freedom, and physical confidence and the reclamation of fat futurity. Tosha Yingling (2016) suggests that fat futurity urges us to reflect on how fat bodies experience time, particularly with regard to the future, in light of the harmful associations tied to fatness. These include stereotypes that portray fat bodies as unhealthy, deviant, sexually unproductive, or even sexually undesirable, unless situated within specific fetishistic or kink contexts. Flores and Batts's porn work uses the spectacular to frame the fat body as desirable at all times, not just in moments when the fat flesh is fetishized. In this regard, they recreate time through the spectacular DIY aesthetic that makes desire for the fat body something ongoing, something other than temporary.

Spectacular Participatory Art and Fan Art

Another key component of Flores and Batts's fat feminist avant-garde pornography is the spectacular participatory art they created. Batts considered his film work to be a form of "erotic sex art," a description that shows his intention to move away from the typical porn set, where directors tell the artists what to do, and instead to make filming a collective effort in which the artists also have a say. Take, for instance, the curation of the traveling April Flores Love Toy Art Show, which consisted of using Flores's fat plastic sex-toy pussy as a canvas to mix art, sex, and the fat body. According to *Adult Video News* (2009), one of Flores's "most important contributions to the adult market may well be becoming the first BBW performer to have her genitals lovingly re-created as part of Topco Sales' popular Wildfire Celebrity Series." The first toy was such a success that in 2012 the company molded a second toy, the BBW Cyberskin Pussy Stroker. Flores states, "I am very proud of the toy's success because it proves that there is a need for adult toys that represent a plus sized body, and that there is an audience who wants more diverse body types to be represented." The April Flores Love Toy Art Shows traveled to cities that included Los Angeles, San Francisco, New York City, and Philadelphia, inviting artists in each city to use Flores's sex toy as a canvas.

The idea for this art exhibit emerged from the experience of molding the toy (Lovett 2009). According to Flores and Batts, the process of making the sex toy was similar to the way artists make sculptures, and they wanted to treat the sex toy as a sculpture (EdenTeam 2010). One painting that conjured a fat Latina future is titled *Our Lady of the Labia* by Misha. According to Luz Calvo, the Virgin of Guadalupe is an "ominipresent" symbol in Chicana/o spaces: "the sorrowful mother, a figure who embodies the suffering of Chicano/a and Mexican populations in the context of colonization, racism, and economic disenfranchisement" (Calvo 2004, 201). Although the Catholic Church often deploys her image to signify regressive sexual politics, in *Our Lady of the Labia*, Misha has transformed the Virgin into a fat sex goddess who lives on Flores's fat pussy. Through the art and the penetration the toy is meant for, Flores is transformed into a cyborg, simultaneously an organism and a machine.

Other Chicanas have used the body of the Virgin of Guadalupe to imagine a different future for themselves (e.g., Alma Lopez, Yolanda Lopez, Ester Hernández). In her short story "Guadalupe the Sex Goddess," Sandra Cisneros (1996) expresses her anger toward the Virgin of Guadalupe, who represents passivity, obedience, marriage, and motherhood. Cisneros's narrator once saw La Lupe as a "Goody Two-Shoes" who would doom her to marriage and motherhood. In her writing, Cisneros reimagines La Virgen de Guadalupe as a sex goddess who feels good about her sexual powers and sexual energy and who speaks through the vulva. Her reimagining of La Virgen allows her to see her as a deity who is "cabrona," who knows her body and is comfortable in it. Cisneros ends her piece with an anecdote about watching porn. Her narrator remembers being terrified by the panocha of a white porn star, whose vagina Cisneros described as "pink, shiny like a rabbit's ear." She was terrified because her own panocha did not resemble that at all. The narrator's panocha was "dark as an orchid, rubbery and blue-purple as pulpo, an octopus." Even her nipples were not little or pink but, rather, big and brown like coins. Now, when the narrator sees La Virgen de Guadalupe, she wants to lift her dress to see if she is wearing underwear, if her panocha looks like hers, and if her nipples are brown too. The narrator is certain that they are: After all, La Lupe is the goddess of all Brown girls.

The art toy exhibit and Flores's participatory art shows also welcomed fan art. One piece that is in direct conversation with *Our Lady of the Labia* is the Bay Area artist Rio Yañez's depiction of Flores as a "sex-positive super hero" (Yañez 2009). Fans Yañez and Mariela had attended a San Francisco event called the "April Flores Love Toy Art Show and *Glamazons* DVD release party," where we can see an example of Flores's mission to give fat women confidence and power. As the son of the late Chicana artist Yolanda Lopez, who famously reimagined the Virgen de Guadalupe in her artwork, Yañez extended this legacy by presenting Flores as the Guadalupe Goddess. In doing so, he connected Flores to a broader lineage of Chicana feminist art, one that embraces a sex-positive perspective and works to destigmatize sex work.

The participatory aspect of Batts's work is also captured in the films he produced with Flores. Take, for instance, the inclusion of the art show scene in the film *April Flores World* (2012), where we are transported to a live painting of Flores's nude fat body. This vignette in the film is edited using a montage technique that transports us between two different places: the live nude painting and Flores undressing for the camera, ready to suck a thick, veiny white dildo. In a teasing manner, before any toys are introduced, we see several cuts between the live art-making and Flores's caressing of her body. The montage is filmed as if Flores is undressing to the beat of the music and as if the process of someone painting her is what is inspiring and driving her erotic play. From a high angle, we then see Flores lifting her boobs away from her bra. Once her boobs are out and free, Flores holds them, and the camera transitions to a low angle that allows us to see the texture of her nipples up close. A cut to the live painting occurs, and then we are back to seeing Flores holding the dildo with her orange-colored nails.

Flores sucks the dildo so hard that the trace of her red lipstick marks the girthy head. In between the sucking and live art-making, we see a tilting-medium shot of Flores's body. The only thing remaining on her body is a pair of purple lacy underwear and one pearl necklace. As the camera tilts down, Flores caresses her soft body, moving from her love handles to her thick thighs. We are taken one last time to the live painting, which is now a complete painting of Flores. After seeing the matching red tones in her live painting, we see a close-up of Flores's face, and someone asks her, "So you are an exhibitionist, right?" Flores responds, "Yes, I am, yeah," and she continues to suck on the dildo. After the dildo is in her mouth, there is a cut, and we are moved to the next scene, titled "Bizarre Shoot," where we watch Flores behind the scenes in a plus-size photo shoot.

April Flores World is a seventy-one-minute docu-porn film that documents Flores talking on film for the first time; it is a nontraditional autobiographical film. The opening scene invites the viewer to reflect on their positionality with regard to sex workers. The scene starts with Flores talking about her first job, as a customer service representative and receptionist at an internet startup company in the early 2000s. Flores is wearing a black fitted dress, with a red bra that matches her red lipstick and nails. Her red hair is accompanied by large, beautiful silver hoops. As she is sharing her first job story, Flores places her hands on her fat waist and tells the audience, "When people say that porn is degrading for women, I always, kind of, *mmm*, that offends me, because my opinion is that, I am a woman and if I am doing it don't tell me that it is degrading, because I am choosing this and I am enjoying it. I am having fun, so I get a little bit pissed off." The audience starts clapping, and in response, Flores claps softly too. She continues, "I always flash back to my most degrading job, which was this job at this company in an internet startup. I was the receptionist there and it was in downtown LA at the Gradbury, which is a beautiful building, I don't know if any of you have been there before but it's beautiful. . . . It was really beautiful but they treated me like shit. I was just in the front office, and I worked with a lot of programmers" (C. Batts Fly 2013). Flores shares how she went unnoticed during her time there: She would say good morning and nobody would respond to her. Flores was offended at this lack of acknowledgment, which she felt was an instance of their treating her "sub-humanly." With this scene, Batts guides the viewer to view Flores as an agent of her life, instead of victimizing her, as anti-porn feminists might do (Dworkin 1981). The spectacular participatory aspect of the documentary shows us that in *April Flores World*, her self-representation will reverse the anti-porn gaze and instead she will stare at the camera to promote a new system for valuing the fat racialized Latina body.

The Fat Cyborg Sexual Monster

Flores's enjoyment of the spectacular invites us to consider how the spectators of her films make sense of their desire for her. We witness the politics of consuming her and her cyborg plastic vagina in an episode of *Caso Cerrado*, the Latinx version of *Judge Judy*, which sets up fictional scenarios inspired by real-life events. The episode, titled "Vagina Plastica," was broadcast on November 13, 2012. In this episode, a heterosexual married couple, Raul and Rebecca, are on trial for a sexual dispute (carlitrosfmtj 2012a, 2012b, 2012c). Raul, a Flores-obsessed husband, has sued Rebecca, his thin Latina wife, for stealing his April Flores Voluptuous Cyberskin Pussy. During his testimony, Raul explains that his decision to purchase the sex toy was due to Rebecca's absence from the household, as she has to travel a lot for work. His logic is that fucking the fat pussy toy prevents him from cheating. In fact, according to Raul, Rebecca was in favor of the idea, and the $800 toy was purchased with her credit card. Raul also testifies that they have both watched porn, particularly Flores's videos, as a couple. Rebecca angrily interrupts him and clarifies that she only has accepted watching that type of porn because he enjoys it—she does not. If Flores was in the videos they watched, we can safely assume that "that type of porn" means fat pornography. The judge chimes in with the comment that Rebecca's version of the story is familiar, as there is a stereotype that Latina women never enjoy watching porn and only do so for the pleasure of straight Latino men.

In this scenario, Raul is portrayed as a "fat admirer" with a pathological and perverse fetish for "Mamita," the name he gives the fat plastic pussy. Unlike Mamita, Rebecca is thin. Rebecca doesn't understand why her husband prefers to fuck the fat plastic instead of her and publicly accuses her husband of being selfish and in need of a psychological intervention. According to Rebecca, Raul not only fucks Mamita but also eats her out, sleeps, reads, talks, and watches TV with her. During her testimony, Rebecca repeatedly yells, "O la vagina o yo?" (the plastic pussy or me?). However, Raul is so addicted to Mamita that if Rebecca does not return the fat toy, he prefers to divorce her. In this melodramatic episode, Flores's body has doubled: Beyond her original body, she has become a fat cyborg sexual monster that is fantasized with and is prioritized and desired over a thin human. This episode, which features a spectator who has become obsessed with Flores's fat cyborg body, flips the normative idea that thin bodies have more value than fat ones. In *A Cyborg Manifesto*, Donna Haraway argues that "a cyborg world might be about lived social and bodily realities in which people are not afraid of their joint kinship with animals and machines" (Haraway 2016, 15). Cyborgs—the combination of organism and machine and the play between imagination and material reality—appear where the boundary between human and animal or machines is transgressed (11). In our example of Flores's plastic pussy as a cyborg, the toy becomes a kinship of her body and the plastic replica that negotiates the desire for her fat body.

"Vagina Plastica" puts a spicy, dramatic Latinx spin on the way BBW porn is encountered, negotiated, and fantasized. This melodramatic marriage dispute has much to tell us about the politics of desiring a fat Latina body. When Flores makes a surprise appearance in the episode, Raul cannot contain his excitement and calls her "Mamita." This recognition by Raul tells us that the sex toy, the soft technology of the fleshy pussy, truly did stand in for Flores's fat body. Flores offers him a night of sex to help him get over his obsession with her cyborg. The wife feels offended, and the judge is so surprised by the invitation that the producers cut Flores's segment short. As viewers, we are unsure what motivated the cut: Was it that Flores offered her sex work to address the obsession, or is it the idea that fat sex can never be perceived as more desirable than thin sex? In this episode, Mamita is a cyborg plastic monster that is an extension of Flores. Her fat body and the desire for it have moved beyond her embodied self. It is in this moment—in the obsession of the fan with her body that transforms the spectacular relationship between desire and desiring with seen and being seen—and in the co-performances of these dynamics that futurity can be felt in the here and now.

Conclusion: Fat Spectacular Futures

In this essay, I have analyzed Flores's early porn work, and in particular the collaboration between her and her late husband. I have shown that their collaborations created a fat spectacular aesthetic in the porn genre of Big Beautiful Women. Their work is significant because it projected a fat confidence mediated by a fat Latina aesthetic that queered mainstream ideas about Latina bodies. A major component of the fat spectacular aesthetic is that it resignifies the fat body within a different value system. Fat here is not a fetish to be gazed at; instead, the fat body is a desiring unit.

Since Batts's unexpected death in 2013, Flores has continued their collaborative mission by finishing some of the projects they had envisioned and directing her own films. Flores's early work is foundational to understanding the contemporary fat pornography genre. By using an artistic lens, their collaboration created an avant-garde aesthetic of the fat grotesque spectacular that used the fat body to facilitate transformation, healing, freedom, and agency through exhibitionism. Flores understood confidence as a two-step process that took place first through representation and later through the desiring of fatness. For Flores, this confidence encompassed showing off the flesh and using it to embody a positive sexual energy that, she hoped, would shift the way fat women feel about themselves.

Yessica Garcia Hernandez is assistant professor of Latinx sexualities, popular culture, and performance studies in the Department of Chicana/o and Central American Studies at UCLA. She is also an award-winning ethnographic filmmaker, humanistic social scientist, and experimental autoethnographer. Her research examines how Latinx and Mexican communities use vulgar performances as ways to refuse respectability and assimilationist politics. Her first book project, *Vulgar Feminism*, is currently under contract with Duke University Press and dives into the gendered politics of late Chicana singer Jenni Rivera. Expanding the study of vulgar pleasures, her future book manuscripts focus on the representation, labor, and reception of Latinas in the pornographic archive and fat Latina sexual economies. You can reach her at yessicagarciah@ucla.edu.

Notes

1. In her reading of Vanessa del Rio's autobiography, Juana Maria Rodríguez (2015) argues that the book disrupts our understanding of literary genres and racialized sexualities and reflects on how images and text complicate the triggers of identification, traumas, and desires in the history of Latina sexuality. *Fat Girl* also distorts the conventions of autobiography, documentary, testimonio, and pornography. I approach *Fat Girl* in a similar manner, taking the visual as seriously as the textual.
2. *Voluptuous Life* does experiment with text for autobiographical storytelling and captures the dialogues of a drag queen who is training Flores in how to be a diva, but the rest of the film is mainly the soundtrack. In *Voluptuous Life,* we go on a tour with Flores to different cities and locations.
3. See *Jim and Tom* (1978) by Robert Mapplethorpe; *Oxidation* and *Piss Painting* (1977 and 1978) by Andy Warhol, and *Piss Christ* (1987) by Andres Serrano.

Works Cited

Adult Video News. 2009. "April Flores." Accessed March 15, 2016. https://avn .com/profiles/april-flores-161277.

Bakhtin, Mikhail Mikhailovich. 1984. *Rabelais and His World*. Translated by Hélène Iswolsky. Bloomington: Indiana University Press.

Batts, Carlos, and April Flores. 2013. *Fat Girl*. Rare Bird Books.

Calvo, Luz. 2004. "Art Comes for the Archbishop: The Semiotics of Contemporary Chicana Feminism and the Work of Alma Lopez." *Meridians* 5 (1): 201–24. http://www.jstor.org/stable/40338654.

carlitrosfmtj. 2012a. "Caso Cerrado desde Los Angeles Martes 15 de Noviembre 2012. Parte 3 de 5." YouTube, November 15. https://www.youtube.com/watch?v=E5gVq8-3ElE&feature=relmfu.

carlitrosfmtj. 2012b. "Caso Cerrado desde Los Angeles Martes 15 de Noviembre 2012. Parte 4 de 5." YouTube, November 15. https://www.youtube.com/watch?v=vZ5s720buVs.

carlitrosfmtj. 2012c. "Caso Cerrado desde Los Angeles Martes 15 de Noviembre 2012. Parte 5 de 5." YouTube, November 15. https://www.youtube.com/watch?v=wrWNLt78kJQ.

C. Batts Fly. 2013. "My First Job, a Scene from April Flores WORLD." YouTube, March 2. https://www.youtube.com/watch?v=yLiv-AUVo70.

C. Batts Fly Productions. n.d. *April Flores World*. https://www.hotmovies.com/3317702/april-flores-world-porn-video.html.

C. Batts Fly Productions. 2006. *Alter EGO*. https://www.hotmovies.com/1458257/alter-ego-porn-video.html.

C. Batts Fly Productions. 2007. *Voluptuous Life*. Adam and Eve Studios. https://www.hotmovies.com/2968242/voluptuous-life-porn-video.html.

C. Batts Fly Productions. 2009. *Glamazons*. Heartcore Studios. https://www.hotmovies.com/1509580/glamazons-porn-video.html.

C. Batts Fly Productions. 2011. *Artcore*. https://www.hotmovies.com/3330660/artcore-porn-video.html.

Cisneros, Sandra. 1996. "Guadalupe the Sex Goddess." In *Goddess of the Americas: Writings on the Virgin of Gudalupe,* edited by Ana Castillo, 46–51. New York: Riverhead Books.

Dahmane, Benanteur, and Chloe des Lysses. 1998. *Porn Art 2*. Alixe Press.

Dworkin, Andrea. 1981. *Pornography: Men Possessing Women*. New York: Perigee Books.

EdenTeam. 2010. "April Flores and Carlos Batts NY Interview." YouTube, January 19. https://www.youtube.com/watch?v=TkrJvKfh-iM.

Garcia Hernandez, Yessica. 2024. "The 'Big Beautiful Women' Awards: Fat Latinas in the Porn Industry." In *Sex Work Today: Erotic Labor in the Twenty-First Century*, edited by Bernadette Barton, Barbara G. Brents. and Angela Jones, 94–107. New York: New York University Press.

Goddard, Michael. 2007. "BBW: Techno-Archaism, Excessive Corporeality and Network Sexuality." In *C'Lick Me: A Netporn Studies Reader*, edited by Katrien Jacobs, Marije Janssen, and Matteo Pasquinelli, 187–95. Amsterdam: Institute of Network Cultures.

Haraway, Donna J. 2016. *Manifestly Haraway*. Minneapolis: University of Minnesota Press.

Hester, Helen. 2016. "Echoing Flesh: The 'Voluminous Body' in Heterosexual Hard Core." *Sexualities* 19 (8): 945–61.

Isthisnormalshow. 2011. "'Is This Normal?': Featuring April Flores and Carlos Batt Pt 3." YouTube, August 29. https://www.youtube.com/watch?v=Aq3fJBEReGk.

Kipnis, Laura. 1999. *Bound and Gagged: Pornography and the Politics of Fantasy in America*. Durham: Duke University Press.

Long, Julia. 2021. *Anti-Porn: The Resurgence of Anti-Pornography Feminism*. London: Zed Books. https://doi.org/10.5040/9781350218512.

Lovett, Tony. 2009. "April Flores' Voluptuous Cyberskin Pussy: What Took Us So Long?" *AVN*, December 1. Accessed August 21, 2018. https://avn.com/business/articles/novelty/april-flores-voluptuous-cyberskin-pussy-what-took-us-so-long-375886.html.

Millett-Gallant, Ann. 2010. *The Disabled Body in Contemporary Art*. New York: Palgrave Macmillan.

Perry, Gillian. 2007. *Spectacular Flirtations: Viewing the Actress in British Art and Theatre, 1768–1820*. New Haven: Yale University Press.

Rodríguez, J. M. 2015. "Pornographic Encounters and Interpretative Interventions: Vanessa del Rio; Fifty Years of Slightly Slutty Behavior." *Women and Performance* 25 (3): 315–35.

Sin TV. 2013. "Interview with April Flores." YouTube, September 28. https://www.youtube.com/watch?v=5PY5R1Lv2f0.

Tidgwell, Tracy, Jen Rinaldi, May Friedman, Emily R. M. Lind, and Crystal Kotow. 2022. *The Future Is Fat: Theorizing Time in Relation to Body Weight and Stigma*. New York: Routledge.

UCTV. 2013. "Feminist Porn Mini Con." Youtube, October 9. https://www.youtube.com/watch?v=DLpwNFAvJiA.

Yañez, Rio. 2009. "April Flores." Flickr, February 28. https://www.flickr.com/photos/elrio/3317242748/in/photostream/.

Yingling, Tosha. 2016. "Fat Futurity." *Feral Feminisms*, no. 5 (Spring): 28–43. https://feralfeminisms.com/wp-content/uploads/2020/08/ff_Fat-Futurity_issue5.pdf.

Tejano Drag Kings: Reclaiming Space, Place, and Culture Through Performance

Meagan Solomon

Abstract: This essay theorizes Tejano drag king performance as a critical source of resistance to state repression and cisheteronormative cultural standards. While drag kings in general, and Latino drag kings in particular, remain marginalized subjects in popular drag discourse, I spotlight the work of Tejano drag kings and theorize how their embodied performance and parody of masculinity serves as a vessel for feminist worldmaking. Offering the language of "queer Tejano camp," I critically examine how Tejano drag kings queer familiar and culturally relevant forms of masculinity through and with their queer and trans Brown bodies on stage. Drawing on queer of color critique, queer performance studies, and decolonial/women of color feminisms, I argue that Tejano drag kings embody transformative visions of masculinity that subvert machismo and challenge dominant representations of drag focused on cis white queens. Through a radical blend of queer and Tejano aesthetics, Tejano drag kings reshape the popular contours of drag and model how camp can serve as a source of both play and political intervention. **Keywords:** lesbian, queer, performance, camp, drag, Latina/o/e, Tejana/o/e

Accessing our full authentic selves is precious. It is healing, and it is everyone's fundamental human right. To restrict drag, an art form, in any way is a direct attack on my fundamental rights as an American and as a performer.
—Bobby Pudrido

I begin with the words of Tejano drag king Bobby Pudrido,[1] who testified before Texas legislators on March 23, 2023, in opposition to Senate Bill 12 (SB12), which sought to criminalize drag "on the premises of a commercial enterprise, on public property, or in the presence of an individual younger than 18 years of age" (Texas Legislature Online 2023a). Despite the moving testimony of Bobby and other drag performers, Texas lawmakers passed SB12 in June of 2023, with plans to begin enforcing it in September of the same year. However, on September 26, 2023, U.S. District Judge David Hittner declared SB12 unconstitutional and blocked the State of Texas from enforcing it. Despite the court's injunction of SB12, Texas lawmakers would go on to successfully pass and enforce a related bill, SB14, which restricts trans youth from receiving gender-affirming procedures and prohibits the use of public funds for gender-affirming care (Texas Legislature Online 2023b). Targeting queer and trans people of all ages, SB12 and SB14 contribute to a long history of LGBTQ repression in Texas. While the landmark Supreme Court case *Lawrence v. Texas* essentially legalized gay sex in 2003 after John Geddes Lawrence Jr. and Tyron Garner were arrested for having sex in their own Houston apartment, bills like SB12 and SB14 signal the state's active agenda to criminalize and erase queer and trans existence today. Of course, for as long as there has been state-sanctioned repression of queer and trans Texans, so too has there been queer and trans resistance. Drag is one such mode of resistance queer and trans Texans take up against ongoing oppression, inviting audiences to embrace the liberatory capacity of gender as performance amid ongoing assaults on queer and trans humanity. As José E. Muñoz writes in the opening pages of *Disidentifications: Queers of Color and the Performance of Politics*: "With hate crimes *and* legislation aimed at queers and people of color institutionalized as state protocols, *the act* of performing and theatricalizing queerness *in public* takes on ever multiplying significance" (1999, 1). Drag is one form of queer public performance that yields more liberating worlds in Texas.

In this article, I am particularly interested in Tejano drag king performance as a distinct form of cultural resistance and worldmaking. My use of "Tejano" signifies Texans of Mexican descent, who have cultivated and sustained our own culture in the U.S. through regional-specific dialects, traditions, food, fashion, and music since the nineteenth century (Benavides 2017). Tejano drag kings represent a unique history of resistance to the layered violences of colonialism, white supremacy, homophobia, and transphobia in Texas. While these violences are clearly evident in the state's social and political landscape, they are also commonly internalized within mainstream Latino/a communities.

It is thus crucial that cis and straight Latino/as, including Tejano/as, embrace queer and trans embodiments as natural and culturally relevant forms of being rather than products of Anglo assimilation. Despite a long history of fighting against Anglo oppression in the United States, many Latino/as uphold the gender binary and heterosexuality as the only natural or religiously sanctioned modes of existence rather than recognizing them as extensions of European colonialism. In "Heterosexualism and the Colonial/Modern Gender System," María Lugones explains how European colonizers classified gender and sexual diversity among Indigenous peoples of the Americas as unnatural in order to justify their colonizing mission (2007, 186). Europeans superimposed the gender binary and heterosexuality as a means of social stratification and control, often framing adherence to such systems as the only righteous path under Christianity. This colonial legacy continues. As Susy Zepeda argues, "We [Chicano/a/es] have increasingly become disconnected through state-imposed assimilative categories (e.g., 'Hispanic') and Eurocentric requirements that normalize the Western"—including, in this case, attachments to the gender binary and heterosexuality as the only culturally acceptable modes of being (2020, 228–29). This disconnection is true not only for Chicano/a/es but for all Latino/a/es impacted by colonialism.

What does it mean, then, for Tejano drag kings to perform and parody gender against a political backdrop of ongoing repression and misguided familial attachments to cisheteronormativity? How do Tejano drag kings embody and preserve culture *through* their queer and trans bodies, not *in spite* of them? How do Tejano drag kings model new and liberating modes of existence, and to what ends? In this article, I argue that Tejano drag kings embody what I name "queer Tejano camp," as a radical reclamation of space, place, and culture in response to ongoing state repression and cisheteronormative community structures. In what follows, I will not attempt to neatly define Tejano drag or approach it as a monolith but will instead focus on a selection of drag kings in Central Texas who contribute to a larger culture of queer Tejano camp and embody its liberatory possibilities. I begin first with a brief overview of drag king culture in the United States and then develop a working definition of queer Tejano camp through an analysis of select performances by Tejano drag kings Bobby Pudrido and Los MENtirosos. I conclude by asserting the cultural and political implications of queer Tejano camp within and beyond Texas borders.

Historicizing Drag King Culture in the U.S.

Historically known as "male impersonators," drag kings typically perform or parody masculinity or "maleness." According to Meredith Heller, male impersonation "refers to a gender-bending act popularized in British and U.S. stage entertainment during the nineteenth and twentieth centuries" (2020, 41). Heller also notes that, in these early eras, "the novelty [of male impersonation] was that a middle-class White woman (occupying a racial-sexual position of social respectability) performed as a White man" (2020, 41). The art of male impersonation, later known as drag, has always been racialized and classed but not always connected to same-sex desire or genderqueer identities. Straight and queer women alike have taken up the art of male impersonation for a variety of reasons throughout history, including performing for entertainment, gaining access to white assigned-male spaces, passing as men to safely express same-sex desire or masculine gender presentation, and more. Today, drag kings are often lesbian, queer, and trans; however, the art of drag is not limited to any particular gender identity or sexual orientation. The art of male impersonation and drag kinging, regardless of identity, contributes to a long history and culture of gender-bending that is distinctly queer in its rejection of gender as static or biologically determined. In other words, cis and straight performers who engage in male impersonation or drag kinging contribute to a culture of gender fluidity that is queer in nature, regardless of their individual identities or sexual orientations.

While drag has largely moved from an underground art form to a mainstream source of entertainment, drag kings have yet to receive the same level of attention drag queens have. RuPaul Charles, often referred to as the "Queen of Drag," helped popularize the art form with his own drag persona and hit television series, *RuPaul's Drag Race* (2009–), which now has over fifteen seasons. With an exclusive focus on drag queens, *Drag Race*—the longest-running drag TV series—disregards drag kings as equally talented artists worthy of screen time. Not only has the show failed to feature drag kings as contestants, but *Drag Race* has also never featured drag kings as guest judges or in other visible roles on the show. While other shows like *Drag Me to Dinner* (2023–), *House of Drag* (2018–), and *The Boulet Brothers' Dragula* (2016–) have featured drag kings, they still remain few and far between compared to the more popular representation of drag queens. This marginal representation and erasure of drag kings in popular culture not only communicates a widespread disregard of drag king talent, but it also highlights opportunities for scholars and cultural workers to offer a more complete history of drag.

Jack Halberstam is perhaps the most prominent scholar to address the history and work of drag kings.[2] In his essay, "Mackdaddy, Superfly, Rapper: Gender, Race, and Masculinity in the Drag King Scene," Halberstam observes that "the histories of both male impersonation and the drag king act are quite difficult to map out, if only because they tend to be subsumed under the larger categories of female drag and impersonation" (1997, 112). In response, he traces a long history of drag king performance across the twentieth century through ethnographic and archival research focused on queer and racialized masculinities performed by Black blues singers like Gladys Bentley and Ma Rainey in the 1920s and 1930s to Black, Brown, and white lesbian drag kings in the 1990s. Observing the racialized and often segregated nature of contemporary drag spaces, Halberstam argues that "it would be foolish to pretend that racial differences and racial disharmonies do not affect drag king cultures" (128). While Halberstam references Latina and Asian drag kings in his study, he specifically focuses on (non-Latina) Black drag king performances and subcultures to underscore distinctions among women of color and white women in the 1990s drag scene.

In *Female Masculinity*, Halberstam expands on his earlier study of queer masculinities and drag kings. Tracing differences in public reception of drag queens versus kings, Halberstam astutely observes:

> Current representations of masculinity in white men unfailingly depend on a relatively stable notion of the realness and the naturalness of both the male body and its signifying effects. Advertisements for Dockers pants and Jockey underwear, for example, appeal constantly to the no-nonsense aspect of masculinity, to the idea that masculinity "just is," whereas femininity reeks of the artificial. Indeed, there are very few places in American culture where male masculinity reveals itself to be staged or performative. (1998, 234)

Drag kings challenge the common essentializing of maleness and masculinity through performance and parody. Because hegemonic conceptions of maleness and masculinity are so tethered to whiteness, Black and Brown drag kings embody particularly subversive expressions of gender. Halberstam also notes that "although white masculinity seems to be readily available for parody . . . black masculinities or queer masculinities are often performed by drag kings in the spirit of homage or tribute rather than humor" (1998, 235). I would add that many drag kings actually rely on humor to express appreciation and even attachment to cultural figures, traditions, and tropes. While some drag performers may reinscribe essentialist gender codes in their work, the art of drag kinging itself serves as a rich source for resisting and reimagining toxic masculinity. Butch drag kings, whose daily expressions of gender already transcend hegemonic conceptions of masculinity, are particularly keen in creating and performing liberatory forms of masculinity that directly challenge cisheteronormative standards.

Halberstam's work has helped shape and inspire subsequent research on drag kings in a world where queens remain the primary focus of drag discourse. Published in 2002, *The Drag King Anthology*, edited by Donna Jean Troka, Kathleen Lebesco, and Jean Bobby Noble, is the first edited collection to center on drag kings and offer an expansive representation of drag king expressions, performances, and cultures. *The Drag King Anthology* critically examines how kings "perform, subvert and interrogate race, class, gender, ability, sexuality and body size" in order to "increase the political potency of drag king culture" (2002, 8). Genevieve Berrick's 2008 essay "Drag King: Camp Acts, Queer Bodies, Desiring Audiences" zeroes in on the erotics of drag king performance, audience desire, and the disruptive capacity of drag king camp, while Jae Basiliere's 2019 essay "Staging Dissents: Drag Kings, Resistance, and Feminist Masculinities" focuses on drag king resistance to hegemonic gender codes and fleshes out understudied expressions of feminist masculinity. Baker A. Rogers's *King of Hearts: Drag Kings in the American South* (2021) highlights the history, identities, and issues of drag king communities in the southeastern U.S., drawing attention to drag kings who perform outside more urban and popular enclaves. There have also been public-facing projects and conferences devoted to the study of drag kings in recent years. In 2018, drag kings Mo. B. Dick (Mo Fischer), Ken Vegas (Kendra), and Flare (Clare Bradley-Smyth) launched *Drag King History*, a website that chronicles and preserves drag king figures and cultures through the centuries, and in 2019, Javier Guerrero and Nathalie Bouzaglo organized *Drag Kings: An Archeology of Spectacular Masculinities in Latino America*, a series of presentations and discussions centered on Latino and Latin American drag kings hosted at Princeton University.

Despite growing scholarship on drag kings, there remains little research centered on Latino drag kings and even less on those who are Tejano. Among those listed above, Guerrero and Bouzaglo are the only scholars to focus specifically on Latino drag kings, while others only marginally discuss them, if at all. Tejano drag kings, like other drag performers across the Southern U.S., are geographically and culturally situated in unique ways. The politically conservative landscape of Texas makes drag kinging a fraught enterprise for all, but especially for Black and Brown drag performers who also remain targets of the state's racist and homophobic hegemony. Tejano drag kings also negotiate respectability politics, religious mandates, and hypersexualization within and beyond their own communities, which bears direct influence on their drag and its public reception. Given the geographic vastness of Texas, there is also significant variance among Tejano drag king cultures and performances. While there are similar threads among those living under the same state's laws, restrictions, and general conservatism, there are also important differences that deserve recognition. Tejano kings in large cities like Austin, Dallas, Houston, and San Antonio—which are each unique in their own right—have different experiences than those in more rural cities in the eastern and western wings of the state or those based in the Rio Grande Valley, the southernmost region of Texas that borders Mexico. Tejano drag, in other words, is vast and varied. Given my own geographical proximity to the drag scene in Central Texas, my analysis below only accounts for a fraction of the larger drag king scene in Texas. However, it is my hope that this essay will motivate continued research on the ways Tejano drag is shaped by and shapes other regions of the state, especially those with less visibility.

Queer Tejano Camp

Tejano drag kings often engage in what José E. Muñoz (1999) calls "disidentification," or the process of minoritized subjects working with, and ultimately refashioning, elements of dominant culture as an act of subversion. This process allows those in marginalized positions, such as queer people of color, to strategically use the tools of dominant culture to radically reconstruct it. In one example, Muñoz reads Marga Gomez's 1992 performance "Marga Gomez Is Pretty, Witty, and Gay" as an act of disidentification. In this piece, Gomez performs a monologue in a bedroom setup, bringing queer interiority into public view. In one scene, she embodies her eleven-year-old self watching an episode of David Susskind's *Open End* that featured a panel of lesbians. She recalls how her mother expressed homophobic views in response to the episode, which she then mimicked, despite internally feeling joy and intrigue watching lesbians on screen. Gomez then transitions into a performance of the lesbian panelists, who had anonymized their names and identities in the TV program out of fear of losing their jobs as truck drivers. In her performance, Gomez "luxuriates in the seemingly homophobic image of the truck-driving closeted diesel dykes," reclaiming this stereotype from a source of shame to one of pride (3). As Muñoz explains, "[Gomez] performs her disidentificatory desire for this once toxic representation. . . . The images of these lesbian stereotypes are rendered in all their abjection, yet Gomez rehabilitates these images" (3). Gomez's performance highlights the subversive nature of disidentification, where marginalized queer subjects appropriate stereotypes or symbols originating from the dominant public sphere and give them alternative meaning.

Through disidentification, Tejano drag kings similarly fashion new worlds through and with familiar expressions of masculinity modeled after heteronormative figures who would not otherwise serve as queer symbols. This might mean dressing like popular male figures, performing heteronormative songs, and parodying machista, or hypermasculinist, tropes. As Muñoz explains, "disidentification is a survival strategy that works within and outside the dominant public sphere simultaneously" (1999, 7). Rather than reinscribe heteropatriarchal expectations, these practices of disidentification offer a vessel for drag kings to remix multiple worlds through their queer and trans Brown bodies without compromising their feminist commitments. This is not to say that all Tejano drag king performers are inherently feminist or free from reproducing harm. As Judith Butler explains in *Bodies That Matter*, "Drag may well be used in the service of both the denaturalization and reidealization of hyperbolic heterosexual gender norms" (1993, 125). Indeed, no one from a marginalized positionality is inherently absolved from perpetuating oppressive ideals. However, the practice of disidentifying from dominant masculinities without entirely abandoning those with cultural resonance creates pathways for queer and trans Brown subjects to embody connection to their cultures and feminist ethics in unexpected ways.

Camp is one such mode of performance that allows drag kings to fashion subversive expressions of masculinity. While difficult to neatly define, camp is a predominantly queer form of visual culture and performance that welcomes the mixing of divergent worlds. This includes people, films, and aesthetics that parody or perform elements of mainstream culture with extravagance and humor. As a queer sensibility and style, camp is often illegible to those who make up or are invested in maintaining mainstream culture. As Susan Sontag remarks in "Notes on Camp," "The essence of

Camp is its love of the unnatural: of artifice and exaggeration" (2013, 275). Drag performance provides the perfect landscape to enact camp, as it invites expansive modes of embodiment that often disrupt strict gender codes and other social norms. Importantly, camp "doesn't argue that the good is bad, or the bad is good. What it does is to offer for art (and life) a different—a supplementary—set of standards" (Sontag 1964, 9). These different standards enable subversive play and possibility for Tejano drag kings. As Muñoz explains, these public performances enable the creation of counterpublics that assert queer existence within, and despite, a homophobic culture (1999, 1). For queer and trans Brown bodies actively under attack, queer Tejano camp provides a vessel for drag kings to subvert both interpersonal and systemic forms of repression.

In my formulation, queer Tejano camp is a mode of embodiment that fuses queer and Tejano aesthetics through performance and parody. Tejano drag kings often queer cisheteronormative Tejano figures, songs, and cultural references in their performances, allowing their bodies to hold and celebrate supposed contradictions. In a society that frames gender as static and biologically determined, those who expose the malleability of gender, like drag kings, are often outcast as unnatural and deviant. Tejano drag kings reject the naturalization of gender and help us understand that "'reality' is not as fixed as we generally assume it to be" (Butler 1999, xxiii–xxiv). In *Gender Trouble*, Butler asserts that it is not only drag but gender itself that is a form of performance that all humans participate in. Drag simply makes the performativity of gender more explicit. Butler further explains:

> To the extent the gender norms (ideal dimorphism, heterosexual complementarity of bodies, ideals and rule of proper and improper masculinity and femininity, many of which are underwritten by racial codes of purity and taboos against miscegenation) establish what will and will not be intelligibly human, what will and will not be considered to be "real," they establish the ontological field in which bodies may be given legitimate expression. (1999, xxiii)

Here, Butler unpacks how gender norms that uphold biological determinism, heteronormativity, and white supremacy also serve to legitimize, or delegitimize, the contexts in which one may "accurately" express gender. In dominant culture, one's gender is most acceptable when it is defined by a biological binary and expressed in service of heterosexuality and whiteness. For Butler, the performativity of drag upends rigid gender norms and in turn challenges the "ontological field" that gender arises from—that is, drag often sets the stage for nontraditional, illegible, and undefinable expressions of gender (1999, xxiii).

While Butler's theory of gender performativity helps elucidate the liberatory properties of drag, some trans studies scholars have taken issue with Butler's neglect of transness. In *Invisible Lives: The Erasure of Transsexual and Transgendered People* (2000), Viviane K. Namaste critiques Butler for failing to address the contexts in which mainstream drag performances occur. According to Namaste, "the drag queens Butler discusses perform in spaces created and defined by gay male culture . . . [where] elements of femaleness and femininity are highly regulated," particularly in ways that erase and exclude trans women (10). By focusing on cis male expressions of drag, Butler not only fails to account for the ways trans people, outside of drag contexts, can embody emancipatory expressions of gender but also neglects trans drag performers whose daily lived realities inform their drag practices. Similarly, in *Masculinity in Transition* (2023), K. Allison Hammer underscores Butler's neglect of trans women in *Bodies That Matter*, where Butler reconstructs the symbol of the phallus from a (cis) lesbian perspective but fails to consider how trans women can also reconstruct the symbol of the phallus as a source of feminine power. Like Namaste, Hammer critiques the cisnormativity of queer theory and calls for a more critical engagement between queer and trans studies from transfeminine perspectives.

Francisco J. Galarte's work connects queer and trans studies with a focus on Brown Chicane and Latine identities and experiences. *In Brown Trans Figurations: Rethinking Race, Gender, and Sexuality in Chicanx/Latinx Studies* (2021), Galarte underscores how Brown trans narratives remain largely invisibilized in popular representations of queer and trans life. Galarte opens the book with an example of trans Latina activist Jennicet Gutiérrez, who interrupted President Obama's 2015 Pride Month speech to critique his treatment of LGBTQ immigrants, demanding their release from Immigration and Customs Enforcement, while others in the crowd booed her. Galarte theorizes "Brown trans figuration" to capture how Brown trans subjects like Gutiérrez disrupt "the social, political, and embodied protocols of normative LGBTQ politics" and are ultimately punished for it (3). It is this social and political rejection that necessitates disidentification as a survival strategy for Brown trans and queer subjects, who are forced to negotiate their place in dominant society. Queer and trans Latines, including those in drag, may work within dominant social structures to express their minoritized subjectivities, ultimately subverting symbols of mainstream culture through and with their Brown bodies.

Below, I examine the performances of transmasculine, queer femme, and butch lesbian Latine subjects whose drag celebrates trans and queer Brown bodies as vessels of self-expression and cultural reclamation in resistance to state-sanctioned repression and cisheteronormative cultural mandates. Through a shared struggle of cultural negotiation and disidentification with respect to queer expression and Tejano culture, Tejano drag kings fuse worlds often deemed separate and co-create new visions for what "queer" and "Tejano" look like. Through the aesthetics and performativity of queer Tejano camp, Tejano drag kings model a playful mode of gender expression that allows them to not only connect to existing cultural traditions but also contribute to shaping new ones.

Bobby Pudrido: Austin's Premier Tejano Drag King

Bobby Pudrido, whose testimony I opened with, is a Tejano drag king from the border town of Laredo, now based in Austin. The name Bobby Pudrido ("Bobby Rotten") is a spin on the name of beloved Tejano singer Bobby Pulido. In drag, Bobby uses he/him pronouns and is often suited in a cowboy hat, boots, and drawn-on facial hair. Out of drag, Bobby is a self-proclaimed transmasculine Tejane dyke who uses they/them pronouns. When testifying against SB12 in March of 2023, Bobby emphasized the personal significance of his queer Tejano drag persona: "Drag has allowed me to connect to, share, and celebrate my Tejano culture and queer identity. It has given me a connection to myself in ways no other art form has before" (Bobby Pudrido 2023). Bobby's testimony and his work as a drag king highlight the significance of drag for queer and trans Brown bodies in Texas, a state that is often written off as a conservative wasteland rather than a place ripe with queer and trans life. While Bobby only recently began his drag career in 2022, he has already made an important and lasting imprint on the cultural and political landscape of Texas through his work as Austin's premier Tejano drag king.

In April of 2024, I witnessed Bobby perform at a queer club in Austin called Cheer Up Charlies, where he was cohosting Puro Pinche 956, a drag event dedicated to uplifting and celebrating queers from the Rio Grande Valley (RGV). "Puro pinche 956" ("pure fucking 956") is a common phrase shared by those from the 956 area code, which represents the southernmost

Bobby Pudrido. Photograph by Reuben L. Atkins.

region of Texas and is over 92 percent Latine ("Ethnicity Data"). This is in stark contrast to the white-dominated city of Austin, where Latines make up only 33 percent of the population (City of Austin, n.d.). Hosting Puro Pinche 956 in Austin not only serves to disrupt the white queer status quo but also carves out a critical counterpublic for queer Latines from the RGV and beyond to gather and take up space. During the April show, Bobby and cohost Venus Rising opened with an RGV roll call, naming various cities from the region and inviting those in the audience to cheer and make their presence known when their city was called. The show exclusively featured drag performers from the RGV, who bonded over familiar phrases, manner-isms, and songs popular among Tejanes and Latines, more broadly.

As the only drag king of the night, Bobby's performances were partic-ularly memorable. Bobby took to the stage dressed like a Tejano singer, complete with a cowboy hat, black shades, a large belt buckle, and an accor-dion prop. In an opening number, Bobby performed "¿Y todo para qué?" by Intocable, a popular Tejano band known for their norteño music. In his performance, Bobby moved around the stage like a real Tejano singer, danc-ing in choreographed motions with the accordion prop bedazzled with his initials, "BP." Later, Bobby performed "Un rinconcito en el cielo" by beloved Mexican singer Ramón Ayala, known as a legendary norteño singer and accordion player. Members of the crowd sang along in Spanish, relishing in the performance of a trans Tejano body queering culturally resonant songs onstage.

Bobby's drag embodies queer Tejano camp by transforming and exag-gerating traditional Tejano aesthetics through queer gestures: wearing makeup to represent a chiseled jawline and facial hair, lip-syncing lovingly to fellow queers in the crowd, using bedazzled stage props, and incorporat-ing queer pride flags in his numbers. In these instances, queer Tejano camp serves as an instrument for connecting with Tejane and Latine commu-nity members through familiar cultural symbols and songs. Yet, rather than reproduce harmful representations of masculinity tethered to heteronor-mativity, Bobby allows traditional Tejano aesthetics to be the vessel from which he affirms his commitment to queer and trans liberation. Bobby's drag subverts heteropatriarchal cultural symbols onstage and helps craft a queer and trans counterpublic for fellow Tejanes and Latines to exist fully and unapologetically in their Brown, queer, and trans bodies.

Through his performance of queer Tejano camp, Bobby also cele-brates queer and trans bodies in resistance to the political hegemony of Texas invested in eradicating queer and trans life. Bobby performs Tejano culture through and with his trans nonbinary body, often displaying his post–top surgery chest. Through his drag, Bobby embodies what Omi Salas-SantaCruz calls a "nonbinary epistemic refusal," which offers "alter-native ways of reading, thinking, and sensing through decolonial methods, trans decolonial theories, and exploring different ways of being within gender coloniality" (2023, 80). While Bobby, as a drag persona, identifies as a man, Bobby's drag performance, enacted by their trans nonbinary body, is itself representative of "nonbinary thinking [that] emerges as a critical epistemic shift for marginalized individuals to counter the ongoing structures that colonize our thought processes" (Salas-SantaCruz 2023, 84). These colonial structures include biologically determined and binary classifications of gender that fail to account for the variance of gender expressions and sex characteristics humans have embodied since time immemorial. Such rigid categories serve as mechanisms of social stratification and control rooted in settler logics of hierarchy, which reject and punish any forms of existence that fall out of line.

As a nonbinary lesbian performing as a man, Bobby models the malleability of gender and challenges colonial modes of thought tethered to binaries. In drag, Bobby does not simply reinscribe rigid or toxic representations of men but rather liberates masculinity from machismo through his fusion of traditional Tejano aesthetics with politically feminist messages invested in queer and trans liberation. Queer Tejano camp also offers Bobby a creative vessel to challenge cisnormative representations of lesbians that exclude those who are nonbinary and trans. This has included Bobby waving a lesbian flag onstage while suited in traditional Tejano clothing—complete with facial hair, a cowboy hat, and boots—and opening his shirt to reveal his top surgery scars with the words "dyke supremacy" written on his chest. Bobby's drag incorporates a fusion of entertainment and political intervention that simultaneously critiques and transforms the white-, cis-, male-dominated drag scene and the heteropatriarchal logics of mainstream Tejano culture.

Los MENtirosos: San Antonio's Drag King Troupe of Tíos y Primos

Performing a similar amalgamation of queer and Tejano aesthetics, Los MENtirosos are a drag king troupe based in San Antonio made up of six active members, including cofounders and couple SirGio and Gacho Marx. Los MENtirosos draw their troupe name from the Spanish term for male liars, emphasizing "MEN" as a clever play on words. They also often shorten their name to "Los Men," a nickname I will adopt for the remainder of this article. In their mission statement, Los Men describe themselves as "a collective of queer and non binary drag entertainers . . . [who] seek to create space for all drag entities outside of the exclusive world of drag that for far too long has excluded kings that don't follow the standards of pageantry" (Los MENtirosos Drag Kings 2019). Fusing play and politics, Los Men regularly perform shows in San Antonio and in Central Texas more broadly, including

Gacho Marx (left) and SirGio (right). Photograph by Reuben L. Atkins.

benefit shows for nonprofits like Familia: Trans Queer Liberation Movement, an advocacy organization for queer and trans Latines, and Lilith Fund,
a Texas-based organization that supports Texans seeking abortions (Jackson 2022). The troupe is also known for hosting bilingual drag storytimes,
making drag and education accessible to people of all ages. Referring to
themselves as "drag king tíos y primos" (uncles and cousins) in their Instagram bio, Los Men are beloved community figures who turn to drag as
an art form that enables cultural expression and community advocacy. As
they explain in their mission statement: "Los MENtirosos bring representation where there is none. We create space for kings regardless of color or
gender, sexual orientation or gender presentation. We believe that all drag
is valid" (Los MENtirosos Drag Kings 2019). Since 2014, Los Men have
been a trailblazing drag king troupe committed to transforming the political
function and face of drag through their performances of queer Tejano camp.

SirGio and Gacho shared their drag testimonies with me in a virtual
plática (conversation), where we spoke on the origins, impact, and goals
of Los Men. Having already built a community network through Zombie
Bazaar, a queer dance troupe Gio directs and performs in, Los Men naturally emerged from a desire to showcase Tejano and Latino drag king talent
and reimagine the political function of drag. When recalling his debut as an
emcee for Los Men, Gacho shared: "I realized, in drag, you have a mic and

two minutes between the last act and next act to say whatever you want to say. And it can be silly shit . . . or you could talk about policy, and you can talk about feminism, and you can talk about misogyny in the drag world."[3] Throughout our conversation, Gacho emphasized the importance of utilizing his drag platform to advocate for collective liberation through a feminist lens. He also explained how this sometimes shocks audience members who don't expect a drag king suited like a traditional Tejano singer to perform a version of masculinity attuned to feminist politics. He shared: "My name is Gacho for a reason, right? They get surprised because what comes out of my mouth is feminist ideology and making fun of misogyny. I like to take the things that are really going to burn men the most and say those things looking like this." Gacho's critique of toxic masculinity while donning traditionally masculine Tejano aesthetics is emblematic of queer Tejano camp: subverting symbols of dominant culture to advocate for marginalized communities.

As "gacho" is slang for "mean" or "rude," Gacho's advocacy embodies a "feminist killjoy" ethos that transmutes traditional modes of masculinity to critique machismo rather than reproduce it. The feminist killjoy trope deems all feminists as unhappy victims invested in ruining the mood by exposing the violence of misogyny, but as Sarah Ahmed writes: "To reclaim the feminist killjoy is not to agree with the negative judgment behind it . . . but to channel the negativity, pushing it in another direction" (2023, 15). As a drag king, Gacho performs queer Tejano camp not merely to entertain but also to offer meaningful critiques of anti-queer, anti-trans, and anti-feminist politics—ultimately transforming heteropatriarchal representations of Tejano masculinity through queer and feminist advocacy. In this way, queer Tejano camp not only transforms traditional Tejano aesthetics from a queer lens but also repurposes drag from a popular source of lighthearted entertainment to a politically conscious and activist-oriented art form.

SirGio similarly breaks boundaries through his performance of Tejano aesthetics that embody both masculine and feminine elements. In our conversation, SirGio explained that his drag king persona embodies "a lot of gender fluidity and gender fucking" as he is often suited in a beard with lipstick and earrings. Having grown up doing folklórico (a traditional Mexican dance form fusing folk dance and ballet elements) and escaramuza (a Mexican equestrian sport for girls and women), SirGio takes inspiration from traditionally feminine aesthetics and fuses them with a masculine flair. In bilingual drag storytime events, SirGio often dresses as a bearded Selena, embodying a recognizable cultural aesthetic of the beloved Tejana singer, with a masculine twist. SirGio's melding of masculine and feminine aesthetics in his performance of Selena serves as a subversive source of queer Tejano camp: Not only does SirGio resist anti-trans and anti-drag politics by performing for youth, but he also transforms hyperfeminine representations of Selena—showcasing that a world beyond the rigid gender binary is possible.

In Texas, legislation like SB12 was crafted to distance children from drag performers through an unnecessary hypersexualization of the art form. As SirGio and Gacho explained, their bilingual drag storytime events enable valuable intergenerational connection with youth, who not only see themselves represented in Los Men's bilingual stories with familiar cultural references but also, for queer and trans youth, in the gender fluidity celebrated by adult figures in the community. Gacho shared: "We really like being for these little Chicanitos [and] Mexicanitos in the community what we didn't have. We didn't have somebody telling us about body autonomy. We didn't have somebody telling us you don't have to hug every member of the family." Through humor, exaggerated costumes, and familiar cultural traditions, drag king tíos Gacho and SirGio embody queer Tejano camp as a critical mechanism for connecting with and educating Tejane and Latine youth on issues of consent, gender variance, bodily autonomy, and more.

Conclusion: Queer Tejano Camp Beyond Borders

While queer Tejano camp is uniquely situated in Texas, it has the capacity to travel across borders and transform dominant conceptions of drag on a transnational scale. During the height of the COVID-19 pandemic, Los Men took to the virtual stage to perform drag for an audience in the United Kingdom, who would have otherwise not had access to Los Men or queer Tejano camp more broadly. In our conversation, Gacho shared that during his U.K. performance, he educated the audience on Tejano history and aesthetics, even teaching them the term "jotería," which describes queer and trans Latines who embody "a complex way of being, relationality, resistant consciousness, and healing pedagogies" (Salas-SantaCruz 2023, 85). Bobby has similarly taken his drag beyond Texas borders, including to the stages of Bushwig, a drag festival based in New York City. Performing to traditional Tejano songs dressed in his typical Tejano attire, Bobby's performance of queer Tejano camp in New York not only introduces a regionally specific form of drag to those who may otherwise never encounter it but also parallels the ethos of border-crossing and boundary-breaking so characteristic of his drag persona.

Tejano drag kings like Bobby and Los Men shatter rigid and static representations of gender, Tejanidad, and the art of drag more broadly. Wielding their queer and trans Brown bodies as instruments of play and political intervention, they fashion new worlds that directly challenge and help to transform the long-standing violences of colonialism, white supremacy, misogyny, heteropatriarchy, and transphobia. Based in Central Texas, Bobby and Los Men contribute to a larger culture of queer Tejano camp across the state that takes shape in a number of diverse and interconnected ways based on varying regional contexts. While more work must be done to offer a fuller portrait of Tejano drag king culture in less urban and popular enclaves, showcasing the transformative talent of Bobby and Los Men invites continued theorizing of queer Tejano camp and its ability to serve as a tool for queer and trans Tejanes to critique oppressive structures and reclaim ownership of our own bodies.

Meagan Solomon is a Tejana Jewish lesbian scholar and educator based in Austin, Texas. She is assistant professor of feminist studies at Southwestern University and the founding director of Malflora Collective, a community project dedicated to preserving the lives and legacies of Latina/e lesbians. Her work focuses on Latina/e feminist, lesbian, and queer forms of relationality and resistance. You can contact her at solomonm@southwestern.edu.

Notes

1. I have omitted the legal names of each drag king, according to IRB standards of confidentiality.
2. The fields of gender and queer studies have long centered the work of white scholars, which has systematically slowed the production and circulation of scholarship by Black and Brown scholars. This structural privileging of whiteness helps explain why white scholars have gained the most prominence in discourse on drag kings but does not indicate that white scholars are the only or primary experts on them.
3. Gacho Marx and SirGio in discussion with the author, August 2024. This plática was later featured on Malflora Podcast. Visit malflora.org/podcast to learn more.

Works Cited

Ahmed, Sarah. 2023. *The Feminist Killjoy Handbook: The Radical Potential of Getting in the Way*. New York: Seal Press.

Basiliere, Jae. 2019. "Staging Dissents: Drag Kings, Resistance, and Feminist Masculinities." *Signs: Journal of Women in Culture and Society* 44 (4): 979–1001.

Benavides, Adán, Jr. 2017. "Tejano." *Handbook of Texas Online*. Last modified January 24, 2017. https://www.tshaonline.org/handbook/entries/tejano.

Berrick, Genevieve. 2008. "Drag King: Camp Acts, Queer Bodies, Desiring Audiences." *Traffic*, no. 10, 207–22.

Bobby Pudrido (@bobbypudrido). 2023. "I testified at the state Capitol against bills targeting drag performers and queer folks." Instagram, March 23. https://www.instagram.com/p/CqKDbLXATWH/.

Butler, Judith. 1993. *Bodies That Matter: On the Discursive Limits of Sex*. New York: Routledge.

Butler, Judith. 1999. *Gender Trouble: Feminism and the Subversion of Identity*. New York: Routledge.

City of Austin. n.d. "Austin Demographics." Accessed June 5, 2025. https://demographics-austin.hub.arcgis.com.

"Ethnicity Data for Region: Rio Grande Valley." 2025. RGV Health Connect. https://www.rgvhealthconnect.org/demographicdata?id=281259 &sectionId=941.

Galarte, Francisco J. 2021. *Brown Trans Figurations: Rethinking Race, Gender, and Sexuality in Chicanx/Latinx Studies*. Austin: University of Texas Press.

Halberstam, Jack. 1997. "Mackdaddy, Superfly, Rapper: Gender, Race, and Masculinity in the Drag King Scene." *Social Text*, nos. 52–53, 104–31.

Halberstam, Jack. 1998. *Female Masculinity*. Durham: Duke University Press.

Hammer, K. Allison. 2023. *Masculinity in Transition*. Minneapolis: University of Minnesota Press.

Heller, Meredith. 2020. *Queering Drag: Redefining the Discourse of Gender-Bending*. Bloomington: Indiana University Press.

Jackson, Jhoni. 2022. "Behind the Parties and Drag Shows that LGBTQIA Latines Call Home." *Refinery29*, October 4. https://www.refinery29.com /en-us/2022/10/11103647/queer-latine-drag-houses-parties-community.

Los MENtirosos Drag Kings (@losmen210). 2019. "Mission." Instagram. https://www.instagram.com/stories/highlights/17983025554222307/.

Lugones, María. 2007. "Heterosexualism and the Colonial/Modern Gender System." *Hypatia* 22 (1): 186–209.

Muñoz, José Esteban. 1999. *Disidentifications: Queers of Color and the Performance of Politics*. Minneapolis: University of Minnesota Press.

Namaste, Viviane K. 2000. *Invisible Lives: The Erasure of Transsexual and Transgendered People*. Chicago: University of Chicago Press.

Rogers, Baker A. 2021. *King of Hearts: Drag Kings in the American South*. New Brunswick: Rutgers University Press.

Salas-SantaCruz, Omi. 2023. "Nonbinary Epistemologies: Refusing Colonial Amnesia and Erasure of Jotería and Trans* Latinidades." *Women's Studies Quarterly* 51 (3/4): 78–93.

Sontag, Susan. 2013. *Against Interpretation*. New York: Farrar, Straus and Giroux. Kindle.

Texas Legislature Online. 2023a. "Bill: SB12." https://capitol.texas.gov/BillLookup/History.aspx?LegSess=88R&Bill=SB12.

Texas Legislature Online. 2023b. "Bill: SB14." https://capitol.texas.gov/BillLookup/history.aspx?LegSess=88R&Bill=SB14.

Troka, Donna Jean, Kathleen Labesco, and Jean Bobby Noble. 2003. *Drag King Anthology*. New York: Harrington Park Press.

Zepeda, Susy. 2020. "Decolonizing Xicana/x Studies: Healing the Susto of De-Indigenization." *Aztlán: A Journal of Chicano Studies* 45 (1): 225–41.

Black Anti-Bodies and the Trauma of Obstetric Racism

Dána-Ain Davis with Bisola Neil[1]

Abstract: This article introduces the concept of Black Anti-Bodies, a framework highlighting the intersection of racism, gender, and medical violence against Black women and birthing people in the United States.[2] Black Anti-Bodies is a diagnostic that refers to the paradoxical treatment of Black women's reproducing bodies as exploited within the American healthcare system and broader society. Black Anti-Bodies are both essential and disposable, relied upon to stabilize the economy and political system, yet subjected to routine medical violence rooted in racist beliefs. Through the narratives of Bisola and a Kreyòl woman whose story first appeared in a news article, we examine the ways medical professionals and the medical complex torment and harm Black bodies. Drawing on Hortense Spillers's concept of flesh and Emily Martin's exploration of flexibility, we show how Black bodies are constructed as "pathological" and subjected to dangerous medical practices. Ultimately, this article aims to critically analyze intersecting dynamics of reproduction, race, gender, and power within medicine. **Keywords:** Black Anti-Bodies, obstetric racism, reproduction, violence

July 2019—New York

In July 2019 Bisola, a thirty-eight-year-old Black woman with a PhD, who already had one child, went to a teaching hospital in New York to give birth. In August, shortly after she arrived home from the hospital, Bisola wrote a letter that began

> Dear Sir or Madam:
> This is a formal complaint regarding care received at MNO Hospital from July 30, 2019, to August 3, 2019. As a research and teaching hospital I had faith my delivery will be safe, uncomplicated and care for my personhood

WSQ: Women's Studies Quarterly 53: 3 & 4 (Fall/Winter 2025) © 2025 by Dána-Ain Davis with Bisola Neil.

would be taken into account. I was also under the impression that as a 38-year-old African American healthy woman extra care would be given to my case for the geriatric nature of the pregnancy, but also due to current research that shows the United States has the highest maternal and infant mortality rates among comparable countries and African American women are 4 x more likely to die from preventable pregnancy related complications. . . .

In the letter, Bisola outlined events that occurred during her labor, birth, and postpartum, an excerpt of which follows, covering just the first seven hours of her experience:

At 40 weeks and 3 days I arrived at the hospital at 10 PM. After completing paperwork, I was taken to an exam room where my vitals were taken. I was checked to determine if I was dilated enough for admission. Although I was having regular contractions and was only 1 cm dilated my blood pressure was unacceptably high—138/95. [Considered to be mild hypertension.] I was admitted to the hospital. Between 11:45 PM and 12:15 AM I was informed by the doctor on duty that due to my high blood pressure, which had risen to 144/93, I would be given medication to increase contractions in order to accelerate the labor. I was then taken to a room which I assumed was the birthing room. It was not. In this room I was placed in a gown, was hooked up to an IV, a contraction monitor [fetal monitor] and blood pressure monitoring machine, I was given the medication by Nurse T, and I waited to dilate beyond 1 cm. At 1:00 AM—I requested an epidural for the birth. I was informed by Nurse S that I could have the epidural at any time, but it was best to wait until I was 3 to 4 centimeters dilated. By 1:57 AM my blood pressure rose to 149/111. At 2:12 AM my blood pressure was 143/108. Between 5:00 AM and 6:00 AM I was in extreme pain and requested an epidural. When the anesthesiologist arrived to administer the epidural, I was asked to stand up and walk to the other side of the bed. When I did so, I screamed out in pain and the Nurse asked is it pain or pressure. I said both. The doctor examined me because if I was in active labor then it would be beyond the point of receiving an epidural. I was at 8 cm. I was escorted to the wheelchair with the intent of being moved to another room. While on the wheelchair I screamed out in pain and said, "I feel the head." But no one listened to me. I repeated it and was told to walk to the bed. When I attempted to stand my water broke and I felt the baby begin to crown. Unable to stand upright, I got down on my hands and knees and crab-walked to the bed. [Bisola gave birth to her daughter in this position and then passed out from pain. She did not witness her daughter's birth nor cut the umbilical cord and was unable to initiate skin-to-skin contact.]

Bisola, who experienced rapid dilation, had a precipitous birth because regular contractions had not started until about 2:00 a.m., but within three to four hours, she had the baby. She fainted from pain during the birth because the contractions were too much. After coming to, Bisola learned that she had a hematoma, which, over two days, grew from the size of a pea (1 cm) to the size of a tangerine or small peach (8 cm). Surgery became necessary. Again, they set her up for an epidural, but after a resident's several unsuccessful and painful tries to insert an IV line before the epidural, the attending took over to administer the insertion. Post-surgery, Bisola saw another doctor, who, she said, never introduced himself and abruptly left the room, having said nothing when she asked questions, and did not return.

Bisola's was a laboring body—to which she felt no one attended, because although she repeatedly said she was in pain, it seemed that people did not take notice. Although Bisola was in agony, she was instructed to stand up and walk to the bed *at the same time* she pointed out she could feel the baby's head emerging. Bisola believed that the inattentiveness of some doctors and nurses, their dismissal of her concerns, and their refusal to listen was because she was Black. Her perception aligns with documented experiences of racial bias in healthcare, where Black patients report feeling discriminated against or judged unfairly by healthcare professionals (Davis 2019). Bisola noted a disturbing fact: despite all the difficulties she underwent, none of the complications were recorded on her chart. Neither the high blood pressure, nor the hematoma, nor the surgery—the only notation was that she had a precipitous labor.

Post-release, Bisola made two emergency room visits; on the second visit, an ultrasound revealed excessive blood in her uterus. What if she had died? Uterine hematomas can be fatal, but, in this case, if there had been a mortality review, there would have been no evidence. The omission of high blood pressure and the hematoma from her medical record essentially means that it did not happen. Bisola's susceptibility to death was a matter of her word against theirs. The absence of documentation underscores the hospital's negligence, which created a vulnerable situation for Bisola. By failing to note her complications, they undermined her credibility and ability to seek legal recourse, effectively silencing her traumatic experience.

February 5, 2021—Florida

On February 5, 2021, a news item came across social media titled "A Black OB-GYN Describes Witnessing White Colleagues Neglect Haitian Patients, Saying, 'You Can't Kill a Creole.'" The article, written by Anna Medaris Miller (2021) for *Insider*, opened with the following paragraph:

> Dr. Jess Robinson's patient was undergoing an emergency C-section when she went into cardiac arrest. The woman had a high-risk pregnancy and needed chest compressions to survive. And yet, Robinson's supervisor, the attending physician, wasn't concerned. He was a white male, and the patient, a Creole-speaking woman from Haiti, was Black. "You can't kill a Creole," Robinson, an OB-GYN of Afro-Caribbean descent who was a resident at the time, told *Insider* she heard him say. Robinson was appalled and "extremely uncomfortable." Without looking away from her computer, she said, "Not cool, guys." As she expected at the hospital with no people of color in leadership and only a few on staff, the small group of clinicians continued to chuckle.

The article continues with Robinson noting that Haitian patients at the Florida hospital were discriminated against because white clinicians sometimes held openly biased beliefs about Black people and their resilience, which can mask complications and delay critical interventions, potentially turning a treatable condition into a life-threatening situation. Dr. Robinson reported that clinicians treated Haitian pregnant patients who presented with preeclampsia with less urgency than white patients, stating, "I would hear comments, such as 'She's Haitian, she'll be fine.'" Being "fine" was not very likely given that, according to the Kaiser Family Foundation, between 2018 and 2021 in Florida, the maternal mortality rate was 26.3 deaths per 100,000 live births (Kaiser Family Foundation 2024) and that in the U.S., Black women are 2.5 times more likely to die from a pregnancy-related cause than white women (USAFacts 2023).

The news story recounts a harrowing situation where a woman in labor faced cardiac arrest, placing her life in imminent danger. According to Dr. Robinson, despite the urgent need for an emergency cesarean section, the attending doctor, in a troubling turn of events, confidently asserted that the woman would not die. In declaring the patient's supposed immunity to death, ironically, the patient was left susceptible to it. This narrative presents a complex interplay of trauma and suffering and also sheds light on the insidious nature of white-controlled medical supremacy. Through the doctor's declaration of the woman's invincibility, what we learn is that compassion for the woman was diminished or nonexistent. Given the role Black bodies have played in the history of medicine and the development of obstetrics in particular, the Haitian woman's experience exemplifies the exploitation and mistreatment Black bodies have withstood over time. Thus, connections can be made between negligent treatment of Black bodies and the vitalization of the medical system. The situation described in the article underscores a problem and raises several questions.

One problem we highlight here is that in Miller's article, the woman emerges as nameless and voiceless: her very anonymity a testament to the erasure of individual identity. She is obscured by the anglicized term "Creole," a word bearing the weight of colonial suppression—in accordance with her heritage, she would be "Kreyòl," a term replete with pride. As a gesture of respect, we refer to her as a Kreyòl woman, an act of linguistic reverence, and an attempt to restore a measure of dignity.

Among the questions raised, we ask: What predetermined notions led to the woman reportedly being subjected to a delay in receiving chest compressions? Could the doctor's comment have been influenced by cultural stereotypes? Perhaps the image of zombies in Haitian folklore was on his mind. Literary scholars Sarah Lauro and Karen Embry (2008) perceptively suggest that zombies are symbols of inferiority and have irreconcilable bodies. If the Kreyòl woman was *imagined* as a zombie by the doctor, she became a metaphor for the consequences that unfold in medical environments. If she was viewed as a zombie with an irreconcilable body, she existed beyond medical resolution. Her treatment, or lack thereof, became embroiled in the medical regime that made her body unacceptable to the promise of care.

Together, Bisola and the Kreyòl woman expose various registers of medical racism that marked their bodies.

Introduction

We purposefully began this article with the stories of two women whose encounters scaffold this discussion of Black Anti-Bodies. The article is structured as such, recognizing that there are stakes in the telling of any story, and in how a story is told. Deploying the two incidents in the service of having the narratives lead to theory, these stories demonstrate how the traumatic experiences resulting from racism and practices in obstetric medicine have contributed to the development of Black Anti-Bodies. The article's primary objective is to unpack the narratives and explain the contours and consequences of racism just as Black feminist anthropologist Leith Mullings and colleagues argued we must do (Mullings et al. 2021, 677). In Dána's work on race, racism, and reproduction and in this article (Davis 2018, 2020), the broad aim is to take up Mullings's prompt to examine what racism *does*.

The concept of Black Anti-Bodies highlights the intersection of racism, gender, and medical violence against Black reproducing women and people in the United States. Conceptually, we emphasize Black Anti-Bodies as diagnostic of how Black women's bodies are exploited and maimed within the American healthcare system and broader society. In lay terms, the medical definition of antibody (with a lowercase *a* and no hyphen) describes protective substances that bind to unwanted substances in our bodies, eliminating them from our system. Although our bodies naturally manufacture these defenders to counteract diseases, this biological safeguard is not the focus of our discussion. Indeed, it is the opposite. Capitalizing the *A* and *B* in "Anti-Bodies" serves as a metaphor for systemic racism. This theoretical and stylistic choice conveys a particular conceptual distinction within the structures of oppression and signifies a macro-level context that aligns with the ways institutions and society foster hostile environments toward particular groups of people. Whereas antibodies identify and neutralize threats, society translates Black bodies into Anti-Bodies, institutionally marginalizing and suppressing them on a scale beyond the actions of individuals.

The term encapsulates the paradoxical treatment of Black women as both essential to and disposable within the nation's social and economic fabric. On one hand, Black women are relied upon as "antibodies" to stabilize the economy and political system. Two examples of the protective mechanisms that Black women possess come to mind: First, by being made to reproduce the labor force during enslavement which upheld the slave economy; second, Black women have been depended upon for their engagement in community organizing and electoral politics. Their voting power has mobilized Democratic voter turnout (Slaughter et al. 2023). On the other hand, they face routine and extreme medical violence, often rooted in racist beliefs about, for example, their pain tolerance. Black Anti-Bodies challenges the notion of Black women's "preternatural immunity" to suffering, instead highlighting how they are *made* vulnerable to suffering through systemic racism and gender-based discrimination—in this case in medicine. Yet the concept of Black Anti-Bodies also emphasizes the transformative potential of centering Black feminist knowledge and recognizing Black women as experts in their own healthcare. This approach challenges the underlying assumptions of white racial superiority and saving logics so often embedded in practices and systems as it identifies mechanisms of change.

This article is organized as follows: the section titled "Flesh, Flexibility, and Fitness" elucidates the role of Hortense Spillers's theory of flesh (1987) and Emily Martin's theory of fitness (1994) in shaping the interpretation of the two stories. "Flesh, Flexibility, and Fitness" is the theoretical anchor for understanding the next section, "Obstetric Racism." In this section, the multifaceted dimensions of obstetric racism are illustrated through the narratives of Bisola and the Kreyòl woman. Owing to the trauma of obstetric racism, the next part discusses the meaning and formation of "Black Anti-Bodies." The term holds diagnostic purchase and helps elucidate that it is an antecedent to and aftermath of obstetric racism. Even so, the concept of Black Anti-Bodies possesses elements of resistance and refusal as mechanisms to address broader concerns for reproductive injustice. In all, the aim is to foster a deeper understanding of the intersecting dynamics of race, gender, and power within medicine broadly and obstetrics specifically.

Flesh, Flexibility, and Fitness

Influenced by Saidiya V. Hartman's *Scenes of Subjection* (1997), we continually grapple with what might lead medical professionals and the medical complex to subject Black bodies to harm. To do so, we center three concepts: flesh and flexibility and fitness. Hortense Spillers's concept of "flesh" (1987; also see Wimbush 2022) and Emily Martin's exploration of bodily flexibility and fitness (1994) illuminate the production and exploitation of Black bodies within medical systems. In "Mama's Baby, Papa's Maybe," Spillers deploys "flesh" as a lens for exploring the existential and ontological dimensions of Black subjectivity. Both Spillers and Wimbush posit flesh as equivalent to illegitimacy, a state in which the body is divested of subjecthood and vulnerable to constant fragmentation. Fragmentation resonates with Black individuals' medical encounters, where their bodies are often objectified, manipulated, and controlled rather than being treated as worthy.

Emily Martin's thinking on flexibility is based on a systems model of the body that is concerned with "fit" individuals, who are supposedly normal and rational (Kirschner and Martin 1999). In her book *Flexible Bodies*, Martin notes that adaptability or flexibility is a prized characteristic that extends beyond the realm of the immune system. It is equally valuable for understanding people and institutions. Those who demonstrate a lack of adaptability are often viewed as less capable of thriving, whether in natural ecosystems or in the competitive landscape of the economy (Martin 1994).

Cumulatively, these concepts help theorize Black bodies as possessing what Spillers calls "zero degree of social conceptualization," which is interpreted here as bodies that are not normal but rather are pathologically fitted or retrofitted on demand—twisted by the history of racial hierarchies that have relegated Black bodies on a continuum of contradictions—located between immunity and susceptibility. That is to say, Black bodies can at once be strong and weak, capable and incompetent, necessary and unnecessary. The medical complex has held and continues to hold Black bodies hostage to this construction, marking them as everything all at once, assigning protean shape-shifting characteristics, smoothly pulling or pushing the Black body from one extreme to another.

Linger for a moment on the implications of racial difference organized as an extension of flesh and flexibility. Two historical examples reveal that medicine imposes a dangerous suppleness on Black bodies as flesh (subhuman) and flexible (fit enough to be manipulated into anything that meets white needs). Yellow fever is a viral example, and pelvic inflammatory disease is a reproductive example, both of which serve as surrogate explanations for Black people's "compulsory difference."

Historian Rana Hogarth (2017) offers insight into how racial differences became structured with the arrival of yellow fever from West Africa in the late seventeenth century. By the eighteenth century, yellow fever had settled in the Americas, gaining a reputation for attacking people along racial lines. Many remarked that it killed more white inhabitants than Black (Hogarth 2017, 18), thus contributing to the medicalization of Blackness. Rationalizing Black people's "low mortality" was rooted in medical authorities' differentiation of Black people, who they believed were innately immune to yellow fever. Physicians publicized the idea of innate Black immunity, and among them was Dr. Benjamin Rush of Philadelphia—the American physician, political leader, member of the Continental Congress, and a signer of the Declaration of Independence, who headed the first abolitionist organization in Philadelphia.

Indeed, it was Rush, Hogarth reports, who wrote to Richard Allen, founder of the African Methodist Episcopal Church, requesting help from

Philadelphia's "Negro" community to meet the needs of sick whites with yellow fever. He said:

> It has pleased God to visit this City with a Malignant and Contagious fever, which infects white people of all ranks, but passes by persons of your color. (Hogarth 2017, 26)

Rush exacted a plea for persons of color to aide in helping whites who were sick—a plea based on the belief there was an "innate" Black immunity to yellow fever. But, as Hogarth shows, Black people who labored in the service of caretaking for whites as nurses, cart drivers, and gravediggers were put directly in harm's way, and 240 "Negroes" died. Despite their deaths, "Negroes" were accused of having stolen from the people they took care of.

In a second example, we find that up until about the 1970s, racially differentiated diagnoses permeated reproductive health (in fact, they still do). Medical historian John Hoberman (1978) invites us to think about the racist implications of a 1938 article reporting that "pelvic inflammatory disease (or PID) is rampant in the colored and is much more frequent and severe than in the white" (Hoberman 1978, citing Williams 1938, 171). Gynecologists believed that Black women were more susceptible to PID, which reduced the likelihood of diagnosing the incredibly painful condition of endometriosis. Endometriosis, as it was associated with "modernity, mobility, and white women's fragility," was not a diagnosis available to Black women, who were (and continue to be) condemned to pathological promiscuity. Hoberman points out that only gradually did physicians come to believe that endometriosis was not just a "white woman's disease." The residual trafficking in Black promiscuity to assume immunity to endometriosis on the one hand and susceptibility to PID on the other, exemplifies the double meaning of flexibility and fleshiness of which Martin and Spillers speak, respectively.

Admittedly, these examples sit squarely in the realm of antiblackness and serve as indispensable examples of how Black bodies are situated outside of boundaries of normalcy. Scholars have delved into questions of antiblackness's relationality to social hierarchies and categories of the human and nonhuman. Laurian Bowles's (2025) work explores antiblackness within social hierarchies among women porters in Ghana. Bowles argues that Blackness is racialized through labor, migratory, and spatial arrangements. Such arrangements mediate women's (in)accessibility to resources as a legacy of slavery and colonialism. Zakiyyah Iman Jackson (2020) insightfully explores antiblackness, challenging that Blackness is not only a site of negation. Jackson emphasizes that the dehumanization of Black bodies through racialized animalization is distinct from the human-nonhuman animal divide. In Jackson's case, it is specifically tied to the systemic marginalization and devaluation of Blackness within human social structures. In other words, antiblackness cannot only be explained by exclusionary and dehumanizing analytics. Katherine McKittrick's (2016) analysis of Sylvia Wynter's *Black Metamorphosis* explicates the conditions undergirding antiblackness in historical context. Through the plantation system, it was violence against Black people that produced nonbeings out of Black people. Cumulatively, these scholars parse antiblackness, rather than conflating it solely with dichotomous human–nonhuman distinctions.

Returning to Bisola and the Kreyòl woman, we have two instances of Black bodies treated as if they are fundamentally outside the boundaries of normalcy: Their bodies are "other bodies," like the bodies Rush wanted to exploit and the bodies gynecologists pathologized. Bisola and the Kreyòl woman's encounters show they were subjected to multiple registers of harm and suffering ranging from neglect, to the absurdity of being forced to crab-walk, to the alleged delay of lifesaving compressions. From this adjacency to antiblackness, we can situate their harms in terms of *obstetric racism* (Davis 2019, 2020).

Obstetric Racism

Transitioning from the broader traumatic history of medical exploitation and discussions of antiblackness described in the previous section, we turn our attention to the production of trauma, through the narrower lens of obstetric racism. Obstetric racism is comprised of beliefs and practices leveled against the reproducing Black body that sit at the intersections of obstetric violence and medical racism (Davis 2020, 57–58). It is the mechanism and practice of subordination to which Black women and people's reproduction are subjected *that track along histories of* anti-Black racism based on ideas of difference that have been worked out through a hierarchy of humanity (the use of anti-Black signals political and structural dimensions of racism). Obstetric racism is a remnant of the afterlife of racial science, a term with resonance to the afterlife of slavery (Hartman 2007). Given that historically, Black women's bodies were used for economic and medical exploitation (Morgan 2021; Hammonds and Reverby 2019), obstetric racism links the emergence of obstetric medicine and Black women's treatment by medical professionals because Black women were central to the development of Western notions of value and race. The legacy of abuse extends beyond individual cases. In the nineteenth century, for instance, medical schools used Black cadavers to supply specimens for dissection (Smith 2024). Thus, medicine has long been animated by the exploitation of Black bodies.

Obstetric racism operates on two crucial levels: as an analytical concept and as a real-world phenomenon. As an analytic, obstetric racism serves as a powerful lens through which we can examine and understand the systemic mistreatment of Black women and birthing individuals in medical settings (Altman et al. 2023). As lived experience, it encompasses a range of discriminatory behaviors, abusive practices, and violent acts perpetrated by medical professionals and institutions against Black patients. These harmful experiences occur across the entire spectrum of reproductive health, including (in)fertility treatments, pre-conception care, conception-related services, prenatal care, childbirth experiences, and postpartum care. Critically, negative experiences are not isolated incidents but rather routine occurrences. The fundamental basis for this mistreatment is the patient's Blackness, highlighting how deeply entrenched racial biases can impact healthcare delivery and outcomes.

Understanding obstetric racism requires recognition that Black women themselves interpret their treatment as racism, illustrating one of the tenets of Black feminist theory—that lived experiences are legitimate spaces of theory-making, a point Patricia Hill Collins (1990) convincingly articulates. Collins emphasizes that power dynamics have sought to control Black women and Black people's humanity. Consequently, there is a convergence of structural control and the medical systems' pathologizing of race and gender. Fictionalizing pathology functions as a mechanism to make subjects vulnerable to extreme neglect or interventions—ultimately forcing Black women into the folds of trauma. The specificities of obstetric racism clearly show the traumas that Bisola and the Kreyòl woman endured.

The trauma of obstetric racism

In outlining the traumas on Bisola and the Kreyòl woman's reproducing bodies, we find both were ensnared by obstetric racism. But what constitutes obstetric racism? Davis (2020) has delineated six dimensions of obstetric racism—diagnostic lapses; neglect, dismissiveness, or disrespect; intentionally causing pain; coercion; ceremonies of degradation; and medical abuse—although this framework is adaptable, and further dimensions or characteristics of each may develop. While most dimensions are defined here using Bisola and the Kreyòl woman's experience as examples, in a different iteration, a specific incident may find its way across multiple dimensions. Given that obstetric racism tracks along historical events, a historical reference is also presented.

Diagnostic lapses occur when clinicians hold unexamined beliefs that Blackness is inherently pathological, leading them to downplay, exaggerate, or overlook a patient's symptoms, thereby resulting in inappropriate or missed diagnoses. Bisola's pain appears to have been viewed as manageable and was thus downplayed, even though she said the baby was crowning. This delayed recognition and diagnosis of her condition may be attributed to the "obstetric hardiness thesis" prevalent in the eighteenth and nineteenth centuries. Obstetric hardiness suggests that Black women are inherently resilient to stress and pains of pregnancy and labor (Bridges 2011). *Neglect, dismissiveness, or disrespect* is the result of medical professionals and staff not paying attention to a person in need of care, treating them with disdain, or both. The doctor's failure to respond to Bisola's questions about the hematoma and his subsequent departure was disrespectful. Regarding the Kreyòl woman, she too experienced neglect and disdain, given the absence of concern about the consequences of the reported delay in cardiac compression. In the past, Black women's reproductive health needs have been neglected, dismissed, and disrespected. For instance, the American Civil Liberties Union (ACLU) published a document of what happened in the 1990s when Norplant, the long-term reversable contraceptive, became available. Six matchstick-size silicone capsules were inserted into the upper arm, releasing small amounts of progestin. Although touted as effective, most women experienced side effects, but among Black women, the implants posed more severe complications. Those complications were dismissed in the interest of policy that sought to control Black women and girls' fecundity when Norplant was viewed as a panacea to decrease the "underclass" (ACLU 1994).

Intentionally causing pain occurs when medical professionals fail to adequately manage pain, often due to racialized beliefs about pain tolerance and a lack of empathy toward Black suffering. The idea that Black people are immune to pain has existed for centuries. Underscoring the historical context, one notorious example is the case of J. Marion Sims, known as the "father of gynecology," who conducted surgeries on enslaved women in the 1800s without anesthesia. Although absence of anesthesia was not the issue, one of Bisola's painful experiences centered on several painful and unsuccessful attempts by a resident to insert an IV line to administer fluids during the epidural—something Dána has heard and witnessed time and again. Infusion therapy protocols suggest restricting IV insertion attempts to no more than two attempts per clinician. According to scholars of nursing practice (Gorski et al. 2021), multiple unsuccessful attempts may cause patients to experience pain or limit vascular access or increase the risk of complications, among other adverse outcomes. To continue, then, is to intentionally cause pain.

While we do not know if the Kreyòl woman was subjected to coercion, Bisola did experience the *coercion domain* of obstetric racism, which arises when medical procedures are performed without consent or when patients are pressured into decisions. Bisola reported that when she was taken for surgery to remove the hematoma, the surgeon said, "You are already thirty-eight, with two children, we may need to perform a hysterectomy. Do you consent?" Bisola felt it was coercive because she was alone. No one contacted her family to discuss the necessity of surgery, and the doctor sought consent while transporting Bisola to the surgical theater.

Working as a doula, Dána has witnessed on-call physicians attempt to coerce birthing people, for example, to agree to a cesarean section by declaring, "Your uterus will fall out," or guilting people by asking, "You want what is best for your child, don't you?" Past examples of coercion include the forced sterilization of Puerto Rican and Black women in the 1930s and 1970s, respectively. Another notable example of coercion includes California's aggressive sterilization program, in which twenty thousand people were sterilized (Stern et al. 2017). *Ceremonies of degradation* involve humiliating or shaming patients, often assessing their worthiness or the perceived threats they or their support persons pose. Sometimes ceremonies of degradation lead medical staff to contact security, police, or other authorities to enforce compliance. Other times it looks like being made to do something that is demeaning. Again, Bisola's degradation originated with feeling worthless when she was commanded to walk, but then had to crawl on the floor on her hands and knees. In her brilliant book *No Mercy Here: Gender, Punishment and the Making of Jim Crow Modernity*, historian Sarah Haley (2019) recounts the innumerable occasions during which Black women had to bear the weight of white supremacy, what she calls racial gendered terror, through Georgia's punishment system in which women were not only subjugated as convict laborers but also forced to serve additional time before being released. *Medical abuse* takes many forms and occurs when professionals and corporations prioritize their own interests or imaginations over the patient's well-being, sometimes through experimental or repetitive actions. In one famous example, in 1951 Henrietta Lacks was diagnosed with cervical cancer. Doctors at Johns Hopkins took samples of her cancer cells without her knowledge, illegally and unethically profiting from her genetic material. A variant thread of abuse is the reported lack of urgency that jeopardized the Kreyòl woman's life due to the report of the attending doctor's delayed chest compression.

Obstetric racism casts a wide net in the ongoing connections between historical medical racism and contemporary medical mistreatment. By examining these individual women's experiences in conjunction with historical examples, we can see the enduring nature of racial subjugation. Broadly, this perspective underscores how Black bodies have been perceived as both distinct and indistinct—different enough to be pathologized, yet not so different as to be excluded from serving the needs of the medical complex. This duality has justified Black exploitation in medical contexts, where physiological characteristics and ideologies can rationalize disparate treatment and experimentation.

Drawing on the women's medical encounters, we now move the discussion of trauma and obstetric racism in relation to the category of Black Anti-Bodies.

Black Anti-Bodies

The experiences of the Kreyòl woman and Bisola illuminate pervasive racism and demonstrate the content of Black Anti-Bodies since both were seemingly subjected to and produced through the construction of what Rana Hogarth calls "Black medicine," revealing how physicians reinforce racial hierarchies by creating a distinct medical approach for Black bodies, perpetuating notions of racial inferiority. The aftermath of slavery in medicine has direct implications for the production and maintenance of Black Anti-Bodies. These cases exemplify how entrenched beliefs and power dynamics in healthcare settings not only shape perceptions and treatment of patients but also actively mold individuals into the category of Black Anti-Bodies, sustaining a racialized social order through medical practice.

What we are wrestling with is that Black bodies are discursively and materially encased in a frame of difference from "normative" white bodies, and are oppositional to what, as Martin describes, constitutes fitness. Fitness differentials are typically viewed to be physiological, mental, cultural, genetic, somatic, raced, and gendered. In other words, white bodies can be and are constructed as societally oppositional to other bodies such that white bodies are the standard body—healthy, alert, refined, sensate, normal, fragile, and worthy, whereas Black bodies are the Anti-Body. They are flawed, unhealthy, careless, slovenly, unfeeling, abnormal, strong, yet also unsuitable. In this way, Black bodies may be leveraged to protect other bodies as they are set apart through the humiliations inflicted by racism.[3]

The term "Black Anti-Bodies" exists within several material relations where corporeal punishment reigns. Black people experience these relations in various complexes—in prison-industrial, educational, and medical complexes. "Anti-Body" is the term meant to identify the rationale of suffering caused by the assaults of policing, policy, and practices—and though some die, others do not. Those that do not die are subjects, living the consequences of the medical complex's ability to master morbidity.[4] Anti-Bodies may be kept close to or severed from possibilities, or both; they can be ushered to and from fatality, and Black Anti-Bodies are formed through the repetition of maiming or harmful practices across time and space. Black Anti-Bodies are captive bodies made porous on demand.

The hospitals and medical personnel held Bisola and the Kreyòl woman captive. They were humiliated, degraded, dismissed, and treated as not-quite-worthy. Both women served as sites of institutional subjugation. One aspect of that subjugation lies in the logic of kinship dispossession. Black kin relations are so often subordinated to white institutions' desire to "shatter bonds," to borrow the title of Dorothy Roberts's 2002 book. Black kinship, as Spillers says, "can be invaded . . . at any given moment" (1987, 218), supporting the idea that Black kin relations are unimportant. For instance, if the outcome of Bisola's experience had resulted in death, her kin would have nothing against which to measure wrongdoing, because there were no records of anything having happened. In the case of the Kreyòl woman, the possibility of her dying would have left her child or children motherless and been a loss for her family. Neither woman was treated as if her body was evidentiary of a life with kin who would miss them.

Black Anti-Bodies seem to hold medical curiosity, an artifact of white medical supremacy's desire to induce extreme intervention or extreme neglect. Together, science and medicine's racist choreography create a political crisis and rationalization of Black difference, diagnostic lapse, and medical abuse, alongside interpretive logics of superhumanness—the ability to hold contradictions. Malleable Black bodies encompass paradoxical assessments of possibility and impossibility, enlisted by medical power as a central point of governance. The way Black bodies are treated keeps them in an unlimited cycle of regulation, neglect, and intervention. When race and class become pliable in the interest of biopolitics, we have a situation in which the Black body can be anything at any time—even if the thing it is at one moment contradicts what it was at another.

What Rests in the Space Around the Hyphen?

While it is incumbent upon Black feminism to explore the contradictory spaces where the bodies of Black people, Brown people, and those treated as nonnormative are forced to inhabit, showing how extreme attributes reinforce or expand domination, it is equally important to examine how Black Anti-Bodies engage in resistance, refusal, and mitigation. Such practices challenge extraction and erasure, justifying the hyphenated form of *Anti-Bodies*, which also signifies a form of resistance.

Drawing from Christina Sharpe's (2012) meditation on the hyphenated term "anti-blackness," the term *Black Anti-Bodies* signals degradation, but the hyphen signals possibility. Sharpe makes the case that "the hyphens mark a not irresolvable distinction, and they are a holding at bay, a horizontalization of relations, a holding on to" (7). Hyphens do not foreclose other openings; they suggest a break. And because there is space around the hyphen, there is the possibility of resolution. In other words, while the medical complex may be adept at producing or treating Black bodies as Anti-Bodies, Black bodies also push back against the violence of that system, as the historical record has shown.

Rachel Dudley is among the scholars whose work has illuminated Black women's resistance, and she provides crucial historical context for enslaved African American women's ongoing resistance. Dudley (2023) situates African American women as the foremothers of modern gynecology. Through her examination of four decades of Black feminist scholarship, art, and activism, Dudley resists victimization narratives, instead highlighting the agency and resistance of enslaved women. She reveals how bondwomen and enslaved midwives developed holistic practices to circumvent exploitative hospital treatments, laying the groundwork for contemporary birth movements.

Resistance manifests as acts of defiance against medical mistreatment and systemic racism. For instance, Bisola's documentation of her hospital experiences serves as a powerful example. Bisola anticipated that racism would define her labor and hospital treatment. Bisola wrote a letter in which she meticulously chronicled what happened while she was in the hospital. Bisola felt her treatment was the result of being Black and shared her sense that doctors and some nurses viewed her as unworthy of being listened to.

To counteract the silence often forced upon Black voices, Bisola made herself audible and made her laboring body "speak" by preparing the nineteen-page timed and color-coded chronology of the events (her daughter's father helped with the timekeeping). The colors represent a ranking of the degree of risk each event posed to her well-being high, medium, or low. In the last column, accompanying many of the events, were links to academic sources—scholarly evidence showing racial differences in outcomes and treatment between white versus Black women during labor and birthing. Think about this for a moment. Bisola came to the hospital prepared to note what happened to her.

The hyphen in *Anti-Body* signifies a second possibility within the context of systemic degradation. It represents a break in the narrative, allowing space for possibility and resolution, for life rather than silence or closure. This mark suggests that while Black bodies may be treated as "Anti-Bodies," they are sites of refusal against institutional violence, challenges to prevailing norms, and agentic assertions. Refusal is the act of rejecting the power of medicalization. Refusal, in this case, is informed by a clear sense that one rejects the possibility of coercion, medical abuse, and disrespect. It understands the implications of both doing and *not doing* something.

Refuse is what Dr. Robinson did. She refused to shy away from confronting Black women's treatment and the legacies that label us as pathological. She is, like so many of the Black reproductive workers Dána has spent time with—doulas, midwives, reproductive justice activists, and yes, some doctors and nurses—fundamentally in some way challenging medical sovereignty. They, and Dr. Robinson, betray the system. By telling the Kreyòl woman's story, Dr. Robinson, in our opinion, refused to comply with silencing a Black woman's denigration, by acting against the logics of medical supremacy.

Robinson, like other birthworkers, reproductive advocates, obstetricians, midwives, and doulas, engaged in labor challenging the inadequacies of the current system of maternal and infant health care. They labor in pursuit of justice by acting collectively for social change. Attending to the everyday activities that emerge out of prenatal care, pregnancy, labor, birthing, and postpartum care, they amplify and translate their care activities to make claims for reproductive justice precisely because Black birthing people live through agonizing encounters in medical spaces (Davis 2022).

Thus, the labor of reproductive care that many radical Black birthworkers provide is often linked to anti-racist political praxis. The article states that Dr. Robinson left that hospital in Florida, and other Black physicians have also left hospitals to write in the service of educating the public about their experiences of racism in hospital settings. Dr. Karen A. Scott, who identifies as a "recovering" OB/GYN, has designed the PREM-OB Scale of Obstetric Racism detailed in her book *SACKRED Birth: Mobilizing a New Quality Paradigm in Obstetric Care* (2025). Dr. Uché Blackstock, emergency physician and author of the book *Legacy: A Black Physician Reckons with Racism* (2024), examines systemic racism in healthcare and provides training to eradicate health disparities.

Due to the expectation of encountering racism in medical environments, individuals and collectives proactively undertake measures to counteract its potential effects. Within what I term "racial reconnaissance," there are preemptive efforts to identify medical settings and professionals that prioritize and respect bodily autonomy and integrity. This may involve a vigilant search for spaces aimed at minimizing the likelihood of experiencing racism. The overarching objective is to reduce vulnerability to racism by actively decreasing the possibility of facing racism.

Conclusion

The narratives of Bisola and the Kreyòl woman are stark and unyielding, serving as potent reminders of enduring injustices. Their experiences as subjugated Black Anti-Bodies are etched onto their lives. Through this concept, we have illuminated the paradoxical treatment of Black women's reproducing bodies as both indispensable and disposable. Pernicious stereotypes and racist ideologies have served as fodder of medical advancement, particularly in obstetrics and gynecology. The legacy of how Black bodies have animated these fields has straddled a form of obstetric pathology. The declaration of the Kreyòl woman's supposed invincibility in the face of cardiac arrest, and the dismissal of Bisola's pain during childbirth, are haunting reminders of how deeply racism can compromise care and cause harm.

Still the concept of Black Anti-Bodies is not only a lament. It is an urgent call to dismantle the structures of the white body as supreme and the Black

Anti-Body logics that pervade the terrain of medicine. We must ask: How does centering whiteness within the medical system perpetuate the formation of Black Anti-Bodies? Whose needs are prioritized when policies are shaped and practices are standardized around whiteness? Intentionally or not, the well-being of white women is often prioritized at the expense of others, making the greater success of white women's health inherently linked to the system that denies Black women and birthing people the same standard of care or disrupts their access to it.

Black women and birthing people live with representational and ideological inheritances in which medicine marks us as pathological, and although we have wounded relationships with medical systems and policies that control our reproduction, we enact everyday forms of resistance, refusal, and racial reconnaissance challenging the very systems that seek to define them.

Beyond these individual narratives and the institutional critiques already discussed, the implications of this framework emphasize the urgent need for comprehensive reform and deeper discussions. A pivotal moment in expanding this discourse occurred during the 2024 American Educational Research Association (AERA) panel "What Is the Black Maternal Health Crisis and What Is It Doing in a Nice Field Like Education?"[5] During the discussion, it was clear that education can play a vital role in societal transformation. The panelists' collective scholarship illustrates how educational frameworks can be important in dismantling the systemic oppressions that permeate healthcare. Furthermore, "Centering Black Women's Voices," by Brailey and Slatton (2024), calls for a reevaluation of healthcare systems, advocating for a model that offers more equitable practices. This aligns with our emphasis on transcending traditional approaches in order to incorporate a holistic understanding of patient experiences—especially those of Black women and birthing people.

As we consider the path forward, it becomes clear that addressing the issue of Black Anti-Bodies requires not only academic attention but also robust legislative action. Policymakers must leverage the insights provided by academic research to craft laws and regulations that genuinely address the highlighted disparities. This involves crafting healthcare policies that are proactive in preventing the perpetuation of inequality, rather than merely reactive. In advocating for these changes, it is imperative that we engage in a continuous dialogue with medical professionals, educators, policymakers, and the communities most affected by these issues. Only through a concerted and unified approach can we hope to dismantle the pernicious structures that currently define medical practices, paving the way for a system that respects and upholds the dignity and health of all individuals.

In conclusion, we are reminded that our responsibility extends beyond the pages of academic journals, into communities, the corridors of hospitals, the halls of legislation, and spaces where policies are shaped. The stories of Bisola, the Kreyòl woman, and countless others who navigate injustice are not just to be studied but to be acted upon. Because we stand at the cross-roads of knowing and doing, we should not only listen to their narratives. We must be active participants in a transformative movement, ensuring people's safety, amplifying their voices, and honoring their dignity.

Dána-Ain Davis is professor of urban studies at Queens College. Davis is on the faculty of the PhD programs in anthropology and critical psychology at the Graduate Center, where she is also the director for the Center for the Study of Women and Society. Davis is the author of *Reproductive Injustice: Racism, Pregnancy and Premature Birth*, which has received several awards, including the Eileen Basker Memorial Prize from the Society for Medical Anthropology and the Senior Book Prize from the Association of Feminist Anthropology. She can be reached at dana.davis@qc.cuny.edu.

Bisola Neil is an assistant teaching professor in the Educational Leadership Department at Montclair State University and a consultant supporting equity-focused curriculum and leadership development. Her research examines the leadership pathways and retention of Black mathematics teachers, using critical theory and QuantCrit to explore issues of equity, voice, and belonging. A former math teacher and school leader, her work focuses on curriculum and leadership practices that affirm the brilliance of Black students and educators. Her work is grounded in both scholarly inquiry and lived experience as a Black woman, educator, and mother committed to justice-centered education. She can be reached at neilb@montclair.edu.

Acknowledgments

The authors deeply appreciate the thoughtful feedback provided by the anonymous reviewers and the editors of *WSQ*, whose careful comments have greatly enriched this work. The authors also thank Emma Banks for proofreading assistance. We thank Laura Briggs; Valeria Ribeiro Corossacz, Sameena Mulla; Chiara Quagliariello; the BBQ+ Program at Johns Hopkins University; Riché Barnes, University of Florida; Maddalena Cammelli and the "F" Word Project at University of Turin; Jennie Gamlin, Paul Gilroy, and the Sarah Redmond Parker Centre for the Study of Race and Racism at University College London; Andrew Kim at UC Berkeley; Annie Menzel at University of Wisconsin–Madison; and Zakiyyah Sorensen at the UW Collaborative for Reproductive Equity.

Notes

1. This article has been written with Bisola Neil, who made the decision to use her real name. An early version of this article was published in *American Anthropologist* under the title "Black Anti-bodies and the Lexicon of Racism: A Thought Piece" in a special section edited by Chelsey R. Carter and Jallicia Jolly, "Antibodies, Anti-body: A Black Feminist Call and Response: Introduction."

2. Where we use the term "Black women and birthing people," we do so in general terms to be inclusive of all individuals who can become pregnant and give birth, regardless of their gender identity. In some cases, though, we refer to "women," for the following reasons: if the subject or issue refers to particular people who identify as such; to maintain the integrity of a scholar's intent; or to reflect language use in historically specific data that did not consider gender identities.

3. I thank Shebati Sengupta, 2023–2024 academic fellow of the BBQ+ program at Johns Hopkins University, who offered this keen observation.

4. Julia Kristeva's *The Severed Head* (2014) explores the symbolism of decapitation and its connection to identity and existence. This concept can be extended to examine the morbid fascination with the Black body in anatomical studies and the history of racial violence. The severed head represents a loss of self and the fragility of human existence, while also serving as a metaphor for the dehumanization and objectification of marginalized groups. This perspective provides insight into the disturbing history of using Black bodies for medical education and research, highlighting the intersection of racism and oppression.

5. This panel was chaired by Dr. Yolanda Sealey-Ruiz and included scholars like Dr. Amber Neal-Stanley, Dr. Qiana Lachaud, and Dr. Kisha M. Porcher (see Neal-Stanley 2024; Lachaud 2024).

Works Cited

ACLU. 1994. *Norplant: A New Contraceptive with the Potential for Abuse.* https://www.aclu.org/documents/norplant-new-contraceptive-potential-abuse.

Altman, Molly R., Kase Cragg, Teresa van Winkle, et al. 2023. "Birth Includes Us: Development of a Community-Led Survey to Capture Experiences of Pregnancy Care Among LGBTQ2S+ Families." *Birth* 50 (1): 109–19.

Blackstock, Uché. 2024. *Legacy: A Black Physician Reckons with Racism in Medicine.* New York: Viking Press.

Bowles, Laurian. 2025. *Headstrong: Women, Porters, Blackness and Modernity in Accra.* Philadelphia: University of Pennsylvania Press.

Brailey, C., and B. C. Slatton. 2024. "Centering Black Women's Voices: Illuminating Systemic Racism in Maternal Healthcare Experiences." *Journal of Health Disparities Research and Practice* 17 (1): 123–42.

Bridges, Khiara. 2011. *Reproducing Race: An Ethnography of Pregnancy as a Site of Racialization*. Berkeley: University of California Press.

Collins, Patricia Hill. 1990. *Black Feminist Thought: Knowledge Consciousness, and the Politics of Empowerment*. Boston: Unwin Hyman.

Davis, Dána-Ain. 2018. *Reproductive Injustice: Racism, Pregnancy, and Premature Birth*. New York: New York University Press.

Davis, Dána-Ain. 2019. "Obstetric Racism: The Racial Politics of Pregnancy, Labor and Birthing." *Medical Anthropology* 38 (7): 560–73.

Davis, Dána-Ain. 2020. "Reproducing While Black: The Crisis of Black Maternal Health, Obstetric Racism, and Assisted Reproductive Technology." *Reproductive Biomedicine and Society Online*, no. 11, 56–64.

Davis, Dána-Ain. 2022. "Beyond Birthing: The Labor(s) of Doulas and Black Birth Workers." In *The Routledge Handbook of the Anthropology of Labor*, edited by Sharryn Kasmir and Lesley Gill. London: Routledge.

Dudley, Rachel. 2023. "Honoring the Enslaved African American Foremothers of Modern Women's Health: Meditations on 40 Years of Black Feminist Praxis." *Medical Anthropology Quarterly* 38 (4): 445–61.

Gorski, L. A., L. Hadaway, M. E. Hagle, et al. 2021. "Infusion Therapy Standards of Practice." *Journal of Infusion Nursing* 44 (1S): S1–S224. https://doi: 10.1097/NAN.0000000000000396.org.

Haley, Sarah. 2019. *No Mercy Here: Gender, Punishment, and the Making of Jim Crow*. Chapel Hill: University of North Carolina Press.

Hammonds, Evelynn, and Susan Reverby. 2019. "Toward a Historically Informed Analysis of Racial Disparities Since 1619." *American Journal of Public Health*, no. 109, 1348–49.

Hartman, Saidiya V. 1997. *Scenes of Subjection: Terror, Slavery, and Self-Making in Nineteenth Century America*. New York: Oxford University Press.

Hartman, Saidiya V. 2007. *Lose Your Mother: A Journey Along the Atlantic Slave Route*. New York: Farrar, Straus and Giroux.

Hoberman, John. 1978. *Black and Blue: The Origins and Consequences of Medical Racism*. Berkeley: University of California Press.

Hogarth, Rana A. 2017. *Medicalizing Blackness: Making Racial Difference in the Atlantic World, 1780–1840*. Chapel Hill: University of North Carolina Press.

Jackson, Zakiyyah Iman. 2020. *Becoming Human: Matter and Meaning in an Antiblack World*. New York: New York University Press.

Kaiser Family Foundation. 2024. "State Profiles for Women's Health: Florida Maternal and Infant Health Data." https://www.kff.org/interactive/womens-health-profiles/florda/maternal-infant-health/.

Kirschner, Suzanne R., and Emily Martin. 1999. "From Flexible Bodies to Fluid Minds: An Interview with Emily Martin." *Ethos* 27 (3): 247–82.

Kristeva, Julia. 2014. *The Severed Head: Capital Visions*. Translated by Jody Gladding. New York: Columbia University Press.

Lachaud, Q. 2024. "Navigating the Academic Job Market at the Expense of Processing Birth Trauma: Reclamation for Healing." Paper presented at the American Educational Research Association Annual Meeting, Philadelphia.

Lauro, Sarah Juliet, and Karen Embry. 2008. "A Zombie Manifesto: The Nonhuman Condition in the Era of Advanced Capitalism." *Boundary 2* 35 (1): 85–108.

Martin, Emily. 1994. *Flexible Bodies: Tracking Immunity in American Culture from the Days of Polio to the Age of AIDS*. New York: Penguin Random House.

McKittrick, Katherine. 2016. "Rebellion/Invention/Grove," *Small Axe*, no. 49, 79–91.

Miller, Anna Medaris. 2021. "A Black OB-GYN Recalls Racism on the Job: 'You Can't Kill a Creole.'" *Business Insider*, February 5. https://www.insider.com/black-ob-gyn-recalls-racism-against-patients-of-color-2021-1.

Morgan, Jennifer. 2021. *Reckoning with Slavery: Gender, Kinship, and Capitalism in the Early Black Atlantic*. Durham: Duke University Press.

Mullings, Leith, Jada Benn Torres, Agustin Fuentes, Clarence C. Gravelee, Dorothy Roberts, and Azanet Thayer. 2021. "The Biology of Racism." *American Anthropologist* 123 (3): 671–80.

Neal-Stanley, A. 2024. "Birthing Herstory: Reproductive Labor and Slavey Re-Productions on the Antebellum and Academic Plantations." Paper presented at the American Educational Research Association Annual Meeting, Philadelphia.

Roberts, Dorothy. 2002. *Shattered Bonds: The Color of Child Welfare*. New York: Civitas Books.

Scott, Karen Antoinette. 2025. *SACKRED Birth: Mobilizing a New Quality Paradigm in Obstetric Care*. Lanham: Lexington Books.

Sharpe, Christina. 2012. Response to "Ante-Anti-Blackness." *Lateral: Journal of the Cultural Studies Association*, no. 1. https://ia801602.us.archive.org/34/items/Lateral1/Sexton%2C%20%22Ante-%20Anti-Blackness-Afterthoughts%22%20%28response%20by%20Sharpe%29.pdf.

Slaughter, Christine, Chaya Crowder, and Christine Greer. 2024. "Black Women: Keepers of Democracy, the Democratic Process, and the Democratic Party." *Politics and Gender* 20 (1): 162–81.

Smith, Laura Elizabeth. 2024. "Dissection, Media Portrayals, and Reaction: Black Bodies and Medical Education in Nineteen Century Newspapers." *Clinical Anatomy* 37 (4): 455–65.

Spillers, Hortense. 1987. "Mama's Baby, Papa's Maybe: An American Grammar Book." *Diacritics* 17 (2): 64–81.

Stern, Alexandra Minna, Nicole L. Novak, Natalie Lira, Kate O'Connor, Sioban Harlow, and Sharon Kardia. 2017. "California's Sterilization Survivors: An Estimate and Call for Redress." *American Journal of Public Health* 10 (1): 50–54.

USAFacts. 2023. "Which States Have the Highest Maternal Mortality Rates." https://usafacts.org/articles/which-states-have-the-highest-maternal-mortality-rates/.

Williams, George A. 1938. "Elliott Therapy of Pelvic Inflammations in the Negress." *Southern Medical Journal* 31 (11): 1171–74.

Wimbush, Vincent L. 2022. *Black Flesh Matters: Essays on Runagate Interpretation*. Lanham: Lexington Books.

Criminalizing Sex Work, Criminalizing Mothers: Unpacking the Legal Frameworks Impacting Sex-Working Parents

Regan Moss and Teagan Langseth-DePaolis

Abstract: Despite the variance between workers and across the industry, one thing remains consistent in all workers' experiences: They are forced to navigate the legalities of sex work within the U.S. For many sex workers who are parents, this poses a unique threat, as they must navigate the effects of criminalization on child custody, healthcare quality and access, and support in instances of client-based or partner-based violence. The way forward must be paved in a manner that prioritizes the legalization, or better, decriminalization of sex work on a large scale. Such legal changes must be paired with sex-worker-centered support services to ensure access to adequate healthcare and legal protections against exploitation by opposing parties, police, and discrimination. **Keywords:** sex worker, maternal health, criminalization, surveillance, family policing

The criminalization of sex work has also led to numerous health and human rights violations, including threatening sex workers' relationships with family and impeding their ability to parent.
> —Putu Duff et al., *Sex Work and Motherhood: Social and Structural Barriers to Health and Social Services for Pregnant and Parenting Street and Off-Street Sex Workers*

Introduction

Sex work is the provision of sexual services in exchange for money, goods, or other benefits. While many equate sex work to prostitution (e.g., street-based work, escort services, brothel-based work) or pornography, as they are popularized in media, these are only two forms of a very large and diverse

WSQ: Women's Studies Quarterly 53: 3 & 4 (Fall/Winter 2025) © 2025 by Regan Moss and Teagan Langseth-DePaolis. All rights reserved.

industry (Harcourt and Donovan 2005). There are many faces and forms of sex work (Harcourt and Donovan 2005). Like other occupations, individuals oftentimes engage in sex work in order to make money. Individuals who engage in this industry and are female are identified as FSW—or female sex workers.[1] Though many sex workers were not assigned female at birth (AFAB), discourse and research on sex work commonly uses this binary language.

Present country-level prevalence estimates of FSW within a country vary between less than 1 percent and 7.4 percent: Estimates are greatest in Latin America, followed by sub-Saharan Africa, Asia, and Europe (Vandepitte et al. 2006). The exact estimate of FSW within the United States is unknown. Due to the covert nature of the occupation, and the complexities in which people define their engagement (e.g., formal vs. informal, full-time vs. supplemental, in person vs. online), it has proven difficult to accurately assess the number of women who identify as female sex workers. Further, there are few barriers to entry, unlike with other occupations, which may require advanced degrees or training, thus making the industry more accessible for vulnerable populations. Thus, people may engage spontaneously, periodically, or consistently.

Many workers have children (Sloss et al. 2004), often reporting great joy and pride in their identity as mothers (Dewey 2011; Faini et al. 2020). Despite—though often in tension with—stigmas, many female sex workers report the desire to become pregnant and parent, similar to their non-sexworker peers. The stigma faced by FSWs will be discussed at a greater length later in this analysis, but generally sex workers are confronted with public pressures and political opinions regarding the nature of their work—making it difficult to live exactly how and where they want to, fully and openly. However, legal interventions may restrict the agency they have to express themselves through parenthood.

One of the most surveilled and criminalized forms of sex work, streetbased full-service prostitution, is an occupation predominantly consisting of low-income gig economy laborers. These workers also face a greater risk of policing, partner violence, client-based violence, and homelessness (Elmes et al. 2022). Coupled with the social vulnerabilities that street-based sex workers face exists the reality of extreme policing—such as through high levels of police presence in "red light districts"—and surveillance, as evident in targeted policies like FOSTA and SESTA (Jones 2022). This is largely due to the illegality of sex work. For instance, prostitution is illegal in every state except for Nevada; however, the specific regulations, penalties, and related status can vary considerably by state (see https://decriminalizesex.work/advocacy/prostitution-laws-by-state/).

In addition to the greater exposure to policing and surveillance as a result of their labor, sex workers also experience heightened policing and surveillance due to their increased risk of being impacted by substance use, homelessness, HIV transmission, and gang involvement. This is particularly true for street-based sex workers. For instance, a study conducted in London between 2018 and 2019 with street-based and non-street-based sex workers found that the prevalence of recent engagement with law enforcement was 87 percent among street-based workers as compared to 9 percent among off-street workers (Elmes at al. 2022). While an equity-based lens (i.e., one with attention toward difference in occupational conditions as a result of socioeconomic insecurity or stigma associated with street-based labor) is critical to unearthing the social inequities that shape policing practices in the U.S., it should not be mistaken that all sex workers, or even a majority, are street-based workers or engaged in prostitution. There are a variety of ways in which someone may engage in sex work, diversity of circumstances that lead someone to the occupation, and significant variability in workers' identities and what they experience within the industry and as parents. That is, individuals may engage spontaneously, or the work may fluctuate between part-time and full-time. Work may be web-based or full in-person services. Some workers experience poverty, and others find that the industry allows for financial stability. Despite the variance between workers and across the industry, one thing remains consistent in all workers' experiences: They are forced to navigate the illegalities of sex work within the U.S. This has negative consequences on themselves, their health, and their families.

Methods and Approach to Analysis

Any true study of how criminalization impacts sex workers is incomplete without the input and guidance of sex workers. This analysis, in utilizing documented firsthand accounts of sex workers from secondary sources, aims to center the voices and experiences of sex workers as they navigate the illegality of their labor. Specifically, this paper looks to articles and interviews conducted with sex workers to examine where and how the criminalization of their labor impacts them as parents, as well as their children.

The legal elements of this paper pull from family law cases throughout the United States, the expectations for treatment of sex workers published by international governing bodies, as well as secondary scholarly sources and critiques of the systems as they exist now. Cases were found using keyword searches like "custody," "health," and "prostitution," in addition to searching for articles published by organizations focused on uplifting and decriminalizing sex work(ers). Generally, there is an extensive amount of research left to be done on this topic. Therefore, there were limited existing interviews and firsthand accounts of sex workers' experiences as parents. Even in legal cases that were accessible for the purposes of this publication, the role of sex workers in shaping the lives and well-being of their children is diminished. Rather, these cases discuss the sex work profession solely for the purpose of denigrating the sex workers' character evaluation in custody matters.

With the largest portion of existing research focused on FSWs, our methods aimed to be inclusive of sex workers who were not AFAB, while understanding that existing discourse on this topic tends to operate within the sexual binary. Research on sex work would be utterly incomplete absent considerations of non-AFAB sex workers, and for the reasons set forth here and in the introduction, scholarship regarding the experiences of non-AFAB parent sex workers is an area in need of expansion.

Sex Work, Parenthood, and Health

For many sex workers who are parents, the illegality of their work poses a unique threat, as they must navigate the effects of criminalization on child custody, healthcare quality and access, and support in the instances of client-based or partner-based violence. The exact estimate of the percentage of sex workers who are parents is not clear, but research shows that many of the sex-working women enter and continue sex work to support their families (Basu and Dutta 2011; Bucardo et al. 2004).

Sex workers may experience issues related to child custody and child removal by social services on the basis that they are a sex worker. The prejudice against sex workers leads to child custody loss or removal of a child by social services due to a perception that they are "unfit" to parent or mother (McNamara 2022). For instance, mothers in London reported being accused of not keeping their children safe and "putting them in harm's way" in instances of domestic violence, and their child custody was lost and instead given to their abusive partner (Support Not Separation 2022). Though sex workers contacted social services to receive support for domestic violence, they instead lost custody of their child, which they reported to be on the basis that they were a sex worker (Support Not Separation 2022). Further, actors in social services accused mothers of prioritizing "men" and "money" over their children. This is despite the fact that their income from sex work was providing for their children and that many sex workers see sex as separate from sexual services. Policing the parenthood of sex-working moms causes irreparable harm to the child(ren) and parent(s) involved. Dewey and coauthors (2018) found that workers report a "causal effect between child custody loss and intensified illicit drug and/or street involvement in ways that highlight the shared precarities they face." The forced removal of children on behalf of the state can lead to unhealthy behaviors in the parent and behaviors that make it even more difficult to appease the state's ideas of responsible parenthood.

Custody, Child Protective Services, and the Department of Human Resources

The legal system surrounding child and family disputes exposes sex workers to extreme discrimination as a result of the criminalization of their profession. One potential root of this issue, and of many collateral consequences of the criminalization of sex work, can be traced to the Model Penal Code. The Model Penal Code (MPC) is a set of recommended laws, definitions, and rationales for the criminal legal process published by the American Law Institute in 1962. Though not every state has adopted the MPC in its entirety, at least thirty-seven states have adopted at least some of its provisions (Dubber 2015, 5–6).

MPC §251.2 governs "prostitution and related offenses," deeming it a petty misdemeanor to be an "inmate of a house of prostitution or otherwise engage . . . in sexual activity as a business;" or "loiter . . . in or within view of any public place for the purpose of being hired to engage in sexual activity" (Model Penal Code 1962, §251.2).

One section of the MPC in particular complicates child custody and family law matters most significantly. Subsection four of MPC §251.2 states: "A person, other than the prostitute or the prostitute's minor child or other legal dependent incapable of self-support, who is supported in whole or substantial part by the proceeds of prostitution is presumed to be knowingly promoting prostitution in violation of subsection (2)." Though child custody and family law matters only arise if the child is a minor, the criminalization of not only sex work but being financially *supported* by sex work further stigmatizes sex workers and calls into question their capability as parents on a social level. In fact, even though a mother who is a sex worker may pass inspection with regard to their ability to provide a "loving and stable home" (one variation of a fairly consistent legal standard in these cases), the workers are often "left with the fact that their job is usually illegal—and in the eyes of some on the bench [court], immoral" (Weisman 2018). Thus, even if the child is a minor and not technically subject to the "promotion of prostitution" provisions of laws criminalizing sex work, the judge in any given case has near-full discretion in determining whether a parent who happens to be a sex worker can provide the type of home environment, assessed during custodial proceedings.

Oftentimes, the inherent biases of judges are seen in these cases through their demeanor and rulings against the sex worker (Weisman 2018). Though varied by jurisdiction, family courts consider a variety of factors when determining whether a parent should have custody of a child. Among the factors considered in a custody dispute are histories of domestic violence or substance use by either parent; the financial status and ability of each parent to provide for the child's needs; the stability of the proposed custodial home; and, in some court systems, the "moral fitness" of the parents as it impacts the child.[2] Generally, these determinations are made at hearings considering what is in the "best interest" of the child. As is made clear by the exercise of sweeping judicial discretion in custody cases involving sex workers, "the problem with the moral fitness and fitness factor when conducting [a] best-interest analysis is a lack of judicial consistency and uniformity in applying the facts to the law" (Meyers and Wolf 2024, 52). As Janet Dolgin emphasizes in her piece "Why Has the Best Interest Standard Survived?," the best-interest standard is "vague" and "non-directive," and allows decisions to depend on the "character values, and prejudices of the presiding judge" (Dolgin 1996, 2). The wide discretion given to each individual judge in determining what is in the best interest of a child means that "behaviors viewed by a court as socially marginal may become determinative in custody decisions" (Dolgin 1996, 4). The socially marginalized nature of sex work, combined with its criminalized status, allows judges to make decisions against sex workers purely on moral or personal value grounds.

As stated by Liz Afton, counselor at the Sex Workers' Project, "parents, particularly mothers, who are involved in sex work often have it used against them to separate them from their child" (Weisman 2018). This has been seen in several family court cases in the United States. In *Fleming-Martinez v. New Jersey Div. of Child Prot. & Permanency*, the plaintiff claimed that his minor children were placed with an unfit custodian, Ms. R., who he argued was "living an unhealthy lifestyle and was involved in prostitution" (2022 WL 17850144). Though the plaintiff's case was ultimately dismissed, the court failed to condemn the wielding of Ms. R.'s involvement in sex work as a factor to be negatively considered in the custodial evaluation. Rather, the court dismissed the case because the claims made were not about the Division of Child Protection and Permanency and, procedurally, should have been handled differently between the parties. The weaponization of one's status as a sex worker in these hearings, if not challenged or noted, contributes to the normalization of such behavior within the court system. This case also illustrates an important and devastating trend: the criminalization of sex workers in the criminal legal system seeping into the civil system, legal claims, and parenthood rights in a manner that can strip sex workers of their children and endanger their livelihood.

Similarly, in *Procopio v. Johnson* and *Ambrosio v. Ledesma*, plaintiffs used involvement in and allegations of sex work as evidence that the sex-worker parent was unfit to maintain custody over their children. Again, though the involvement in sex work was not necessarily dispositive in these cases, the instinctual presentation of evidence of sex work as a means to paint the sex worker as an unfit parent illustrates the deep infiltration of criminalization attitudes in all areas of the legal system.[3] Importantly, even though sex work may not be the single dispositive issue in these cases, it is a contributing factor to the court's consideration of whether a particular mother is capable of parenting in a way that is in the best interest of the child.

Though neither of these publicly available cases resulted in a judgment against the sex workers in question, sex workers who are parents are undeniably stripped of their parental rights because of their status as sex workers. For example, in summarizing her interviews, Carrie Weisman (2018) highlights the frequency with which sex workers face loss of custody of their young children. One example in particular involved a sex worker who lost custody of her child due to filming legal sex shows in the home, which, according to the court, "allowed her child too much awareness of the job." According to another interviewee of Weisman's (2018), "every sex worker I know has had their custody threatened." These stories illustrate the catastrophic impact of bringing allegedly "criminal" behavior—which is commonly driven by personal choice or economic need—into civil courtrooms. The possibility of having one's profession impact their ability to have custody over their children exacerbates the widespread marginalization of this working population. Additionally, involving sex work in custodial hearings can extend the discrimination and marginalization to the children and families of sex workers, sometimes regardless of whether the sex worker is an outstanding parent.

Healthcare Access

Under international law, sex workers have a legally recognized right to health. The right to health is safeguarded in multiple parts of international law. Article 25 of the Universal Declaration of Human Rights (1948) lays out the right to health: "Everyone has the right to a standard of living adequate for the health and wellbeing of himself and of his family, including housing and medical care." Additionally, the International Covenant on Economic, Social and Cultural Rights (ICESCR) codifies the right to health in article 12, which lays out the "right to the highest attainable standard of physical and mental health" (ICESCR 1976), including "access to medical care due to a physical, sexual, and psychological violence" (Marshall 2016, 5). Impressively, several UN bodies have taken specific note as to how the right to health of sex workers is impacted in the modern world. In 1999, the Convention on Discrimination Against Women issued a general recommendation calling for "special attention" for the right to health needs of "vulnerable and disadvantaged groups," including "women in prostitution" (Mgbako 2012, 115). Additionally, the ICESCR Committee in General Comment No. 22 called for state parties to "take measures to fully protect persons working in the sex industry," including by ensuring "access to the full range of sexual and reproductive healthcare services" (Mgbako 2012, 115). The most forceful calls for attention on sex worker health have come from the World Health Organization and the Joint United Nations Program on HIV/AIDS, who have both demanded decriminalization of sex work due to the excessive violations of the right to health experienced by sex workers because of criminalization (Mgbako 2012, 116).

As part of the Universal Declaration of Human Rights's promise to ensure the inalienable rights of all members of the human family, the declaration must include the rights of sex workers as those which are protected and promoted. Similarly, the ICESCR promises that the right to health guarantees certain protections to *everyone*, as participants in the global economy and social structure requires that sex workers are included as a component of that *everyone*. However, in the United States, where sex work is heavily stigmatized and criminalized, as is the existence and transmission of HIV, sex workers are less able to exercise a full right to health and more prone to criminal charges. Sex workers as a whole experience a higher prevalence of HIV infection (Visawsam et al. 2021, 16). Sex workers as a collective, however, are also well versed and successful at curbing new HIV infections through safety measures and community action (Tago et al. 2021). Because of the prevalence of HIV among sex workers, they, as a group, are more frequently subject to the multitude of criminal laws governing HIV transmission and disclosure.

The relationship between the health of sex workers and criminalization is simple: Criminal laws governing *both* sex work and HIV "significantly impede the ability of sex workers to access services and to live without the stigma and blame associated with being a transmitter of HIV" (Baskin et al. 2016, 355). When sex workers are criminalized for their labor, they are less able to "negotiate safer sex practices with clients and have less access to testing, treatment, and health care in general," making it more likely that sex workers "will not know their HIV status or be able to limit their risk" (Baskin et al. 2016, 361). Not only does the criminalization of sex work decrease sex workers' access to healthcare and safe sex practice, but it also increases the likelihood of transmission of HIV. This is particularly problematic because of laws targeting HIV-positive people, as it compounds the criminalization of sex workers based on their work *and* their HIV status.

Laws that target HIV-positive sex workers can be found in various places in statutes: Sometimes they are within anti-prostitution laws in state criminal codes, other times they are included in a separate part of the law pertaining to HIV. A large trend among statutes that relate to HIV and sex work, though, is that involvement in the sex industry (which is usually charged as a minor crime or misdemeanor under state law) frequently *compounds* with laws criminalizing HIV exposure and HIV testing laws —leading many sex workers to be charged or convicted with a felony offense (Baskin et al. 2016, 363). The severe escalation of the level of crime charged, from misdemeanor to felony, can be seen in several laws still in existence today across the U.S., both its states and territories:

1. In Guam, where prostitution is a misdemeanor offense, a person convicted of prostitution who engaged in such work knowing that

   they were infected with either HIV or AIDS is guilty of a felony in
   the first degree (9 GCA §28.10[b][3]).

2. In Ohio, where solicitation of prostitution is a misdemeanor, no
   person who has knowledge that they have tested positive for HIV
   can engage in sexual activity for hire. If they do so, they are charged
   with a felony in the third degree (ORC Ann. §§2907.24, 2907.25).

3. In Oklahoma, where prostitution is a misdemeanor, any person who
   engages in sex work knowing they are HIV-positive is guilty of a
   felony (21 Okl. St. §1031).

4. In Pennsylvania, where prostitution is a misdemeanor, if a sex worker
   promotes their work knowing they are HIV-positive, they can be
   charged with a felony in the third degree (18 PA.C. S. §5902).

5. In Utah, where prostitution is a misdemeanor, a person who is
   HIV-positive and is convicted of engaging in sex work is guilty of a
   felony in the third degree (Utah Code. Ann. §§76-10-1302, 1309).

6. In Georgia, where prostitution is a misdemeanor, if a sex worker
   engages in a sexual act for money "with the intent to transmit HIV
   without disclosing his/her status" or "consenting to perform the
   sexual act when such an act has a significant risk of transmission,"
   such a worker is guilty of a felony (O.C.G.A. §16-5-60).

7. In Missouri, where prostitution is a class B misdemeanor, if a sex
   worker engages in "prostitution" knowing that they are HIV-positive,
   such sex work would be considered a class B felony. Importantly,
   the "use of condoms is not a defense to this offense" (§567.020 R.S.
   Mo.).

The language of these statutes further criminalizing sex workers fails to take
into account safety precautions taken by the laborers surrounding their
HIV status (aside from Missouri law, which explicitly states that the use of
prophylactics like condoms is *not* a defense to the felony charge of engaging
in sex work while HIV-positive). The lack of consideration for the precautions taken by sex workers in managing their HIV diagnosis, treatment, and
potential for transmission further minimizes the autonomy of sex workers and their ability to execute their labor safely and considerately. These
laws fail to take into account the success of antiretroviral therapy and HIV
prevention measures that reduce transmission risk (Lehman et al. 2014,
997). Further, such laws are problematic due to their failure to take into
account how difficult it is to prove causation with transmission, the fact

that HIV is not easily transmitted, and that other means of transmission may yet be found to exist (Lahey 1995, 86–87).

Given that sex workers are already criminalized for their profession, the criminalization of engaging in their work while HIV-positive only serves to move healthcare and treatment of HIV into the shadows, further jeopardizing the health of sex workers and their clientele. While laws criminalizing engagement in sex work while HIV-positive serve to further criminalize sex workers—triggering the collateral consequences on sex workers and their families that accompany criminal convictions—laws exist on the global scale that explicitly criminalize the ability of people who are HIV-positive to provide for their child.

HIV-Transmission Breastfeeding Laws
The criminalization of HIV onsets prior to infancy or early childhood, and FSWs may experience criminalization of HIV during pregnancy. This is true especially for workers who use substances. FSWs who are injecting drug users have lower rates of condom use with clients as compared to non-injecting drug-using FSWs (Lau et al. 2007). Pregnancy after HIV is associated with antiretroviral therapy interruption, knowledge of mother-to-child transmission, and negative perceptions of care provider(s) (Cernigliaro et al 2016). Thus, without HIV testing and treatment (continuity) within family-planning clinics as well as through perinatal care provision (Schwartz et al. 2015), workers may breastfeed while being HIV-positive. Given the barriers to seeking care and associated stigmas of HIV, workers may be at risk of facing criminalization due to HIV-transmission breastfeeding laws.

In addition to laws criminalizing HIV transmission in the United States, several countries have laws targeting people living with HIV for acts that are deemed a "transmission risk," like breastfeeding (Symington et al. 2022, 1). As of 2022, there has been a wave of criminal cases against women living with HIV for breastfeeding (Symington et al. 2022, 2). Women living with HIV experience "surveillance judgment and limitations on autonomy and decision-making in relation to childbearing and infant feeding" (Symington et al. 2022, 1). There have been at least twelve prosecutions of women living with HIV worldwide in relation to breastfeeding or comfort nursing, in countries such as Malawi, Uganda, Kenya, Zambia, Canada, Austria, Botswana, and Russia (Symington et al. 2022, 3–5). These prosecutions typically occur under laws requiring people who are HIV-positive to take all reasonable measures and precautions to prevent the transmission of HIV to others and avoid placing another person at risk of contracting HIV (Symington et al. 2022, 5). Under these laws, a person who is HIV-positive and breastfeeding is considered to be "willfully" exposing the child to HIV, which is viewed as an "offense against the child's health and their future" regardless of the risk of HIV transmission actually being fairly negligible (Symington et al. 2022, 6). While the aim of such laws is typically to reduce parent-to-child transmission, in reality, laws that criminalize transmission in this manner worsen health for both parents and children. The fear of criminalization in these situations may deter parents who are HIV-positive from "communicating honestly with their service providers, . . . potentially putting their child at increased risk of acquiring HIV or suffering other health problems" (Symington et al. 2022, 6). Given that scientific evidence suggests the risk of transmission through breastfeeding is low, this criminalization simply represents "discrimination on the basis of positive HIV status" (Symington et al. 2022, 7). Notably, as many of these prosecutions have taken place in low- and middle-income countries (LMICs), this is in direct opposition to guidance from the World Health Organization, which has issued guidance on the value of breastfeeding in LMICs among moms living with HIV who are food insecure.

Stigma and Policing

Due in part to the criminalization of sex work, workers face significant stigma associated with being pregnant or parenting and in sex work. Further, FSWs frequently face unethical provider discrimination that may contribute to delays in seeking care (Moore et al. 2023). Provider discrimination such as violations of patient confidentiality, assumptions of being "infected," and social exclusion from other mothers impact the well-being of sex-working moms (Dewey et al. 2022; Beckham et al. 2015). In some instances, workers feel the need to avoid disclosing their occupation entirely, which can complicate the provision of care (Beckham et al. 2015).

The conditions of the industry at large, such as difficult clients and unsafe working conditions, which are associated with incarceration, victimization, and police harassment, are also contributing barriers to care (Sloss et al. 2004). Duff and colleagues (2015) found other social barriers to care during pregnancy among FSWs. Factors included sex work stigma, homelessness, educational attainment, poverty, policing, and fear of child protective services (CPS). Fears of CPS are rooted in historical precedent, whereby children of sex workers are taken away and occupational status is used as a means to criminalize parenthood.

Violence against workers by police, within the workplace (i.e., from clients or pimps), and from intimate partners warrants adamant attention toward safety, especially considering elevated rates of intimate partner violence during pregnancy within general populations, and high rates of violence toward sex workers even when not pregnant (Duff et al. 2015). However, there is a dearth of information on violence against pregnant female sex workers. Further, due to economic instability and food insecurity, FSWs report engaging in sex work late in pregnancy and returning early in the postpartum (Reno et al. 2020). This is critical context in light of the effects of abuse at later gestational ages. Due to the discrimination of workers from police and CPS, workers face challenges in seeking support for violence against them. Workers also report being turned away from victim services when seeking out care because they are sex workers. This may pose challenges for workers with child custody, even during early postpartum. For instance, workers report child custody being threatened when trying to seek support for sexual assault. Thus, the safety of workers is weaponized by legal actors.

In addition to their custodial rights and family access to healthcare being threatened by the criminalization of their profession, sex workers are also subject to increased policing and compounding criminalization. One of the primary ways in which sex workers are more policed, more surveilled, than the average laborer is through sex offender registries. Though we do not see many states explicitly requiring people with prostitution convictions to register as sex offenders, there are several states in the U.S.—namely Arkansas, Louisiana, Ohio, South Dakota, and Tennessee—that require people who have been convicted for intentionally transmitting HIV to register (Center for HIV Law and Policy 2017). Given the aforementioned prevalence of HIV among sex workers, laws that require people to register for transmission of HIV inevitably and disproportionately affect sex workers.

The registration of sex workers as sex offenders, even if implicitly done through HIV criminalization, creates a slippery slope for the registration of sex workers as offenders as a whole. Until 2012 in New Orleans, prior to the Louisiana Supreme Court deeming such a law unconstitutional, workers convicted of prostitution-related offenses were required to register as sex offenders. The reasoning behind the unconstitutionality of the statute involved the impact on sex workers' housing and employment. In addition, sex workers faced increased stigma, marginalization, and violence within their communities as a result of their registration. This can pose further harms to sex workers, who may be being exploited or stalked by clients, as the stigma compounds and legal services may be difficult to access, putting them and their children in danger. Individuals who are on sex offender registries in the U.S. have their addresses made public. As a result, they are harassed, stalked, and physically harmed. When sex workers are put on the registry, they and their families are at an increased risk for discrimination and violence. Individuals who are labeled "sex offenders" by law have significant challenges in obtaining custody rights in order to protect children. As sex workers are not sex offenders, registering them as such can impact their ability to have custody of their children. Therefore, any kind of association between sex offender registries and sex workers should receive severe skepticism and reform.

Conclusion

Laws criminalizing sex work do not follow scientific evidence. For instance, criminalization of breastfeeding while HIV-positive is in direct opposition to guidance from the World Health Organization. Further, criminalization is shown to have harmful health outcomes toward sex-worker mothers and their children, rendering these policies more harmful than helpful. The laws described here need to be revisited and amended or abolished. While many of these laws have incidental or collateral consequences on workers, the general criminalization of sex work is associated with negative health outcomes. Criminalization of sex work leads to poor health outcomes among workers, including sexual and mental health outcomes and also maternal-child health outcomes. Contrastingly, countries that have legalized or decriminalized sex work demonstrate better health outcomes (McCann et al. 2021).

Many scholars and research have observed that sex workers are more likely to seek healthcare and see improvements in their sexual health in settings where sex work was legalized or decriminalized (McCann et al. 2021, 7). Ultimately, the criminalization of sex work does not have an isolated impact. Rather, the impact is compounded with the ongoing criminalization of homelessness,[4] addiction, poverty, and HIV status. Sex workers have complex social and physical needs that domestic and international policy must reflect. The way forward must be paved in a manner that prioritizes the legalization—or better, decriminalization—of sex work on a large scale. Such legal changes must be paired with sex-worker-centered support services to ensure access to adequate healthcare and legal protections against exploitation by opposing parties, police, and discrimination.

Regan Moss, MPH (she/her), is a graduate of Columbia University and a doctoral student at Tulane University. Her research integrates social and legal epidemiology, feminist theory, and behavioral science to examine how cultural ideas of morality and criminality surrounding m/otherhood and womanhood drive health inequities. Recognizing the impact of legal inequities on personhood, she examines the embodiment of such health inequities through maternal and reproductive psychology frameworks on maternal and reproductive identities and experiences of womanhood and m/otherhood. She can be reached at rmoss3@tulane.edu.

Teagan Langseth-DePaolis is a recent graduate of Northeastern University School of Law, currently working in criminal defense in Boston, MA. Teagan's work is driven by her passion for sex-worker justice and the devastating collateral consequences of the criminalization of sex work. Teagan seeks to continue to highlight and change the discrimination, marginalization, and criminalization sex workers face, through ongoing projects and activism. She can be reached at teaganlangsethdepaolis@gmail.com.

Notes

1. While many individuals who engage in the sexual commerce industry may have children and not identify as "mothers" and likewise many individuals may not be AFAB, cisgender, and/or don't identify as women, the largest body of evidence and documentation on criminalization of the parenthood of workers is on AFAB individuals who identify as mothers. Thus, our work is focusing on the experiences of these workers. We believe it's crucial that future research highlights the experiences of individuals who are parents in the industry and are not cisgender women, especially given the marginalization of transgender individuals in the industry.
2. *F.T. v. L.J.* 194 Cal. App 1, 28 (4th Cir. 2011); *Matter of Fiore v. Gima*, 227 A.D. 1071, 1073 (A.D. 3d. 2024); *In re Marriage of Winternitz*, 235 Cal. App 644, 658 (4th Cir. 2015).
3. *Procopio v. Johnson*, 994 F.2d 325 (7th Cir. 1993); *Ambrosio v. Ledesma*, 227 F.Supp. 3d 1174 (D. Nev. 2017).
4. *City of Grants Pass v. Johnson*, 603 U.S. 520 (2024).

Works Cited

American Law Institute. 1962. *Model Penal Code.*

Baskin, Sienna, Aziza Ahmed, and Anna Forbes. 2016. "Criminal Laws on Sex Work and HIV Transmission: Mapping the Laws, Considering the Consequences." *Denver Law Review* 93 (2): 355–88. https://heinonline .org/hol-cgi-bin/get_pdf.cgi?handle=hein.journals/denlr93&section=12.

Basu, Amber, and Mohan J. Dutta. 2011. "'We Are Mothers First': Localocentric Articulation of Sex Worker Identity as a Key in HIV/AIDS Communication." *Women & Health* 51 (2): 106–123.

Bucardo, Jesus, Shirley J. Semple, Miguel Fraga-Vallejo, Wendy Davila, and Thomas L. Patterson. 2004. "A Qualitative Exploration of Female Sex Work in Tijuana, Mexico." *Archives of Sexual Behavior* 33 (4): 343–351.

Center for HIV Law and Policy. 2017. "State-by-State Chart of HIV-Specific Laws." The Center for HIV Law and Policy. https://www.hivlawandpolicy .org/sites/default/files/State-by-State%20Chart%20of%20HIV -Specific%20Statutes%20and%20Prosecutorial%20Tools.%20%28final %208%2023%2017%29.pdf.

Cernigliaro, Dana, Clare Barrington, Yeycy Donastorg, Martha Perez, and Deanna Kerrigan. 2019. "Patient-Provider Communication About Pregnancy and HIV Among Female Sex Workers Living with HIV in Santo Domingo, Dominican Republic." *BMC Pregnancy and Childbirth* 19 (1): 427.

Dewey, Susan. 2011. *Neon Wasteland: On Love, Motherhood, and Sex Work in a Rust Belt Town.* Berkeley: University of California Press. https://doi.org/10.1525/9780520948310.

Dewey, Susan, Kirsten Brown, Jessica Hankel, and Tonia Anasti. 2022. "'I Was Already in the System from the Start': How Substance-Using Women in the Street Sex Trade Make Decisions About Pregnancy." *Drugs: Education, Prevention and Policy* 29 (2): 150–59.

Dolgin, Janet L. 1996. "Why Has the Best Interest Standard Survived? The Historic and Social Context." *Children's Legal Rights Journal*, no. 16: 1–2.

Dubber, Markus D. 2015. *An Introduction to the Model Penal Code.* 2nd ed. Oxford: Oxford University Press.

Duff, Patricia, Jane Shoveller, Joti Chettiar, Catriona Feng, Roberta Nicoletti, and Karen Shannon. 2015. "Sex Work and Motherhood: Social and Structural Barriers to Health and Social Services for Pregnant and Parenting Street and Off-Street Sex Workers." *Health Care for Women International* 36 (9): 1039–55.

Elmes, Jocelyn, Rachel Stuart, Pippa Grenfell, Josephine Walker, Kathleen Hill, Paz Hernandez, Carolyn Henham, et al. 2022. "Effect of Police Enforcement and Extreme Social Inequalities on Violence and Mental Health among Women Who Sell Sex: Findings from a Cohort Study in London, UK." *Sexually Transmitted Infections* 98 (5): 323–31.

Faini, Diana, Patricia Munseri, Muhammad Bakari, Eric Sandström, Elisabeth Faxelid, and Claudia Hanson. 2020. "'I Did Not Plan to Have a Baby. This Is the Outcome of Our Work': A Qualitative Study Exploring Unintended Pregnancy Among Female Sex Workers." *BMC Women's Health* 1 (20): 1–13.

Harcourt, Chris, and Bridget Donovan. 2005. "The Many Faces of Sex Work." *Sexually Transmitted Infections* 81 (3): 201–6.

Jones, Angela. 2022. "FOSTA: A Transnational Disaster Especially for Marginalized Sex Workers." *International Journal of Gender, Sexuality and Law* 2 (1): 73–99.

Lahey, Karen E. 1995. "The New Line of Defense: Criminal HIV Transmission Laws." *Syracuse Journal of Legislation and Policy* 1 (1): 85–95. https://heinonline.org/hol-cgi-bin/get_pdf.cgi?handle=hein.journals /syracujlpo1&section=6.

Lau, J. T. F., Shara P. Y. Ho, X. Yang, Eric Wong, H. Y. Tsui, and K. M. Ho. 2007. "Prevalence of HIV and Factors Associated with Risk Behaviours Among Chinese Female Sex Workers in Hong Kong." *AIDS Care* 19 (6): 721–32.

Lehman, J. Stan, Meredith Carr, Allison Nichol, et al. 2014. "Prevalence and Public Health Implications of State Laws That Criminalize Potential HIV Exposure in the United States." *AIDS Behavior* 18 (6): 997–1006. https://pubmed.ncbi.nlm.nih.gov/24633716/.

Marshall, Rachel. 2016. "Sex Workers and Human Rights: A Critical Analysis of Laws Regarding Sex Work." *William & Mary Journal of Women and the Law*, no. 23, 47.

McCann, J., Gregory Crawford, and Jessica Hallett. 2021. "Sex Worker Health Outcomes in High-Income Countries of Varied Regulatory Environments: A Systematic Review." *International Journal of Environmental Research and Public Health* 18 (8). https://doi.org/10.3390/ijerph18083956.

McNamara, Molly. 2022. "Sex Work, Social Services, and the Needs of Mothers and Their Children." *openDemocracy*, March 22. https://www.opendemocracy.net/en/5050/sex-work-social-services-mothers-children/.

Meyers, Ariana, and Gabrielle Wolf. 2024. "Policing Morality: The Inconsistent Application of the Moral Fitness and Fitness Factor." *Children's Legal Rights Journal* 44 (1). https://lawecommons.luc.edu/cgi/viewcontent .cgi?article=1284&context=clrj.

Mgbako, Chi. 2012. "Why the Women's Rights Movement Must Listen to Sex Workers." *Huffington Post*, June 1. https://www.huffpost.com/entry /sex-workers_b_1561428.

Moore, Brandi E., Lauren Govaerts, and Farzana Kapadia. 2023. "Maternal Health and Maternal Health Service Utilization among Female Sex Workers: A Scoping Review." *Women's Health* 19. https://doi.org /17455057231206303.

Reno, Rebecca, Sharvari Karandikar, Rebecca J. McCloskey, and Megan España. 2020. "Structural Vulnerabilities and Breastfeeding Among Female Sex Workers in Mumbai." *Maternal & Child Nutrition* 16 (3): e12963.

Schwartz, Sheree, Erin Papworth, Marguerite Thiam-Niangoin, Kouame Abo, Fatou Drame, Daouda Diouf, Amara Bamba, et al. 2015. "An Urgent Need for Integration of Family Planning Services into HIV Care: The High Burden of Unplanned Pregnancy, Termination of Pregnancy, and Limited Contraception Use among Female Sex Workers in Côte d'Ivoire." *Journal of Acquired Immune Deficiency Syndromes* 68 (March): S91–S98.

Sloss, Christine M., Gary W. Harper, and Karen S. Budd. 2004. "Street Sex Work and Mothering." *Journal of the Association for Research on Mothering* 6 (2): 102–15.

Support Not Separation. 2022. "Stop Punishing Sex Worker Mums by Taking Kids Away, Demand Activists." *Support Not Separation* (blog), July 28. https://supportnotseparation.blog/2022/07/28/stop-punishing-sex -worker-mums-by-taking-kids-away-demand-activists/.

Symington, Alison, Nyasha Chingore-Munazvo, and Svitlana Moroz. 2022. "When Law and Science Part Ways: The Criminalization of Breastfeeding by Women Living with HIV." *Therapeutic Advances in Infectious Disease* 9 (September). https://doi.org/20499361221122481.

Tago, Achieng, Lyle R. McKinnon, Tabitha Wanjiru, Festus Muriuki, Julius Munyao, Gloria Gakii, Maureen Akolo, et al. 2021. "Declines in HIV Prevalence in Female Sex Workers Accessing an HIV Treatment and Prevention Programme in Nairobi, Kenya over a 10-Year Period." *Aids* 35 (2): 317–24.

United Nations. 1948. *Universal Declaration of Human Rights.* https://www.un.org/en/about-us/universal-declaration-of-human-rights.

Vandepitte, J., R. Lyerla, G. Dallabetta, F. Crabbé, M. Alary, and A. Buvé. 2006. "Estimates of the Number of Female Sex Workers in Different Regions of the World." *Sexually Transmitted Infection* 82 (3): 18–25.

Viswasam, Nikita, Justice Rivera, Carly Comins, Amrita Rao, Carrie E. Lyons, and Stefan Baral. 2021. "The Epidemiology of HIV among Sex Workers Around the World: Implications for Research, Programmes, and Policy." In *Sex Work, Health, and Human Rights: Global Inequities, Challenges and Opportunities for Action,* edited by Shira M. Goldenberg, Ruth Morgan Thomas, Anna Forbes, and Stefan Baral. Springer.

Weisman, Carrie. 2018. "The Right to Mother and Do Sex Work." *In These Times,* February 12. https://inthesetimes.com/article/presumed-guilty-of -bad-mothering.

The Fermented Subject: Bodily Survival and Kinship-Building in Grace M. Cho's *Tastes Like War*

Aimee N. Jurado

Abstract: This paper close-reads Grace M. Cho's memoir *Tastes Like War* to describe an Asian American subjectivity that is fermented under the pressures of immigration, assimilation, and Americanization. This fermented subjectivity is analyzed through the experiences of Korean military brides like Cho's mother, Koonja, whose integration into U.S. society in the twentieth century exemplifies a specific transformation of the Korean body, its identification, and its use. The fermented subject describes one whose subjectivity holds a past and present form simultaneously, while also remaining expansive and in flux. As such, Asian American assimilation is punctuated by the persistence and resiliency of the fermented subject. **Keywords:** assimilation, immigration, Americanization, Asian American identity, Korean War, fermentation

Grace M. Cho dedicates her memoir *Tastes Like War* to "all of my mothers, each of whom fed me in her own way." While we as readers don't know these mothers that Cho refers to, "mothers" is understood here to mean more than one's biological mother, and that to be fed is to be nourished by each person Cho has felt mothered by. This dedication precedes her chapter "Kimchi Blues," in which Cho describes how food, and kimchi specifically, is situated in her bodily memory. "Kimchi Blues" is also a reflection on the domestic ramifications of assimilation, displacement, and war for twentieth-century Korean immigrants. Simultaneously, Cho's memoir reminds us that the presence of brutality does not mean an absence of tenderness, and that to be "fed in her own way" is to signify a nourishment that is one's own.

While the historical timeline of an occupied Korea is relatively concrete, the timeline Cho grounds her text in is anything but linear. Jumping back and forth between her mother's life and her own memories, Cho offers a

WSQ: Women's Studies Quarterly 53: 3 & 4 (Fall/Winter 2025) © 2025 by Aimee N. Jurado. All rights reserved.

memoir and family history that sees the effects of Japanese and American occupation in Korea as a fluid component in the lives of Koreans, Korean Americans, and Korean "military brides" especially.[1] Across her chapters, Cho comes to terms with her mother Koonja's schizophrenia diagnosis by way of close-reading Koonja's memories that resurface alongside the historical events that coincide with these resurgences. Thus, Koonja's developing schizophrenia intertwines with a muddled history that necessitates a nonlinear analysis to match the nonlinear text, paying close attention to the intimate spaces between time, family, history, memory, and place.

While Koonja's marriage and immigration happen in the 1970s, her experiences still reflect early, pre–Korean War experiences of Korean military brides, and to ground her text in this history, Cho interweaves pertinent moments of Ji-Yeon Yuh's *Beyond the Shadow of Camptown* into "Kimchi Blues," contextualizing the historical circumstances that brought American men and Korean women together and naming the specific tensions that arose in and around these unions. Specifically, Yuh highlights the nearly one hundred thousand Korean military brides that immigrated to the United States between 1950 and 1989, and the Korean-American marriages brought forth by American occupation prior to the Korean War (Yuh 2002, 3). It's this history that informs Koonja's relationship to war, her marriage to Cho's American military father in 1971, and her relationship to the United States.

Alongside Yuh, my close reading is informed by Grace M. Cho and Hosu Kim's "The Kinship of Violence," which analyzes the Korean war as a site of simultaneous destruction and creation. In their text, Cho and Kim analyze specific productions of American occupation in Korea and the making of a new kind of citizen: the mixed-race Korean American child born from "camptown women" and American GIs, whose conception is disapproved of in Korea and whose Korean-ness makes them an outsider in the United States. I use Cho and Kim's way of carefully naming this production, in terms neither good nor bad, to theorize Cho's focus on kimchi in "Kimchi Blues" to suggest that assimilation into the United States, like the process of fermentation, changed the Korean military bride socially and bodily, thus producing a new kind of identity and existence for these women. Likewise, the Korean military bride's role in mixed-race American homes produced a new kind of kinship and family dynamic that, like the unwieldy bubbles of fermentation, needed to be controlled in and out of the Korean American household.

Theorizing Cho's use of the metaphor of kimchi is not to understand Korean military brides' assimilation into American culture in concrete terms. Rather, it's to further ideas that Lisa Lowe puts forth in *Immigrant Acts,* where she analyzes the complex history of Asian American citizenship throughout the nineteenth and twentieth century and names the Asian American as an alternative site to Americanization. Lowe writes:

> Rather than attesting to the absorption of cultural difference into the universality of the national political sphere as the "model minority" stereotype would dictate, the Asian immigrant—at odds with the cultural, racial, and linguistic forms of the nation—emerges in a site that defers and displaces the temporality of assimilation. . . . Rather than expressing a "failed" integration of Asians into the American cultural sphere, this distance *preserves* Asian American culture as an alternative site where the palimpsest of lost memories is reinvented, histories are fractured and retraced, and the unlike varieties of silence emerge into articulacy. (Lowe 2012, 6; italics added)

Lowe's presentation of Asian American identity is purposeful and warrants a close reading. For an Asian body to assimilate into American culture, it is not enough to integrate; it's not even enough to emulsify; one must be *absorbed*, swallowed, into a universality dictated by the "national political sphere." However, the Asian body in the United States is rewarded not for its absorption but for its *trying* to be absorbed, further reinforced by the model minority myth, Lowe says. When an Asian body does not fully dissolve its Asian-ness, as it's encouraged to do but is never allowed, this is seen as a "failed integration" and further justification for seeing the Asian body as "other." And yet, Lowe suggests, if Asian bodies never arrive at full integration, perhaps the place they do occupy disrupts this domination. It's in this space, or rather having this *distance* from Americanization, that Asian Americans preserve, retrace, and articulate a "palimpsest of lost memories" and their histories.

Lowe's vision inspires what I call a "fermented subject," which in this context is the Asian American citizen produced but never "completed" under the pressures of U.S. assimilation. I italicize Lowe's use of the word "preserve" to highlight fermentation as useful language for describing components of identity that preserve some point of origin but are dynamic and changing, holding both past and present in the fermented subject. But also, the fermented subject complicates Lowe's use of the palimpsest and its function in preservation. Lowe's palimpsest theorizes what it means to simultaneously hold an attempted erasure while retracing an Asian subject's individual and collective memory. Where the palimpsest and the fermented subject differ is in *how* they preserve and reinvent an Asian identity. For

Lowe and her use of the palimpsest, preservation is an act of protection, ensuring and maintaining what lies under the surface and acknowledging its existence within the palimpsest. Whereas the fermented subject offers a site for the past to not only be present but nourished; where the past is alive and fed by the present and by ongoing, dynamic interactions with other organisms, systems, pressures, and communities.

Lowe herself attends to this dynamism in her chapter "Heterogeneity, Hybridity, Multiplicity: Asian American Differences," where she offers the terms "heterogeneity," "hybridity," and "multiplicity" to examine different axes of Asian American identity. In thinking about essentialized versus universal understandings of Asian American identity, Lowe argues that rather than imagining Asian American identity as something definitive, it would be more productive to focus on "Asian American cultural practices that produce identity" and how these practices are constantly in relation to historical, generational, and other material differences within Asian America (Lowe 2012, 67). Thus, Lowe offers her terms as an approach to Asian American identity that can remain in flux and yet specific. In a similar way, fermentation is a transformative process, recognizing that the entanglements of heterogeneity, hybridity, and multiplicity demonstrate transformation in motion.

If we are thinking about body matters as the bodies who matter and issues of the body, Espiritu's *Body Counts* and Cho's *Haunting the Korean Diaspora* lay out plainly that bodies, Asian bodies, matter in the aftermath of U.S. imperialism and militarization. How these bodies and their ghosts are read and handled matters not only in our memories but in how such figures are re-membered in collective and individual memories (Cho 2008, 3–4). I situate the fermented subject in the context of Asian immigration into the United States, due to a history of Asian bodies being marked as perpetually "other" and "alien." In ways both structural and social, Lowe points out how despite the ever-changing categorization of Asian and Asian American immigration and citizenship that haunts the "national memory" of the United States, an understanding of Asian and Asian American identities is far less dynamic (Lowe 2012, 6–10). Asian immigrants and Asian Americans continue to be defined in proximity to that which is alien, a "yellow peril," and forever foreign due to past legislation and wars that marked them as a threat to, and being outside of, American society.

In and out of Lowe's academic scope, fermentation and its relationship to contamination is informed by a dedication to purity and "pure blood" that continues in the United States, impacting Asian and non-Asian Americans alike. Purity, as Sandor Ellix Katz says, is a fantastical concept, and contamination is not only inevitable but has likely already happened, as no subject arrives at an interaction in a pure state, free from their own muddled history (Katz 2020, 41). This same rhetoric around contamination and fear of its spread characterizes a history of Asian people and their immigration to the United States, showing up as things like the "Yellow Peril" or "China Virus" that inform Asian American identity to this day. It's this history, as well as fermentation's proximity to contamination, that makes the fermented subject a relevant theoretical lens to study Asian American subjectivity. However, Katz's alternate description of fermentation as a force that cannot be stopped and that "recycles life, renews hope, and goes on and on" can be a tool for centering persistence and resistance as opposed to trauma and displacement. Reading fermentation as having a rebellious spirit that is "allied with purpose, but can just as well be petty, peevish, or personal" (Katz 2020, 85–86) allows a reading of Asian American experience that exists outside the realm of complacency, the model minority myth, or survival. It's this rebellious spirit that is reminiscent of Lowe's describing Asian America as a site of resistance and possibility and makes way for the one who "fails" to integrate into American society. And while the palimpsest is helpful in studying an Asian American identity written and revised, the fermented subject attempts to unflatten the palimpsest.

Just as fermentation is an incremental and somewhat invisible process, the transformation of a fermented subject is observable through the intimacies of daily life. Cho's memoir illuminates these intimacies by way of making her mother's story visible while still contextualizing it with Korean American history and critical feminist thought. To articulate how these intimacies form the fermented subject, I close-read Cho's "Kimchi Blues" to study the theme of kimchi and how foodways relate to the fermented subject. In this close reading, I attend to Cho's integration of *Beyond the Shadow* into her chapter, noticing how she literally layers the text within her memoir and differentiates Yuh's work from hers with italics. By doing so, Cho engages Yuh's ideas and makes *Beyond the Shadow*'s influence clear, inviting readers to see her memoir in conversation with Yuh and the analysis that she puts forth. Given how central *Beyond the Shadow* is to Cho's memoir, I include a close reading of Yuh's text to better understand the assimilationist pressures put on Korean military brides, and I incorporate a variety of intimacies, like oral histories and domestic experiences, in this reading of a fermented subjectivity.

My aim is to imagine through "Kimchi Blues" what a fermented subject could be and how fermented subjectivity illuminates sites of transformation for Korean military brides and Korean immigrants more generally. I begin by analyzing how ingesting food changed for Korean military brides upon coming to the United States. For these women, food altered from something commonplace to a necessary component of physiological and social survival. I think about how kimchi, a fermented Korean side dish, is central to the story of transformation in body and community that both Yuh and Cho highlight. From here, I transition into not only the circumstances that necessitated such changes to Korean families and communities but also the specific kinship and familial dynamics that emerged from Korean-specific displacement. I discuss identity in this section to consider the ways Korean mothers were active participants in the home but simultaneously relegated as the other, further differentiating these women from their biracial children. While the idea of a fermented subjectivity is certainly not applicable to Korean Americans alone, my hope is that this paper can study one specific event, the integration of Korean military brides into the American home, to argue that the identity of Asian Americans exists in motion with what Lowe names heterogeneity, hybridity, and multiplicity. In this way, the fermented subject is complex, dynamic, and a site of transformation.

Cho begins "Kimchi Blues" by revisiting a story of Koonja's relationship to kimchi. Separated from her family as a child and left to feed herself, Koonja rationed the "earthenware jars of kimchi that [her] grandmother had buried in the backyard" (Cho 2021, 90), demonstrating the scarcity that war brought forth and defining the kind of survival it necessitated. Rationing her food at a young age, Koonja is an example of how Koreans adapted in a state of war and, specifically, how scarcity changed food and familial practices. Korean relationships to food became further complicated by the introduction of American food on military bases stationed in Korea, which, as Cho points out, oftentimes became one of the few reliable sources of food for Korean refugees. Reflecting on Koonja's transition from Korea to Chehalis, Washington, Cho writes, "As a child, I never imagined that it was so hard on my mother to have limited access to Korean food, because there had always been American foods she enjoyed. She loved hamburgers and hot dogs, and any kind of meat, foods that had colonized the collective taste buds of South Korea during the American occupation and war" (Cho 2021, 96). Koonja's relationship to food and her literal gastronomy were not only complicated but colonized; her altering tastes being a direct result of American occupation and necessity. And while American society warns against contamination brought forth by Asian immigration, these warnings are contradicted by the U.S. occupation of Korea. What Cho's memoir makes apparent is that colonization of Korean bodies began even before one's immigration to the United States and that for Koonja and other Korean refugees, their bodies were primed for Americanization by way of associating American GIs with the taste of satiation.

Food, of course, is only one way in which Koonja's body experienced American occupation. Cho discloses in her memoir that her mother's survival included being a "camptown woman" for American GIs, offering sexual services for compensation. "I would learn," Cho writes, "that the prototypical Korean birthmother looked a lot like my mother—the camptown woman of the 1950's and 1960's—and then I'd remember her complaining that the birth control pills she used to take hadn't worked" (Cho 2021, 100). While this paper focuses primarily on the relationship between food and the changing body, the experiences of camptown women are an important consideration in the relationship between Korean and Korean American bodies and fermentation under American influences. It's this way of relegating the Korean body to a means of American satisfaction in Korea that gives way to another kind of relegation for the Korean body in the United States.

American occupation and the Korean War spurred the creation of an altered Korean body that assimilationist efforts could build upon. However, similar to Koonja's reliance on kimchi to survive Japanese occupation in Korea, kimchi acted as symbolic refuge for Korean military brides in the face of Americanization. To understand the ways food, and specifically kimchi, was a mode of survival, it's important to first understand the circumstances that caused Korean military brides distress and isolation in the United States.

Yuh argues that not being fluent in English, not having access to Korean food, and being discouraged from finding Korean community amplified the discrimination Korean women faced in the United States and negatively altered the domestic space for these women. Specifically, her chapter "Immigrant Encounters" emphasizes the struggle for Korean military brides to function in American society, due in large part to their not being fluent in English. That "in a largely monolingual environment where English is the ruling language, lack of fluency in English means not only the inability to fully communicate, but also the inability to function *with confidence.* . . . Language differences brought more than ridicule or humiliation. They prevented women from receiving proper service, medical care, education, jobs and other necessities" (Yuh 2002, 93–96; italics added). As Yuh suggests, America's monolingual ideology not only daunts a non-native speaker but is purposeful in maintaining a culture and environment that revolves around "proper" American English and, in turn, American culture and thought. When these language barriers permeate into larger social structures like healthcare, academia, the workforce, and more, it becomes expected that American language is needed to function in these spaces, lest you face "ridicule or humiliation." But even if these women could speak English, it's not always enough to feel *confident* in communicating their needs. Lacking language, but specifically lacking language in a monolinguistic culture, makes the mouth unreliable in meeting and communicating one's basic needs and thoughts.

Losing language compounded "the burden of adjustment [placed] almost entirely on the shoulders of women. This is true not only for language, but for virtually every area of daily life, including food, child rearing, housekeeping, and work" (Yuh 2002, 96). Throughout her text, Yuh analyzes the significance of controlling Korean women's language and consumption of food, arguing that these domestic battles paralleled American propaganda that pushed for an erasure of Korean culture in favor of American culture. She writes, "Language and food are two mediums through which Korean military brides are pressured to act American. . . . Likewise, American food was dominant in most homes while Korean food was only minimally present. . . . It is also a way for husbands to assert their authority and preside over an 'American' family, a way to contain the racial-cultural other that they have brought into the family through marriage" (Yuh 2002, 99). Where English was necessary to function in the public sphere, "American-ness" was necessary to function in the domestic sphere.[2] More than this, American expectations of the home allowed American husbands to maintain power, as they would always have the closest proximity to American-ness, thus having the most authority over how an American home "should" be. In this dynamic, American households could maintain their "American" qualities while containing "Korean" ones, further defining the home's "racial-cultural other" and assigning a specific identity to Korean wives. By doing so, expectations of an American wife are laid bare, and especially the expectations of a *Korean* wife *when in America*.

With this in mind, we revisit Cho's reflection on her mother's survival among her new family: "My father's family, too, was wary of my mother. Little by little, she chipped away at their fear by learning to cook their familiar foods and hosting all-American Thanksgiving dinners in which green Jell-O concoctions made an appearance on the table" (Cho 2021, 94). Food maintained power over Korean wives and vice versa, acting as a site for

Korean wives to prove their American-ness and that they were trustworthy. For Koonja, conceding to "green Jell-O concoctions" and other American foods meant lessening family tensions and regaining safety amid hostility. In Cho's memory, we see the uneven power dynamic between American and Korean family members that leads to an absence of Korean food and culture. As a result, the domestic sphere changes from a place of refuge to an additional place of contention for Korean women like Koonja.

But if the mouths of Korean women could no longer communicate or eat their desires, what becomes of them? It's perhaps because of this question that Cho includes an epigraph from Kyla Wazana Tompkins's *Racial Indigestion*: "The double function of the mouth—both in processing food into digestible matter and in producing sense—sutures that space to the domestic and civic production of language, of storytelling" (Cho 2021, 62). Tompkins analyzes the mouth's ability to ingest and "produce sense," meaning that for fermented subjects, manipulation of the mouth is to change how and what the body ingests and makes sense of. In conjunction with Tompkins, an analysis of oral histories demonstrates how losing access to language, in and out of the home, changed the body's use of the mouth, as it was no longer a reliable site for communication and nourishment.

However, language was only one way assimilationist efforts manipulated the mouth to serve American preferences. Upon their arrival in the United States, Korean military brides were met with the absence of Korean food and an abundance of American food. This jarring change in the gastronomical landscape forced an immediate detox of the body's Korean-ness by way of starvation and an immediate adoption of American-ness through American foods. Despite this "powerful force for Americanization," Yuh says that "the women not only longed for Korean food, they also searched for it, invented ways to replicate it, and gave it an emotional loyalty they never developed for the American food they ate out of necessity" (Yuh 2002, 128). Yuh's description parallels the scarcity of food that Koonja faced in Korea. Of course, the absence of Korean food and the absence of food altogether are different circumstances, but the absence in both changed how Korean food was seen and consumed. For Korean military brides, inventing replicas of Korean food not only signaled survival but a change in food practices, and makeshift Korean food signaled a medium through which Korean military brides *created* ways to satiate more than their hunger. As Yuh points out, the relationship between food and kinship interconnects in the social-psychological survival for Korean military brides. The specifics of the relationship between food, kinship, and identity will be further analyzed, but it would be remiss to analyze survival without acknowledging how kinship makes survival possible. What Yuh points to, and what Cho's memoir observes, is a nourishment found in community intertwined with food and food practices. Reliance on community made access to food possible and fed the Korean body and Korean kin.

The oral histories in Yuh's text prove that survival through community was necessary in navigating the pains that displacement and assimilation created. As discussed previously, efforts to streamline Korean military brides' assimilation into American culture targeted language and food, and, similar to how American culture revolved around the English language, American foods were expected of American homes. Yuh cites sociologist Marjorie DeVault (1991) when she writes that "feeding the family literally produces the family. It is at meals that the unity of the family is expressed and reinforced, that the individual members feel themselves to be part of a whole. Thus women's work of feeding the family is more than just nourishing bodies, it maintains a particular social unity, the family" (Yuh 2002, 138). This newfound responsibility oftentimes meant American husbands discouraged their Korean wives from keeping Korean foods in the home, or from cooking and ingesting Korean foods at all. For these women, a failure to uphold American-ness meant a failure to uphold the family, and thus failing as a wife. Furthermore, the Korean wife is tasked to produce a family that they themselves are not seen as a part of because they're Korean, forcing them to find refuge in alternative ways as the domestic becomes an extension of Americanization.

For these women, being Korean in the mixed-race household resulted in inner and outer conflict. Yuh writes that the enforcement of English and American foods not only impacted the mixed-race family's interactions with each other but also their way of seeing each other: "Their [military brides'] own family becomes the terrain for intercultural encounter, struggle, and negotiation. . . . The husband, the biracial children, and the family itself are defined as American, while the wife, however accultured she may be, is defined as Korean" (Yuh 2002, 98). Yuh notes a contradiction similar to the one Lowe points out, which is that while the Asian body is encouraged to assimilate, it is simultaneously seen as a perpetual other. Where enforcing English and American food asserted dominance over Korean women, the isolating consequences of this enforcement reinforced such dominance.

A lack of language meant literally boxing Korean mothers out of their mixed-race family's conversations and intimacies, and "instead of becoming a bilingual family, they have become a primarily monolingual family.

. . . Even those who said that they had little trouble communicating with their husbands also said that they were not able to satisfactorily communicate their innermost thoughts. . . . Sometimes they feel left out when their husbands and children speak to each other in English" (Yuh 2002, 99–102). Just as a lack of language disallowed military brides from meeting their public needs, a lack of *satisfactory* language disallowed a deeper connection with family. In this way, what ferments in the Korean American home is not just a convergence of racial identities, languages, and customs; also feelings; isolation, disconnect, and misunderstanding become part of these familial relationships and the Korean American domestic sphere more broadly.

The mixing of Korean and American cultures in the home, however, was not isolated in the United States, nor was it a consequence of Korean military brides' immigration only. In their cowritten essay, Cho and Hosu Kim name "The Kinship of Violence," detailing the effects of the Korean War on kinship ties in and out of Korea. In this essay, Cho and Kim argue that the Korean War, also called the "Forgotten War," literally altered Korean bodies and communities through destruction, but that from this destruction also came new kinds of bodies that weren't so easy to categorize. Specifically, they break these bodies into literal and abstract categories: First are bodies that adopt a new identity characterized by their newfound need for care. These persons would include those made into orphans, widows, disabled people, and homeless people as a direct consequence of war. Second are what Cho and Kim refer to as "'excess bioproduct' [referring] to the new bodies that are born of militarized occupation and war, such as that of camptown prostitution. Camptown sex workers and biracial children who were fathered and abandoned by American soldiers . . . presented a very special kind of population problem for South Korea" (Kim and Cho 2014, 35). For both full and, especially, mixed-race Korean children, the effects of the war and U.S. involvement made Korea a place of precarity and contention, usually before they were even old enough to experience such. The feelings Korean people had about mixed-race children conceived in this time were also not subtle, as illustrated by the sentiments of Korea's first president, Syngman Rhee: "We are most anxious to send as many orphans to the States as possible. In particular we desire to have adopted those children of Western fathers and Korean mothers who can never hope to make a place for themselves in Korean society" (Kim and Cho 2014, 37). Rhee summarizes a culture and mentality towards mixed-race children in Korea that led Korean mothers to relinquish their children to the United States, hoping that they would find acceptance. Cho and Kim's analysis of postwar kinship offers framing to consider Korean American homes and Korean–American kinships that are not only complicated by U.S. occupation and the Korean War but also forge new, nonheteronormative relationships.

The history that Cho and Kim provide nuances the relationships that Cho and Koonja forge with other Korean people in the U.S. Reflecting on her mother's time in Chehalis, Cho writes about how Koonja recognized the needs of other displaced Koreans and took action by sharing kimchi with them. She recalls her mother consoling two Korean adoptees that had moved to Chehalis and were crying uncontrollably. After visiting these neighbors and offering herself as a translator, she explains: "'Mrs. Anderson was fermenting some cabbage, you see, and the poor children thought it was kimchi but it was sauerkraut.' She held her disappointment in her heart for a moment. . . . She immediately recognized them as mouths to feed, and for a brief moment, she became the Korean mother these children had lost" (Cho 2021, 99–100). Koonja does not say out loud what she recognizes in these children, nor does she explicitly say what is so disappointing about the cabbage turning out to be sauerkraut. Only through the context Cho provides is it clear that what Koonja holds in her heart is an understanding that these children are starving for something that is absent in America, and that this need is invisible to the Americans around them. It's starvation, both of Korean food and Korean-ness, that makes assimilation and displacement even more brutal.

Cho observes from this memory how Koonja stepped into a mothering role for these children and "recognized them as mouths to feed." Again, mouths are centered as a part of the Korean body that endures a forced change, a force that went unnoticed in homes like the Andersons'. Despite the dominating pressure of Americanization, Koonja's efforts to care for the children should not be dismissed, as her interjection is both an act of care and a disruption to assimilation by reintroducing what's been lost to the children. As such, defining a fermented subject cannot be thought of as a practice of adding and subtracting components of one's identity but rather of understanding that what has been lost and what is new both exist as change and do not necessarily negate each other. Similar to how Cho and Kim analyze the "excess bioproduct" created from war, Cho's memoir sees the community that Koonja creates with other displaced Koreans in Chehalis as forged from displacement and isolation, but kinship nonetheless.

In response to the Korean adoptees being teased by sauerkraut, Koonja does the "one reasonable thing" she can think to do and decides to make kimchi for the children. Cho describes how Koonja's body moves and labors through the ritual of kimchi making:

> She went to the kitchen and took baechu out of the refrigerator, mixed a bath of warm water and salt in a huge metal mixing bowl, laid a cutting board on the floor, and got to work. She squatted down, quartered the heads of cabbage, and slid them into the brine. Next she pounded a fine paste of garlic with the handle of her knife. . . . She packed the seasoned leaves into the jars, and put them back in the attic to ferment. (Cho 2021, 99–100)

This moment pauses to watch Koonja engage her whole self into this act by squatting, pounding, and preparing the ingredients for fermentation, demonstrating how the body's preparation of food is to make care tangible. Furthermore, by offering kimchi to others, Koonja offers an extension of herself, detailing a relationship between the body, food, and kinship that feeds the fermented subject.

While Korean culture was suppressed in and out of the domestic, Yuh offers a counter-thought: "A child's taste for rice and kimchi, a mother's eruption into Korean when angry, a wife's insistence on sending money to her family in Korea, these can all be reminders that the Koreanness of the wife and mother has not been erased and that the identity of the family must somehow take this into account" (Yuh 2002, 105). Yuh observes how Korean-ness ferments in the Korean American domestic space and how "the family must somehow take this into account." While Americanization acts as a powerful force within these fermented subjects, resilience is a competing force, made visible through intimacies like a taste for Korean food. And if the Korean military bride will always be seen as the "Korean mother" in the otherwise American family, her children will always contradict the "American-ness" of this family.

Towards the end of her chapter, Cho details her earliest memory: "[Koonja] brings the little pieces to me and feeds me with her hands. 'Not too spicy, Grace-ya?' she asks. I eat. 'Oh kimchi jal mung-neh! Good girl!' She is smiling, pleased that I am developing a taste for kimchi. . . . 'Ja. Kimchi deo mu-ra. Grace-ya, we are survivors. You can endure anything'" (Cho 2021, 104). Holding kimchi in her hands and bringing it to Cho's mouth, Koonja recognizes the mouth as a medium for bringing culture into one's body. She understands that her daughter is a continuation of her own body; that they are both survivors.

Throughout this text, I've centered Korean military brides as an example of a fermented subjectivity, studying their transformation through a mixture of historically recognized events, such as the Korean War, and more general assimilationist pressures specific to Asian people in the United States during the twentieth century. This reading considers food as a site for studying these subtle changes in and out of the Korean American home, as well as its proximity to the body. While these developments in body and kin are certainly connected to loss, this reading suggests that fermented subjects do not relent to American assimilation, even when pressured to only speak English or detox themselves of Korean food. In putting these authors together, it becomes clear that where violence is both a site of destruction and creation, the fermented subject is a site of multitudes where identity is expansive.

In the larger context of Asian American studies, this article draws from the work of Kandice Chuh, who introduces "subjectlessness" as an anti-essentialist tool, highlighting the dangers and limitations of a multicultural sentimentality currently existing in Asian American literary critique. As Chuh points out, multicultural structures and ideologies essentialize Asian American subjectivity and emphasize "authentic" Asian American identity as opposed to the multifaceted, expansive experience that reflects a globalized world operating within multiple axes of power. Thus, it's fitting that Chuh pulls from Lowe's analysis of Asian Americans existing in a space elsewhere from this assimilated idea of who Asian Americans are. Chuh writes,

> Deconstruction is a state of becoming and undoing in the same moment. "Asian American" is/names racism and resistance, citizenship and its denial, subjectivity and subjection—at once becoming and undoing—and, as such, is a designation of the (im)possibility of justice, where "justice" refers to a state as yet inexperienced and unrepresentable, one that can only connotatively be implied. . . . Justice is understood here as not the achievement of a determinate end, but rather as an endless project of searching out the knowledge and material apparatuses that extinguish some (Other) life ways and that hoard economic and social opportunities only for some. (Chuh 2003, 8)

In other words, Asian American studies' goal of justice falls flat if an essentialized reading of Asian American being is made the goal as opposed to an ongoing commitment to honoring difference in one's reading and critique. What this text attempts to do, then, is respond to Chuh's call for anti-essentialist, dynamic readings of Asian American identity that honor the differences and axes of power that multiculturalism oftentimes ignores.

Chuh's phrasing of deconstruction as simultaneous "becoming and undoing," Espiritu's insistence that "bodies—Vietnamese bodies—should *count*" (Espiritu 2014, 2–3), and Lowe's vision of a palimpsest that preserves the Asian American are all at the heart of this text, which attends to their vision of studying Asian American subjectivity as one that thinks beyond the bounds that currently contain understandings of Asian American identity, subjectivity, and epistemology. In this text, I've theorized the role of kimchi, language, the mouth, and the body in "Kimchi Blues" to understand a relationship between food, survival, and kinship built among Korean military brides in the United States. In doing so, the "fermented subject" is realized to be a theoretic lens and language that combats the Asian body's consumption by centering its resilient transformation. Countering U.S. tendencies to relegate Asian bodies as consumable and containable, a fermented subject is not defined by the aspects of their culture and identity that have been lost but rather the ever-changing form their identity takes. Thus, what fermented subjectivity allows is not dismissal of the losses in collective and individual experiences but framing for how these trajectories are read and re-membered in Asian American literature and studies more broadly. Moreover, fermented subjectivity holds two aspects of subjectivity simultaneously: First is the way that history is a composing part of the self and individual experience. But also, there is recognition that monolithic transformation is impossible across the many different containers that subjects ferment in. How this text contributes to Asian American studies specifically is by offering a version of studying the Asian American body, its difference and transformation, and what an imagined otherwise could be—not reminding oneself that Asian American subjectivity is dynamic but treating it as such. While I see the fermented subject in relation to foreignness and contamination, a status historically placed onto Asian bodies, fears of contamination continue to expand beyond this context. As such, the fermented subject's definition continues to expand and, ideally, supports the nourishment of multitudes.

Aimee Jurado is a literature PhD candidate at the University of California, San Diego. Her research focuses on twentieth- and twenty-first-century Asian American and multiethnic literature, and she writes about immigrant household dynamics, persistence narratives, and cultural fermentation. She can be reached at ajurado@ucsd.edu.

Notes

1. This text utilizes Ji-Yeon Yuh's term "military brides," as opposed to "war brides," when describing the Korean women who married American GIs and immigrated to the United States around the time of the Korean War.
2. I continue Yuh's use of "Korean-ness" and "American-ness" not to reinforce binaries but to discuss cultural differences used to define Korean people as outside American society.

Works Cited

Cho, Grace M. 2008. "Intro." In *Haunting the Korean Diaspora: Shame, Secrecy, and the Forgotten War*. Minneapolis: University of Minnesota Press.

Cho, Grace M. 2021. *Tastes Like War*. New York: The Feminist Press at CUNY.

Chuh, Kandice. 2003. "Introduction: On Asian Americanist Critique." In *Imagine Otherwise: On Asian Americanist Critique*, by Kandice Chuh, 1–30. Durham: Duke University Press. https://doi.org/10.1515/9780822384427-002.

DeVault, Marjorie L. 1991. *Feeding the Family: The Social Organization of Caring as Gendered Work*. Chicago: University of Chicago Press.

Espiritu, Yen Le. 2019. "Critical Refuge(e) Studies." In *Body Counts: The Vietnam War and Militarized Refugees*, by Yen Le Espiritu, 1–23. Berkeley: University of California Press. https://doi.org/10.1525/9780520959002-003.

Katz, Sandor Ellix. 2020. *Fermentation as Metaphor*. Chelsea, VT: Chelsea Green Publishing.

Kim, Hosu, and Grace M. Cho. 2014. "The Kinship of Violence." In *Mothering in East Asian Communities: Politics and Practices*, edited by Patti Duncan and Gina Wong. Ontario: Demeter Press.

Lowe, Lisa. 2012. *Immigrant Acts: On Asian American Cultural Politics*. Durham: Duke University Press.

Tompkins, Kyla Wazana. 2012. *Racial Indigestion: Eating Bodies in the 19th Century*. New York: New York University Press. https://doi.org/10.18574/9780814738375.

Yuh, Ji-Yeon. 2002. *Beyond the Shadow of Camptown: Korean Military Brides in America*. New York: New York University Press. https://doi.org/10.18574/nyu/9780814789018.

SECTION III. **CLASSICS REVISITED**

Colonial Residue on the Body: Making Sense of Puta Life

Aracely García-González

Juana María Rodriguez's *Queer Latinidad: Identity Practices, Discursive Spaces*,
New York: New York University Press, 2003

Juana María Rodríguez's *Puta Life: Seeing Latinas, Working Sex*,
Durham: Duke University Press, 2023

I begin this revisitation and rumination on the body with a question that is central to the *Body Matters* special issue call for papers. How does the physical body redefine feminist scholarship? With the sex wars of the 1980s still haunting academic studies of sexuality and sexual labor, it is perhaps a mandatory endeavor to revisit and review Juana María Rodríguez's contributions to our understanding of the racialized body in scholarship. More importantly, though, to think about how we might continue to broaden our intellectual engagement with sex work beyond a binary of exploitation and empowerment, to do proper justice to a more pertinent question in sex work: Who has the right to own their sexual labor and sell it under capitalism?

In *Queer Latinidad: Identity Practices, Discursive Spaces*, Rodríguez provides a road map to understand the urgency of unbounded, undisciplined ways of being and knowing that extend beyond the confines of academic knowledge production: "Whether in single-author texts or edited volumes on queer Latino sexuality and identity, traditional disciplinary boundaries become inadequate containers for subjects whose lives and utterances traverse the categories meant to contain them" (2003, 30). Discursive spaces are sticky and tricky, often rendered illegible by structured ways of knowing. Yet it is in these elusive spaces that transgressions create a punctum that shifts paradigms of knowing. Similarly, puta life represents a commitment to methodological interventions that free oneself from expectation, from traditions, and from being contained. Puta life encompasses a disinterest in the neatness of being bounded. Puta life gestures toward underground codes in which we learn to communicate deviance, otherworldliness, and

WSQ: Women's Studies Quarterly 53: 3 & 4 (Fall/Winter 2025) © 2025 by Aracely García-González.

refusal. These elements are the heart of a puta methodology that can transform the world.

Puta Life: Seeing Latinas, Working Sex begins with whispered murmurs of larger questions in Latina sexuality studies: How can intellectual engagements with sex work help us articulate a fight for bodily autonomy that encompasses new frameworks for labor studies within Latinx studies? How can we honor the working of sex that has long been written on the Latina body? Through archival interventions and close reading of images, Rodríguez divides the book into two parts to reconfigure how archives of *putería* are constructed and visited. The first part presents a historical overview and offers visual genealogies of puta life to argue the ways that "the convergence of empire, technology, and statecraft" inform societal views on sex work (2003, 37). Chapter 1 "turns to one of the earliest archival records of sex work in the Americas," *Registro de mujeres públicas de la Ciudad de México, de acuerdo con la legislación de V. M. El Emperador*, created in 1865. Rodríguez connects Foucault's biopolitics with archival research and the use of registries as surveillance mechanisms that turn "working sex" into state business. This chapter begins to outline how feelings of disgust and shame are unnaturally braided into the image of sex workers. Disgust serves as a state-sanctioned apparatus that frames sex workers as criminals needing to be captured and documented. Although this registry was created as a tool for sexual surveillance, Rodríguez analyzes the evasion of capture that is so deliciously embedded in puta life through archival encounters: "Carlota, who rebuffs the camera's gaze, women who refuse to look back.... Her desire to elude capture, to refuse the options available to her, to escape the archive, to be a fugitive from history" (2023, 55–56). This evasion of capture reflects the ephemeral nature of queer Latinidad, the ever-moving figure that refuses categorization.

Chapter 2 interrogates what Rodríguez calls "colonial echoes," the residue of coloniality on the body. Colonial echoes think through how non-white racialized women of color are often imbued with discourses of sexual excess and sexual labor. Puta is always written on the Latina body through these colonial echoes. Rodríguez invokes speculation as an analytic to track the "origins of the visual tropes that remain attached to the figure of the puta" (2023, 70). In *Queer Latinidad*, Rodríguez analyzes Marcelo Tenóro's political asylum case to understand how occupying specific spaces, such as San Francisco's Castro District or Rio De Janeiro's gay neighborhoods, writes a story on queer bodies: "It is both the body and space that are coded and read" (2003, 91). Tenóro cannot remove the queerness nor the Blackness from his body. With the invocation of interpellation and hailing, she teases out the various ways that identity is a relational process. Similarly, in *Puta Life*, Rodríguez introduces the concept of "working sex," which begins to define how colonial echoes are etched onto the body and are made productive by Latinas. However, in the case of colonial echoes on the Latina body, spatial context isn't as flexible. You can be anywhere in the world, and the story inscribed on your body travels with you. "Working sex" is the most significant contribution of the book's first half. To work sex is to work the colonial echoes tattooed onto your skin. To take the productive labor that has been written on your body, previously monopolized by colonial dreams of accumulation, and to bask in the fruits of your labor. The surveillance of the selling of sex documented through the *Registro* is also a story about the surveillance of Latinas who make colonial echoes written on their body (self) productive under capitalism. Making their sexual excess profitable for themselves warrants hunting and capture.

The second half of the book focuses on specific self-proclaimed putas who have been captured, sometimes by the self, through photography and film. Their racialized excess is a spectacle to consume and to assign meaning to. The second half of the book asks: How does the racialized body speak back to these voyeuristic entitlements? If photography is a technology of control, how do agency and voice in self-representation disrupt it? This methodological decision mirrors a political choice made in *Queer Latinidad*, where bringing into focus the ways subjects are "continually involved in speaking back to contest and reimagine subjectivity through individual and collective self-representation" (2003, 48) is essential to writing about fugitives of history.

Chapter 3 centers on adult film star Vanessa del Rio's multimedia life narrative, *Vanessa del Rio: Fifty Years of Slightly Slutty Behavior* (2007). Vanessa del Rio's autobiographical account makes clear that "both the pleasure she takes in sex and her right to define the meaning of her own puta life" (2023, 108) are crucial to her autonomy. Chapter 4 interrogates the function of photojournalism and a genre and focuses on two photography books, *Las amorosas más bravas* (Desrus and Gómez Ramos 2014) and *The Women of Casa X* (Vencille and de la Rosa 2013) and does a comparative analysis with the film *La muñeca fea*, directed by Claudia Lopez and George Reyes (2016). Rodríguez integrates self-reflective writing to discuss the social anxieties of femme aging but, most importantly, to think critically about the voyeuristic elements of photojournalism. These perspectives are blended to provide readers with a portal of possibility to think about two populations abandoned and made into spectacles: the elderly and sex workers. The critique in this chapter is how photojournalism as a genre further alienates sex workers and the elderly to garner pity, incite shame, and provoke relief in only being able to peek in from the outside. This voyeurism functions as a disciplinary component that works to obscure the fact that elderly people are discarded when they are no longer productive, and sex workers are relentlessly viewed as tragic subjects. At the end of the chapter, Rodríguez provides a remarkable narrative by centering a collaborative film project, *Plaza de la soledad*, by Maya Goded (2016). This documentary takes a holistic approach that refuses the voyeuristic gaze and instead emphasizes the immense networks of care built by sex workers globally. Chapter 5 turns to the self-curated social media archive of Adela Vázquez to locate the central topic of the book: Latinas working sex. This chapter is the culminating moment where the reader witnesses how Latinas understand the colonial echoes written on their bodies and how they play with, refuse, and make friends with these ghosts. While Vásquez only briefly worked as a sex worker, she articulates the various ways she "learned that sex and beauty were power" (2023, 186) and how she exerted that power throughout her life. This, too, is a form of working sex, of working coloniality and gender regimes.

Queer Latinidad, like *Puta Life*, flirts with the potentiality of evading categorization and pushes us to continue to create homes at the threshold of various worlds. At the end of both books, the reader is left with exciting questions to consider as the body becomes recentered in our scholarship. The physical body communicates various histories, and for the Latina in particular, histories of imperialist desire. Her body creates cultural labor of iconicity that is co-opted for larger projects of conquest and economic expansion. The colonial echoes Rodríguez defines are colonial echoes of ownership over the constructed sexual excess written on the body. The body of women of color is in constant limbo; it is constantly a site of tension over ownership. Therefore, if the racialized body is always already owned, she cannot possibly own her own sexual labor nor sell it under capitalism because this labor is not hers to sell. If she does, the state will criminalize her and recruit ideological warfare tactics, often stemming from knowledge production sites like the university, that further isolate and shame her. By interrogating "working sex," we can think critically about how the body is constantly speaking back to power. Further scholarship must continue this conversation on what it means to work sex and the various ways that working sex offers glimpses of deeply transgressive approaches to bodily autonomy under capitalism.

Aracely García-González received her PhD in Chicana and Chicano studies at the University of California, Santa Barbara. She is an interdisciplinary feminist scholar and is a postdoctoral research fellow at the Effron Center for the Study of America at Princeton University. Her research focuses on the connections between histories of colonialism, global capitalism, gender, and economic vulnerabilities in marginalized communities. Her book-length project "Flirting with Sexual Economies" outlines how Latina sexualities reflect U.S. capital accumulation and are integral to how capital moves, particularly in the Americas. She can be reached at ag4163@princeton.edu.

Works Cited

Desrus, Bénédicte, and Celia Gómez Ramos. 2014. *Las amorosas más bravas.* Mexico City: Libros del Sargento.

Goded, Maya, dir. 2016. *Plaza de la soledad.* Mexico City: Pimienta Films.

Hanson, Dian, ed. 2007. *Vanessa del Rio: Fifty Years of Slightly Slutty Behavior.* Cologne: Taschen.

Venville, Malcolm, and Amanda de la Rosa. 2013. *The Women of Casa X.* Amsterdam: Schilt Publishing.

Lessons from Precolonial Yorùbá Society in the Age of "Anti-Gender"

Tèmítópé (Temi) Fàmọdù

Oyèrónkẹ́ Oyěwùmí's *The Invention of Women*, Minneapolis: University of Minnesota Press, 1997

As I sit in Budapest, Hungary, where Prime Minister Viktor Orbán's current political rhetoric intensifies a national conversation about gender, Oyèrónkẹ́ Oyěwùmí's *The Invention of Women* holds an urgent contemporary significance. My fieldwork, which considers the experiences of Nigerian students who have migrated to postsocialist geographies, initially included a question about how "gender operates" in diasporic contexts and has been delightfully revised thanks to consultation with this classic. In *The Invention of Women*, Oyěwùmí takes us to precolonial Yorùbáland. Here, the colonial, Western gender episteme had not yet been imposed. People's identities were not based on their anatomy. The Yorùbá language and society did not include specific differences around gender, there existed no gender hierarchy, and, to put it simply, Yorùbá didn't "do gender" in the manner of the (American) context under which I had been socialized. So why should I assume that my frame of reference was a universal phenomenon? And how could I, the child of a Yorùbá, be so unfamiliar with these ways of being?

Oyěwùmí reminds me that I am in good company, as Western and Yorùbá scholars alike have fallen into the trap of articulating experiences from the perspective of the imperial core, perpetuating the notion that gender is universally understandable, proving that Western ideas are still at the center of African studies. The "man" and "woman" binary, and the assumed power dynamics that accompany it, have been written into history time and time again as translatable relations that exist similarly in all cultures, across all time. Oyěwùmí calls for an undoing of this assumption by way of presenting historical material about the relational experiences of Yorùbá in precolonial Nigeria in what she posits as a Yorùbá "world-sense." The existence of

WSQ: Women's Studies Quarterly 53: 3 & 4 (Fall/Winter 2025)

this world-sense provides fertile ground for considering the contemporary implications of colonial reorganization of indigenous relationalities, and, crucially, the possibilities of their undoing.

Thinking with *The Invention of Women* in Hungary, at a time when Orbán has declared that "there is no gender" in Hungary, echoed in his infamous slogan "no gender, no migration, no war," invites a conversation with Oyěwùmí's critique of if and how gender is shaped, imposed, and erased. For Orbán, rejecting what he calls "gender ideology" is about affirming the "purity" of Hungarian identity and preserving the means of production of the male-female-children construction of the nuclear family. With falling birthrates and fear of replacement by "migrants," Orbán relies on pronatalist strategies such as "family credits" to boost the ethnic Hungarian population and stave off demographic anxieties. These tactics are similar to colonial endeavors that impose rigid frameworks on indigenous societies in the name of producing an "ideal" population, while exploiting a racialized and gendered other. Oyěwùmí's work challenges these reductive narratives by laying bare another way of understanding how bodies, relationships, and identities have been historically encoded, and how they might yet be reimagined. Oyěwùmí argues that in Yorùbáland, gender did not serve as the foundational principle for social organization; rather, social roles were negotiated through factors such as age hierarchy (seniority) and lineage. Relational responsibilities were structured around peoples' age instead of gender. Lineage, conceived for Yorùbá as the "living, the dead, and the unborn" (143), underscores the propensity for Yorùbá cosmology to transcend the physical, present-tense body as the only meaningful unit of social relation. In so doing, Yorùbá ontology prompts us to envision a world in which imposed binaries had not yet existed.

Gender, as defined by Western colonial powers, was imposed as part of a broader project to reshape social relations and control the bodies of colonized peoples. In Britain, access to power was gender-based, whereas Yorùbá society respected both male and female chiefs. Britain's indirect rule of Nigeria administered processes of alienating women from politics and implementing patriarchal power structures. Oyěwùmí argues that the creation of "woman" as a category was one of the first accomplishments of the colonial state (124) and was solidified by a twofold process of racial inferiorization and gender subordination. The "invention of women" is thus a construction, not an inevitability. Through the violent processes of Christianization and British imperial legal systems, colonization flattened the complexities of Yorùbá social structures. Knowing that these categories were not naturally occurring or predestined, we can hold them accountable for their resultant controlling and organizing of populations. Further, these Western discourses on gender are not just about the body—they are about power and control, about how relations are mediated and how labor is produced. The very concept of a "gendered division of labor," even in its apparent uses toward attempts to repair social bonds, is a colonial prescription. In precolonial Yorùbáland, all bodies were represented in all occupations (71), despite misunderstood claims of a universal "feminine subjugation." This misunderstanding has led to an assumption that motherhood domesticated childbearers in Yorùbáland, when in reality, childbearing did not imply independent child-rearing. The responsibility for raising children was shared between mothers, fathers, eldest children, and other members of the community.

In rejection of the colonial and academic urge to apply the workings of foreign gender categories to precolonial Yorùbá lifeways, Oyěwùmí argues that a Western cultural sense is not a universal "worldview." She takes to task the idea of a "worldview" and claims that it is often steeped in predispositions of societal ordering that may not be mappable onto indigenous ways of being. The West's fixation on the body, particularly on the anatomical difference between "man" and "woman," was not part of Yorùbá's genderless society, but is certainly a part of Orbán's "no-gender" political project. Hungary, often figured in local political imaginations as exempt from the colonial project, is not spared from its clutches when aggressively imposing this binary, inviting us to reconsider what we think we know about the "naturalness" of gender categories. After all, there is nothing "natural" about the colonial project or authoritative rulings on bodily expression and relations.

Revisiting Oyěwùmí's work while I do fieldwork in Hungary, I am struck by how both Orbán and other heads of state, such as U.S. President Donald Trump, push for the enforcement of a naturalized gender binary and attempt to fix gender roles within a state-backed framework. Orbán's call for a return to "traditional values" around gender aligns with colonial strategies of stabilizing social order by enforcing gender distinctions. The consequences of such policies have material impacts, such as the shuttering of gender studies programs in Hungary, as well as the removal of gender-related language in laws and regulations and funding for minority groups in the U.S. Just as colonial powers imposed their own views of gender on the societies they colonized, Orbán's government is attempting to define and control the "natural" order of gender for Hungarian citizens in order to erase the possibility of alternative gendered experiences. However, as Oyěwùmí reminds us, colonial impositions are never inevitable. While Orbán may argue for a return to a fixed gender order, Oyěwùmí's work challenges us to recognize the multiplicity of relations outside of body-centric gender logics that both existed before colonialism and could yet be mobilized against colonially coded politics today. If gender logics can be wielded as a means of controlling a populace, rejecting these logics might strengthen the kinds of relational bonds we desire.

In Oyěwùmí's analysis, the insistence on a universal, fixed gender system and its mediation of labor production were—and remain—part of a broader project to impose European capitalist models onto African societies. Orbán's and Trump's political moves to reinstate a binary gender order are just the latest iterations of a long history of colonialism that sought to control not only the bodies of colonized peoples but also their ways of relating to one another, to the land, and to the world. As Oyěwùmí observes, Western gender ideologies are deeply tied to the historical processes of racial capitalism, regulating who does what kind of work and under what conditions. Land, in precolonial Yorùbá society, was not a commodity to be bought and sold. It was a plentiful, collective resource, bound to lines of lineage. The colonial project imposed a shift from communal land models to a private property model. The disruption of this system by colonial powers reinforced not only capitalist economies but also patriarchal systems of control, with land mobilized as a form of capital to be owned and exploited.

In one of Budapest's public archives, I now sift through documents that detail resistance to neofascist regimes and am reminded that the fight against oppressive forces, whether they seek to control gender or erase marginalized histories, has always been part of a larger struggle for liberation and bodily autonomy. The archival material before me serves as a reminder that, just as communities in the past have resisted colonial impositions, today's movements continue to write and rewrite their truths into history. These claims have the potential for both bolstering and challenging structures of power that seek to define them. As we witness the ongoing struggles for gender equality and LGBTQIA+ rights around the world, Oyěwùmí's call to reject the false naturalization of gender—both as an ontology and an epistemology—is urgent and important. By revisiting her work, we can learn not only about the history of colonialism but also what it has tried to stamp out: ways of organizing social relations beyond the limits of colonial and capitalist logics. Understanding how these systems were imposed, and how they continue to be enforced today, is a crucial part of resisting them. Thinking from a Yorùbá world-sense, on their terms, we may take this work as an opportunity to interrogate how, and from where, we know what we know; how we might be entangled in the reproduction of, or resistance to, colonial logics. We might then work toward sensing possibilities of resistance beyond the frames of inherited colonial worldviews.

Tèmítọ́pẹ́ (Temi) Fàmọdù is a PhD candidate living and researching in Budapest, Hungary, through the Fulbright program. They aim to understand everyday matters of place-making among Nigerian and other African students who have migrated to Hungary through state-sponsored scholarship and recruitment programs. They question prevailing conceptions and productions of gender at both personal and state registers. Working with students, organizers, and everyday people in Hungary's capital and the university town of Debrecen, their research takes up themes of belonging, Blackness, gender, and livingness in the postsocialist context, from the point of view of students from predominantly postcolonial countries. They can be reached at tfamodu@uci.edu.

Manufactured Obsolescence:
Writing Centers Through the Lens of Housework

Raquel Coy

Angela Y. Davis's *Women, Race and Class*, New York: Random House, 1981

A version of this paper was written and presented as part of the April 11, 2025, panel titled "Repurposing Women, Race and Class *by Angela Y. Davis as Inspiration for Rhetorical B-Sides" at the 2025 Conference on College Composition and Communication Annual Convention. My copanelists included Professor Shereen Inayatulla (York College), Professor Michael T. MacDonald (University of Michigan–Dearborn), and Professor Andrew Heerah (York College). Our panel's overarching theme offered "a rereading, a revisiting, and a remixing of* Women, Race and Class *by Dr. Angela Y. Davis, a text that continues to shape the way we experience and perceive the gendered, racialized, and rhetorically constructed world around us." My fellow panelists presented outstanding explorations on the ways in which Davis's work persists throughout the years and transcends the original context straight into today's concerns of women's suffrage, radical feminist readings, and archiving in the face of data disinformation. In my own presentation, I reflected on the ways the college writing center, in many ways, paralleled Davis's analysis of housework.*

When I read chapter 13 of *Women, Race and Class*, Angela Davis's critique of domestic labor felt eerily familiar—not only in its analysis of invisibilized work but in how those same dynamics echo in the academic spaces I move through daily. In "The Approaching Obsolescence of Housework: A Working-Class Perspective," Davis explores the notion that housework, though essential, is being phased out or rendered obsolete by technological and social change. Importantly, this idea of obsolescence is rooted not in the elimination of our societal need for housework but in a shift in who is expected to do the work, under what conditions, and with how little recognition. This chapter becomes a powerful lens through which to examine the institutional realities of academic support systems, especially writing centers. These spaces, like the domestic sphere Davis describes, are essential yet consistently undervalued. In my own experience as a first-generation college student—and later as a tutoring center administrator—student support services, especially the writing centers, provide crucial intellectual and emotional labor: They foster critical thinking, support multilingual writers, and nurture students' academic voices. Yet their work is often seen as supplementary and marginal: a kind of academic housework that runs in the background, keeping everything functional but rarely being honored as potentially vital to students' academic experiences.

In this chapter, Davis tracks the creation and fossilization of the ideological figure of the "housewife" out of the redefinition of women's labor during industrialization, outlines the societal devaluation of "housework," while it also warns of its impending obsolescence due to women's demand for equality in the workforce. According to Davis, this "virtually invisible" work is essential in a capitalist society, not through the direct contributions to capitalism but rather as an assumed precondition to capitalist production (Davis 1983, 128). In her context, this demanded a change to our expectations of who should shoulder that burden, especially in the face of technological advances and capitalist market forces. Rather than shifting the labor of housework from women to men, Davis proposes the socialization of housework as a solution, especially in light of aspects of housework already being capitalized in the marketplace, in forms such as fast-food restaurants.

While not a one-to-one parallel, reading this analysis of housework brought to mind the role of academic support services, in particular writing centers, in higher education institutions. Similar to housework, the work of writing centers is often invisible: "No one notices it until it isn't done—we notice the unmade bed, not the scrubbed and polished floor" (Davis 1983, 128). As Genie N. Giaimo (2024) mentions in her article "The College Writing Center in Times of Crisis," early incarnations of writing centers were often underfunded sites of basic remediation, in response to "enrollment pressures, underprepared students, and the limitations of lecture-style education models." This old model of the writing center was tasked with "cleaning up" students' writing, so that the visible "unmade bed[s]" (Davis

1983, 128) of student academic work were tidied away. Throughout the years, alongside increasing acceptance of transformative teaching practices in composition and the standardized incorporation of peer tutors, writing centers slowly began to embody a history of care and support that often goes unseen.

Today, Giaimo maintains, writing centers "still tend to be a hub for BIPOC and underrepresented students on college campuses"—for those whose backgrounds may make them feel alienated by the dominant use of standard academic English in their coursework. However, rather than merely forcing students to conform to the standard academic English mold via grammar drills, today's writing center largely focuses on building students' "confidence, skills, and metacognition" (Giaimo 2024). Giaimo's observations ring true for me. I've spent ten years at CUNY's York College Collaborative Learning Center (CLC), our campus's tutoring center, first as a peer tutor and then as an administrative assistant. Through my own experience of the tail end of this shift, this emphasis on student-centered learning is very much the norm. In their tutor handbook, new tutors at the CLC are encouraged to use active learning and cooperative learning techniques in order to encourage students "to take ownership of their learning and to hone their critical thinking and analysis skills" (York College CLC 2021). This philosophical approach to tutoring facilitates collaboration and empowers marginalized voices in academia. Yet these efforts seem to be the invisible "scrubbed and polished floor" in our institutions and continue to be framed as remedial. In her article reflecting on her experiences with undergraduate and graduate writing centers, Alexandria Lockett (2019) notes that she felt "ashamed to seek assistance," while Kristi Costello (2021) recounts the not at all infrequent experience of a "colleague across campus [who] calls to complain that a student came to the writing center and 'still has errors in their paper.'" Both sentiments reflect a persistent stigmatization of writing centers despite the intellectually rich, emotionally demanding, and pedagogically complex nature of the work they do.

The idea of writing center work as "approaching obsolescence" becomes a less than apt parallel when we look closely at how these centers are positioned within the modern university. In Bob Jessop's "On Academic Capitalism," he outlines five stages of academic capitalism: commercialization; capitalization; quasicommodification of mental labor, or the separation of intellectual labor from the means of intellectual production;

and financialization due to the finance-dominated system (Jessop 2018, 105–6). His entire analysis is a bleakly succinct breakdown of the shifting contexts of the modern university, made concrete through his expertise in sociology and political economy. Pertinent to this discussion, however, is stage 3, in which we see "the appropriation of traditional knowledge, privatization of the intellectual commons, commodification of teaching materials, scholarship, scientific research, and scientific publications, and, more recently, digitization of lectures enabling their virtually costless reproduction and circulation—while charging consumers for access" (Jessop 2018, 105). Through this trend, we see the value institutions place on efficiency, automation, and cost-cutting, which can render support services expendable. As university administrations steer universities and colleges steadily into the depths of academic capitalism by increasingly adopting market-driven models that position students as consumers and education as a commodified service, writing centers also fall victim to digitization, both in the form of outsourced, off-campus online tutoring series and through the nearly giddy embrace of AI tools unethically trained on data that superficially mimic the feedback of a human tutor. In this shift, we do not see the inevitable march toward obsolescence driven by the organic needs of our students. Instead, what we are seeing is a *manufactured* obsolescence of writing center work.

This trajectory echoes Davis's argument that obsolescence is not about elimination but rather displacement. Instead of displacing the work onto another gender or a socialized institution, writing center work is being displaced onto the faceless, onto the simulacra. Missing from this fevered pursuit for efficiency is the equally invisible yet vital emotional labor ingrained in writing center work. In tutoring sessions, tutors are often compelled to take on a variety of roles ranging from mentor, to confidante, to therapist, and more. Costello (2021), in her article "Naming and Negotiating the Emotional Labors of Writing Center Tutoring," lists a substantial, though nonexhaustive, list of some emotional labors tutors may experience in their work. The category of *performance* is one that stands out the most to me, as it embodies the performing of "emotions (i.e., empathy, compassion, kindness, enthusiasm, politeness) perceived to be 'expected' or preferable when they are contrary to what is actually being felt" (Costello 2021). While burdensome, this performance is usually to the benefit of students, especially marginalized students, in that they create low-pressure spaces on campuses, where they can develop and cultivate their academic identities. Besides the students who use the services of the writing center, peer tutors are frequently also students. Not only can their labor help their tutees, but, as Giaimo (2024) explains, "writing centers can help all kinds of students—those who seek writing support and those who provide it—find community on campus and be more likely to remain in school." Much like the well-intentioned Wages for Housework movement that aimed to compensate women's domestic labor as a means of women's emancipation, AI is put forward now as a proposed solution to the emotional labor in writing centers. However, just as Davis's critique reveals the Wages for Work strategy as reinforcing the very systems it aimed to challenge, it is likewise not certain that AI is the appropriate tool to replace the space writing centers hold in institutions.

Angela Davis's analysis of domestic labor in *Women, Race and Class* offers a striking lens through which to examine the institutional role of writing centers. Like the domestic labor Davis describes, writing center work remains undervalued and rendered invisible despite often being critical to student success. Despite the institutional pressures toward cost-cutting, automation, and commodification, writing center work is far from obsolete. Instead, it has and continues to evolve in ways that nurture student voices and create affirming academic spaces. By rereading Davis's work alongside our own institutional realities, we can uncover and make visible the work of writing centers, which demands recognition, support, and persistence.

Raquel Coy is a lecturer in CUNY's York College English Department and is passionate about composition and rhetoric and writing center pedagogy. She is currently a campus Writing Across the Curriculum coordinator and cochair of the Writing Intensive Advisory Committee. She can be reached at rcoy@york.cuny.edu.

Works Cited

Costello, Kristi M. 2021. "Naming and Negotiating the Emotional Labors of Writing Center Tutoring." In *Wellness and Care in Writing Center Work*, edited by Genie N. Giaimo and Nicole Pollack. Pressbooks. https://ship .pressbooks.pub/writingcentersandwellness/chapter/title-here/.

Davis, Angela. 1983. "The Approaching Obsolescence of Housework: A Working-Class Perspective." In *Women, Race and Class*. New York: Random House.

Giaimo, Genie N. 2024. "The College Writing Center in Times of Crisis." *Los Angeles Review of Books*, February 13. https://lareviewofbooks.org/article/the-college-writing-center-in-times-of-crisis/.

Jessop, Bob. 2018. "On Academic Capitalism." *Critical Policy Studies* 12 (1): 104–9. https://doi.org/https://doi.org/10.1080/19460171.2017.1403342.

Lockett, Alexandria. 2019. "Why I Call It the Academic Ghetto: A Critical Examination of Race, Place, and Writing Centers." *Praxis: A Writing Center Journal* 16 (2). https://www.praxisuwc.com/162-lockett.

York College Collaborative Learning Center. 2021. *Collaborative Learning Center New Tutor Handbook*. CUNY York College.

Revisiting Melissa Febos's *Whip Smart*: BDSM as a Praxis of Care

Ash M. Smith

Melissa Febos's *Whip Smart*, New York: Thomas Dunne Books, 2010

Published in 2010,[1] *Whip Smart* chronicles the author's personal experiences as a professional dominatrix working in a New York City sex dungeon while in college from 1999 to 2003. The book reads as both an autoethnographic excavation of lived experience and a self- (and other-)flagellating confession, as Febos explores themes of power, control, pleasure, pain, desire, and shame, across contexts of BDSM, sex work, substance use and recovery, academic achievement, and interpersonal relationships. In this review, I examine the function and practice of BDSM sessions represented in *Whip Smart,* through the lens of BDSM, sadomasochism, and sex work literature in queer and trans studies, to argue for BDSM as a praxis of care to heal the psychic wounds of trauma and structural oppression and explore identities and social roles of oneself and others.

Through Febos's personal reflections and descriptions of scenes with clients, BDSM sessions emerge as a praxis for political subversion of oppressive power structures, reprocessing damaging past experiences and relationships, and self-exploration. Febos struggles with the personal and political functions of her role as a professional dominatrix. At times, she frames her role as empowering, liberating, and equalizing, but more often she emphasizes the humiliating and oppressive nature of her BDSM sessions. She questions whether BDSM sex work reifies patriarchal power and violence, writing,

> most sessions—if not all—were . . . a kind of inversion of misogyny, the subjugation of women reenacted by men on themselves. Our clients wanted to be dressed in women's clothing and raped, molested, infantilized, humiliated, and physically abused. Did this kind of mimicry reinforce or subvert the power of these paradigms? (Febos 2010, 59)

WSQ: Women's Studies Quarterly 53: 3 & 4 (Fall/Winter 2025) © 2025 by Ash M. Smith. All rights reserved.

Theoretical interpretations of BDSM in queer studies have similarly wrestled with this question. Some radical feminists argue that sadomasochism perpetuates patriarchal, racist, and xenophobic culture (Dworkin 1987; Parker 1993; Linden et al. 1982). Bersani argues that sadomasochism ties structural oppression to "the body's erotic economy" (1995, 90), suggesting an intentional localization of political oppression within an individual in relational contexts. Califia (1994) asserts that the emphasis on consent, negotiation, and intentional exchanges of power subverts structural oppression, allows individuals to reclaim power, and promotes sexual liberation. Examining these theories through the lens of queer temporality, Freeman posits that sadomasochism may facilitate reparative examination and subversion of structural oppression, through an intentional reenactment of historical oppressions and harms that allows for examination of oppression and harm in current individual and relational contexts (2008, 41, 62–63).

Febos provides several examples of how engaging in BDSM scenes functioned as a way for her clients to process past traumatic experiences, interpersonal rejection, and gendered identities and power dynamics. She describes a scene in which a client discloses a fear of water stemming from his experience nearly drowning as a child, and profusely expresses his gratitude after she repeatedly forces his head underwater while he is tied up. Clients regularly ask her to play "mean mommy," scenes where she scolds and punishes the childlike submissive for misbehaving, or the "high school bitch," where she humiliates and bullies them. Febos's portrayal of the function of BDSM for her clients aligns with feminist queer scholars who view BDSM as a way to reclaim consent and power after experiencing sexual trauma, promoting healing after sexual trauma (Hart 1998; Cvetkovich 2003; Barker et al. 2007; Easton 2007). Calling on Simone de Beauvoir's analysis of Marquis de Sade's foundational fictional sadomasochistic writings as a way to symbolically restore sovereignty and feudal power (Beauvoir 1953, 16), Freeman describes sadomasochism as "a form of writing history with the body" (2008, 36). In this way, rather than reinforcing the power structures that subjugate women, the BDSM scenes that Febos enacts with her clients represent a consensual and negotiated practice for confronting trauma, accepting rejection and the loss of power, and subsequently healing psychic wounds.

Febos also shares that clients frequently requested feminization, or forced feminization, scenes in which she pleasures, punishes, or penetrates clients while they wear women's wigs and clothing. Febos describes several scenes with a particular client, called Margie during role-play, in which the client plays a sorority sister punished for "whorish behavior" or a school-girl punished for masturbating. Although the client's very specific session instructions frustrate Febos, the negotiation and enactment of these role-play scenes allow the client to explore gendered embodiment and the resulting power dynamics otherwise inaccessible to a person presenting as a man in their daily life.

Trans and queer communities have long used BDSM as a framework to explore gendered identities and roles (e.g., Bauer 2008; Hale 1997). Through a qualitative analysis of interviews with trans and queer BDSM practitioners, Bauer describes how the interaction of fantasy and bodily manipulation in BDSM offers an opportunity for people exploring their gender to rename body parts or sexual practices based on their personal meanings instead of those circumscribed by society, and simultaneously to reassign their bodies with gendered meanings that oppose the medical assignment of sex (241–42). This renaming and reassigning occurs in Febos's role-play sessions with Margie when, in anticipation of penetrative sex, Margie asks Febos to "call it my pussy" (140). Although Febos never considers the possibility that this client could be a trans woman or trans-feminine, these role-play scenes offer the opportunity for self-exploration and formation of new perspectives, regardless of the client's gender. Bauer explains how self-exploration in role-play builds insight regarding the self and how gender and other social positions function differently for others depending on their position in society, to experience an embodied understanding of where and how their own and others' perspectives are situated (2008, 240–41). From this perspective, role-playing as a gender different from the gender a person typically experiences in society may promote greater understanding about their own gender and how gender interacts with power to impact others' experiences in society, which may facilitate resistance to structural oppression and reparation.

In addition to the positive political and personal functions of BDSM sessions portrayed in *Whip Smart*, Febos explicitly and implicitly compares the function and practice of BDSM sex work to medical and psychological care structures throughout her memoir. The language used to describe "clients" and their "sessions" mirrors that typically used in psychotherapy. The dungeon where Febos starts her career as a pro-domme maintains protocols for assigning clients and maintaining their privacy. In a conversation with her mother, a psychotherapist, Febos explicitly compares her role as a professional domme to the role of a therapist helping clients process trauma. Febos even describes medical BDSM scenes in which dommes dress as doctors or nurses and inflict medicalized torture on clients. Discussing a friend and coworker in the dungeon, Febos writes,

> It's funny but not surprising that she ended up a bona fide nurse. I've known more than one former sex worker who did. Whatever other reasons brought you to it, our work required a patience with the human body—call it nurturance, caretaking, or curiosity—that not all people have and only some can learn. (275)

This quote highlights the inherent nature of sex work as a form of intimate labor, bodywork, and care work. Boris and Parreñas define intimate labor as work that involves bodily or emotional closeness, observing or holding knowledge of personal information (2010, 2). Theoretical (Bateman 2021; Jäger 2023; Wolkowitz 2006) and empirical (Näre and Diatlova 2024; Yeoh et al. 2014) investigation of sex and care worker experiences draw parallels between between sex work, domestic work, and forms of bodywork, like massage, physical therapy, or nursing or other healthcare work. Echoing Febos's observation of former sex workers becoming nurses, Grant highlights the pragmatic fluidity between sex work and other service economies to argue for sex work's decriminalization, explaining that sex work is not only analogous to other commercial services (e.g., healthcare, food, entertainment industries), but that sex workers are often also providing other forms of service and care (2014, 98–99).

By interpreting the functions and practice of BDSM sessions and sex work in *Whip Smart*, Febos's portrayal of BDSM sex work highlights its potential as a form of care that allows practitioners to subvert structural oppression, process trauma, and explore new perspectives on the identities and roles held by oneself and others. As a tangible symbol of how BDSM sex work functions as a form of care, Febos describes how her and her coworkers appropriated the function of a medical device:

> A TENS unit is a small, battery-operated device used to send electrical impulses to select parts of the body. The electrical currents it produces, when mild, can prevent pain messages from being transmitted to the brain and are thought to raise endorphin levels in medical patients. At the end of the wires . . . disposable electrodes could be attached and then adhered to body parts. Conventionally, that would be shoulders, neck, and joints. In our case, it meant nipples, scrotums, and penises. (147)

In both its use on medical patients and sex-work clients and regardless of what parts of the body it is attached to, the TENS unit provides pleasure and relief from pain. The TENS unit example emphasizes how sex work is distinguishable from medical care only in the parts of the body involved. Just as Febos and her coworkers use the functions of a medical device to provide pleasure and pain relief, medical and psychological care providers may leverage the functions of BDSM as a praxis of care to subvert structural oppression, process trauma, and promote self-exploration. Through an interpretive lens informed by queer and trans theories on BDSM, sadomasochism, and sex work, the function and practice of BDSM sex work represented in *Whip Smart* reveals BDSM sex work as a form of care to promote resistance against structural oppression, recovery from the psychic wounds of trauma, and identity exploration, suggesting exciting possibilities for application in medical and psychological care settings and public health initiatives.

Ash M. Smith is a doctoral candidate in the Health Psychology and Clinical Sciences program at the CUNY Graduate Center. His current research leverages community-engaged implementation science to build sustainable community care structures that promote access to gender affirmation and mitigate suicide risk in trans and nonbinary populations. They have been a graduate student researcher at Hunter College's Gender-Based Violence Lab since 2020, earning their MA in psychology from Hunter College in 2023. With a passion for community-based care, Ash is invested in furthering non-exploitative approaches to research and clinical work. He can be reached at asmith3@graduatecenter.cuny.edu.

Note

1. The book contains a number of descriptions based in racism (e.g., characterization of an Asian dominatrix working in her dungeon) and transphobia (i.e., unwarranted use of slurs, gender essentialism), which, although not the focus of the current review, take on new meaning with fifteen years of hindsight, and warrant acknowledgment.

Works Cited

Barker, Meg-John, Camelia Gupta, and Alessandra Iantaffi. 2007. "The Power of Play: The Potentials and Pitfalls in Healing Narratives of BDSM." *Safe, Sane, and Consensual: Contemporary Perspectives on Sadomasochism*, edited by Darren Langdridge and Meg Barker, 197–216. New York: Palgrave.

Bateman, Victoria. 2021. "How Decriminalisation Reduces Harm Within and Beyond Sex Work: Sex Work Abolitionism as the 'Cult of Female Modesty' in Feminist Form." *Sexuality Research and Social Policy: Journal of NSRC* 18 (4): 819–36. https://doi.org/10.1007/s13178-021-00612-8.

Bauer, Robin. 2008. "Transgressive and Transformative Gendered Sexual Practices and White Privileges: The Case of the Dyke/Trans BDSM Communities." *Women's Studies Quarterly* 36 (3–4): 233–53. http://www.jstor.org/stable/27649798.

Beauvoir, Simone de. 1953. "Must We Burn Sade?" Translated by Anette Michelson. In *The Marquis de Sade*, edited by Paul Dinnage, 9–82. New York: Grove.

Bersani, Leo. 1995. *Homos*. Cambridge: Harvard University Press.

Boris, Eileen, and Rhacel S. Parreñas, eds. 2010. *Intimate Labors: Cultures, Technologies, and the Politics of Care*. Palo Alto: Stanford University Press.

Califia, Pat. 1994. *Public Sex: The Culture of Radical Sex*. 2nd ed. Jersey City: Cleis.

Cvetkovich, Ann. 2003. *An Archive of Feelings: Trauma, Sexuality, and Lesbian Public Cultures*. Durham: Duke University Press. https://doi.org/10.2307/j.ctv113139r.

Dworkin, Andrea. 1987. *Intercourse*. New York: Free Press.

Easton, Dossie. 2007. "Shadowplay: S/M Journeys to Our Selves." *Safe, Sane, and Consensual: Contemporary Perspectives on Sadomasochism*, edited by Darren Langdridge and Meg Barker, 1084–99. New York: Palgrave.

Freeman, Elizabeth. 2008. "Turn the Beat Around: Sadomasochism, Temporality, History." *differences* 19 (1): 32–70. https://doi.org/10.1215/10407391-2007-016.

Grant, Melissa G. 2014. *Playing the Whore: The Work of Sex Work*. London: Verso Books.

Hale, C. Jacob. 1997. "Leatherdyke Boys and Their Daddies: How to Have Sex Without Women or Men." *Social Text* 15 (2–3): 223–36. https://doi.org/10.2307/466741.

Hart, Lynda. 1998. *Between the Body and the Flesh: Performing Sadomasochism*. New York: Columbia University Press.

Jäger, Sarah. 2023. "Self-Determined Sex Work as Care Work Between Experiences of Integrity and Vulnerability." *Ethica* 7 (3): 61–74. https://doi.org/10.3384/de-ethica.2001-8819.237361.

Linden, Robin R., Darlene R. Pagano, Diana E. H. Russell, and Susan L. Star, eds. 1982. *Against Sadomasochism: A Radical Feminist Analysis*. San Francisco: Frog in the Well. https://archive.org/details/against-sadomasochism/mode/2up.

Näre, Lena, and Anastasia Diatlova. 2024. "Ageing/Body/Sex/Work—Migrant Women's Narratives of Intimacy and Ageing in Commercial Sex and Elder Care Work." *Sexualities* 27 (5–6): 1146–64. https://doi.org/10.1177/1363460720944590.

Parker, Pat, ed. 1993. *Unleashing Feminism: Critiquing Lesbian Sadomasochism in the Gay Nineties*. Santa Cruz: Herbooks. https://escholarship.org/content/qt4wn4458v/supp/Unleashing_Feminism.pdf.

Wolkowitz, Carol. 2006. *Bodies at Work*. London: Sage.

Yeoh, Brenda S. A., Heng Leng Chee, and Thi Kieu Dung Vu. 2014. "Global Householding and the Negotiation of Intimate Labour in Commercially-Matched International Marriages Between Vietnamese Women and Singaporean Men." *Geoforum*, no. 51, 284–93. https://doi.org/10.1016/j.geoforum.2013.09.012.

SECTION IV. **BOOK REVIEWS**

Review of *Laboring Women: Reproduction and Gender in New World Slavery*

Tuka Al-Sahlani

Jennifer L. Morgan's *Laboring Women: Reproduction and Gender in New World Slavery*, Philadelphia: University of Pennsylvania Press, 2004

In *Laboring Women*, Jennifer Morgan uncovers the reproductive, productive, mental, and emotional labor of enslaved women in early American colonial history. Morgan asserts that enslaved Black women's bodies were crucial factors in the ideological and economic justification for colonialism and the expansion of racial slavery. (Without these gendered, racialized, and othered bodies, racial slavery would not have been feasible for the powers that be.) The emphasis on the racialized and gendered body is important to Morgan because a part of her project is to fill the gap at the intersection of American colonial history, African American studies, and women's studies, where a "slave" is usually male, "women" are usually white, and "fecundity" ignores racialized bodies. Moreover, Morgan is frustrated with the state of research about Black women and advocates for more than "simply an exercise of inclusion but . . . rather a foundational methodology in writing the history of early America" (11). And *Laboring Women* is that—an exercise in what we have come to term as the methodology of feminist archival and recovery work, feminist citation practices, and feminist care work.

Morgan's labor and care work in excavating and documenting the lived experiences of enslaved African women in early American colonial history guide us on an archival journey that spans from 1640 to 1750 and docks on the ports of the coasts of West Africa, Barbados, and North Carolina. Aptly, *Laboring Women* begins with travel narratives. These narratives (alphabetic and visual) by white male travelers dehumanized Indigenous and African women by purporting and cementing two key fantastical ideas about the physical capabilities of non-white and non-European women. One, these other women across the Atlantic were able to feed their children by simply swinging their breasts over their shoulder to nurse the child tied to their

WSQ: Women's Studies Quarterly 53: 3 & 4 (Fall/Winter 2025)

back. Two, these same "over-the-shoulder-breast-feed[ers]" (31) would bathe in the sea immediately after giving birth, then return to complete their chores. The difference between the unearthly superpowers wielded by these Indigenous women and African women versus those of white and European women, who suffered from death postpartum or sent their children to wet nurses, supported the ideological distancing of the delicate human woman who suffers and the beastly woman who endures. The othering of women is the foundation of racial slavery.

Having explored the foundational dehumanizing ideology of racial slavery, Morgan then takes us on a numerical journey. In chapter 2, Morgan analyzes ship logs and finds that most captive African women came from the coast rather than inland and that, despite missing information about their lived experience and the unclear answers as to why some years the number of women was higher or lower than the men captives, the logs provide a point of departure to hypothesize the impact and role of enslaved women in the Americas. One such hypothesis is that these women shared the same language, culture, or both. Morgan suggests that the shared or similar cultures would have assisted women to transfer familial customs and rituals in family planning, caring for a pregnancy or the termination of it, and child-rearing. Although some contraceptives and rituals, like circumcision, were forcibly abandoned due to slavery, their role as laboring women expanded beyond birthing and childcare, and into reproducers of traditions and rituals. (This epistemological labor of women is again cited in chapters 4, 5, and 6, where Morgan investigates the labor of women in creolization, rice culture, and rebellion in the eighteenth century.)

In chapter 3, Morgan takes us through the numbers that cemented the economic advantages for enslavers. Legislative acts, land grants, and probate records solidified the necessity for racial slavery to grow the colonies. This expansion required landowners to inventory, calculate, and divide their property (land, livestock, and enslaved people) to manage their land, obtain land grants, and most importantly, impart their wealth to future generations. Morgan samples probate records that represent the economic significance of Black women's bodies and their fecundity to the generational wealth of the white colonists. The degrading language widely used in probate records includes "the breedings goeth with the mothers" (77) or "Nothing is more to the Advantage of my son th[a]n young breeding negroes" (86). The language of "breeding" and "breedings" does two things: one, dehumanizes Black women by placing them in the same category as breeding livestock, and two, reinforces the legalized hereditary nature of racial slavery. (Morgan notes Black enslaved women can only birth enslaved children, according to a 1662 Virginia legislative act.) This vicious cycle is another reason to explore the relationship of Black women bodies and the institution of slavery. The lived experience of these enslaved women was physically and ontologically different from that of enslaved men and even indentured white women. A Black enslaved man can be free, a white indentured women can be free, but a Black enslaved woman is the source of more enslaved individuals and so even if she was free, she remained the propellant of racial slavery as imposed upon her—what a travesty!

As Morgan stuns her reader with this horrific reality, she begins to explore the other facets of labor (spiritual, emotional, psychological, epistemological, and revolutionary) performed by enslaved Black women. In chapter 4, Morgan asserts that Black enslaved women, especially those who gave birth on Barbados and who witnessed the arrival of newly enslaved women, were the source of creolization. The need to preserve customs and rituals combined with the reality of losing their agency, requiring enslaved women to modify and create rituals to keep spiritual practices afloat and to bequeath their children (and the children of other enslaved individuals, those whose parents had been sold or died) with traditions and a sense of identity and humanity. In chapter 5, Morgan presents an example of the transfer of knowledge by enslaved Black women, which they transmitted not only to children or African newcomers but to the men who cultivated rice. We learn that in West Africa, women were rice cultivators and they carried that knowledge through the voyage. Ironically, this epistemological and physical labor was considered by enslavers to be "easy" work. Because field work was deemed easy work, Black enslaved women were relegated to the fields and could not become "skilled" or artisanal workers. Skilled work was commonly used to earn money to buy one's freedom, but if Black women were free, how could colonists "breed" free laborers? Moreover, free skilled workers could rise and rebel. In chapter 6, Morgan cites a court case where a free Black woman took a white man to court for refusing to pay her, and the court ruled in her favor. Faced with stacked injustices based on their gendered and racialized bodies, enslaved women rebelled by either controlling conception or escaping in groups of women and children to Spanish Florida. Moreover, Morgan suggests, children were a determining factor in rebellions. For example, there were no reported revolts in the eighteenth century, when there was a high birth rate among the enslaved population, thus making a revolt more risky due to the presence of many children.

Jennifer Morgan is akin to an archaeologist who finds pieces of a broken artifact and must reconstruct it from historical knowledge and secondary sources to counter-narrate and inform the public of the artifact's impact and significance. She recognizes the limitations of using the colonizer's archives but imparts on us the need to practice a methodology, albeit grueling, to humanize and give voice to the lived experience of oppressed peoples, especially gendered and racialized bodies. A couple of things struck me while reading *Laboring Women*: one, the labor of the woman author in archiving, researching, writing, and humanizing the enslaved women; and, two, the jarring fact that today we still witness the ceaseless oppression of women and the theft of their agency through legislation and genocide. In 2017, Margaret Atwood, in the introduction to *The Handmaid's Tale*, while addressing her choice to make women the center of the novel, states, "They [women] are not an afterthought of nature, they are not secondary players in human destiny, and every society has always known that.... The control of women and babies has been a feature of every repressive regime on the planet. Napoleon and his 'cannon fodder,' slavery and its ever-renewed human merchandise—they both fit in here.... Who profits by it? Sometimes this sector, sometimes that. Never no one" (xiii). Morgan provides significant evidence of who profited, and profits, by the labor of women, especially enslaved women.

In conclusion, Jennifer Morgan's *Laboring Women* is an example of feminist archival work, care work, and feminist citation, significantly before the time these terms became common in the field of women and gender studies. I would suggest archivists and instructors to include *Laboring Women* as an example of archival methodology.

Tuka Al-Sahlani (she/her/هي) is a rhetoric and composition doctoral student and a GC Digital Fellow at the Graduate Center, CUNY. Her interests include cultural rhetorics, translanguaging practices, and feminist, affective, and digital pedagogy. She is currently working on a digital index titled "Arab American Women Academics," hosted on the CUNY Academic Commons. She can be reached at talsahlani@gradcenter.cuny.edu.

Work Cited
Atwood, Margaret. 2017. *The Handmaid's Tale*. London: Vintage Classics.

Review of *Book Anatomy: Body Politics and the Materiality of Indigenous Book History*

Katrina M. Phillips

Amy Gore's *Book Anatomy: Body Politics and the Materiality of Indigenous Book History*, Amherst: University of Massachusetts Press, 2023

Book lovers know that it's not just the words on the pages that matter—there's also the cover image that catches your eye, the font on the spine, or the way the book looks on the shelf. What's less evident, though, are the many decisions writers, illustrators, editors, and publishers make along the way—and the power structures inherent in those choices. In the beautifully written and powerfully argued *Book Anatomy*, Amy Gore turns to the paratext, the material associated with, but still distinct from, the main body of the book that often remains outside of "the purview of literary criticism" (5). But these paratextual elements, Gore contends, are just as critical as the text itself. *Book Anatomy* examines five books published by Native authors in the late nineteenth and early twentieth century, an era marked at the beginning by the forced loss of Native land through the General Allotment Act of 1887 (also known as the Dawes Act) and the government's dogged determination to strip Native nations of their children through the federal Indian boarding school system.

Each text marks critical milestones in Native history. The first is John Rollin Ridge's *The Life and Adventures of Joaquín Murieta: The Celebrated California Bandit* (1854), followed by Sarah Winnemucca Hopkins's autobiographical *Life Among the Piutes: Their Wrongs and Claims* (1883) and S. Alice Callahan's novel *Wynema, a Child of the Forest* (1891). The final two are *Red Mother: The Life Story of Pretty-Shield, a Medicine Woman of the Crows* (published in 1932 and later renamed *Pretty-Shield*), a collaboration between Frank B. Linderman and Apsáalooke (the autonym for Crow) elder Pretty Shield, and D'Arcy McNickle's *The Surrounded* (1936). Each chapter centers a thematic element, and Gore deliberately contrasts the original publication with at least one reprint, underscoring "the paratextual negotiations present not only within one edition but in multiple editions over time" (6).

This is not, as Gore explains, a comprehensive study of Indigenous book history. While the names of these five authors may ring a bell for some readers, Gore's choice to avoid some of the most well-known Native writers—including Samson Occom, William Apess, Gertrude Bonnin, Luther Standing Bear, Ella Deloria, and Charles Eastman, among others—is a wise move. Even though these authors and their oeuvres showcase a wide range of Native literary prowess from the eighteenth to the twentieth centuries, Gore's decision allows for a deeper engagement with the chosen texts. It's also crucial to note that Native women wrote or contributed to three of the five books.

Gore turns to the issue of copyright in chapter 1 with *The Life and Adventures of Joaquín Murieta*. Written by Cherokee author John Rollin Ridge, often considered the first Native novelist, the book is significant for several reasons. Ridge was the grandson of Major Ridge and the son of John Ridge, two of the "Treaty Party" Cherokee who signed the 1835 Treaty of New Echota—the document that paved the way for the forced removal of the Cherokee from their homelands. The contestations over removal caused deep rifts within the Cherokee Nation, and Ridge was twelve when his father and grandfather were assassinated for signing the treaty. His family moved several times in the wake of his father's death, and Ridge himself fled to California in 1850 after killing a man who sided with those who'd killed his father. The publication of Ridge's novel, though, was plagued by plagiarism allegations and the deliberate dispossession of Ridge from his work. Much of the scholarship on *Murieta* focuses on "the numerous dismemberments in the content and context of the novel" (29). But Gore's riveting analysis of the subsequent publications—including the "paratextual decapitation" of the author by means of copyright in the 2018 edition, coupled with the "discursive violence" of the Library of Congress's classification headings—underscores the deep parallels between the alienation of the Cherokee from their land and the alienation of Ridge from his work (39).

Next, Gore looks to the works of Hopkins and Callahan—the first known books published by Native women—and the question of blank space. Sarah Winnemucca Hopkins was a Paiute woman who served as a translator and mediator, touring the nation to bring attention to the issues Paiute people faced.[1] While she had written periodical pieces for decades, her autobiography was groundbreaking both in its byline and in how its style broke away from the autobiographies by Native men. A Muscogee writer considered the first Native woman novelist, Callahan worked as a newspaper editor and teacher. She had hoped to finish her own education and open her own school in the Creek Nation but died of pleurisy at the age of twenty-six.

Gore's study of strategic rhetorical omissions, chapter and paragraph breaks, and the invitation of the margins within these works invites the reader to more fully understand how Winnemucca and Callahan used the written word—and the blank spaces therein—as a strategic platform in their advocacy surrounding Native issues.[2] Both women's readerships were predominantly white women. Gore's close reading of the chapter and paragraph breaks in Winnemucca's book, for instance, highlights Winnemucca's ability to connect emotional engagement to a call for action. Gore then moves to Callahan's novel, published shortly after the Wounded Knee Massacre of 1890. Here, the paratextual differences between the first edition of *Wynema* and the contemporary edition from the University of Nebraska Press mirror the tensions Callahan faced while writing for a non-Native audience, reminding us of "the multi-faceted nature of reading" the works of marginalized authors (69).

The final two chapters take us into the early decades of the twentieth century, an era marked by the shift in federal Indian policy from allotment and assimilation to reorganization. The penultimate chapter explores a collaboratively created piece first titled *Red Mother: The Life Story of Pretty-Shield, a Medicine Woman of the Crows*. Linderman, a writer and ethnographer, took notes as Pretty Shield simultaneously told her story in Plains Indian Sign Language (PISL) and in the Crow language. While Linderman was fluent in PISL, he asked another Crow woman, Goes Together, to translate the Crow language into English to make sure his notes were correct. Gore traces the changes across multiple editions of the book, seeking to reframe it as a feminist project, an ethnographic collaboration, and an assertion of corporeal agency (74). Gore's additional focus on the paratext surrounding Pretty Shield's thumbprint, which acts as a claim to copyright, offers a compelling consideration of Native women's resistance to the ongoing effects of colonialism and colonization.

The final chapter offers a fascinating analysis of primitive modernism alongside Salish Kootenai writer, activist, and professor D'Arcy McNickle's 1936 novel *The Surrounded*, looking particularly at the ways the "paratextual elements of the novel shape and expose the ethnographical expectations of its non-Native readers during the early twentieth century" (104). While McNickle's debut novel premiered to disappointing sales, its textual and paratextual elements remain a rich source of analysis and conversation among scholars. Here, Gore's paratextual focus moves to the book's "Note" and footnotes, demonstrating McNickle's determination to foreground the Salish oral storytellers who helped shape the novel. Gore's subsequent reflections on the power embedded in a book's citations offers a poignant critique of the challenges that historically excluded and marginalized authors have long faced in academic and trade publishing.

As a historian, I'm used to reading books for the content and the context, for the references and the source bases. But Gore's ability to quite literally read between the lines offers a new way of examining books by Native authors in this era. Gore seamlessly interweaves historical context and contemporary scholarship throughout the book, deftly signaling and signifying how Native books—and Native bodies—have long been read as contested spaces. Gore's sharp eye and careful reading of the paratext in these five books invites readers to more clearly see these texts as sites of resistance, negotiation, and agency. The book itself is a call to action, inviting readers to acknowledge, celebrate, and uphold the power of Native pasts, presents, and futures.

Dr. **Katrina M. Phillips** is a proud citizen of the Red Cliff Band of Lake Superior Ojibwe, and she's currently an associate professor of Native history at Macalester College. She's the author of *Staging Indigeneity: Salvage Tourism and the Performance of Native American History* (University of North Carolina Press, 2021), among other articles and publications. She's also the author of several children's books, including *Indigenous People's Day*; *Indigenous Peoples: Women Who Made a Difference* (Super SHEroes of History series, Scholastic Libraries) and *I Am on Indigenous Land*. She can be reached at kphilli2@macalester.edu.

Notes

1. The original title is *Life Among the Piutes*, and the contemporary spelling is "Paiute."
2. Sarah Winnemucca Hopkins is nearly always referred to as Sarah Winnemucca. Gore notes that Winnemucca's reference to her husband in the text (and the use of his last name in her byline) was a strategic move to highlight her "respectability" for her intended audience.

Review of *A Short History of Trans Misogyny*

Lava Schadde

Jules Gill-Peterson's *A Short History of Trans Misogyny*, New York: Verso Books, 2024

In her book *A Short History of Trans Misogyny*, Jules Gill-Peterson offers us a global history of trans misogyny, uncovering the layered history of a seemingly modern concept. While the book is short, its scope is large, spanning a discussion of hijras in colonial India, enslaved Africans brought to the United States, Indigenous two-spirit people, Black trans femme sex workers in antebellum New York and New Orleans, and the street queens of 1950s Los Angeles. The goal of such a "devastatingly global" history of trans misogyny is to decenter the narrative of trans-femininity emerging in the "progressive" metropoles of the West, to trace instead how the colonial patriarchal forces of Empire *trans-feminized* some of those it subjugated. One of the overarching questions Gill-Peterson poses is why violence against trans women is perpetuated at such extraordinary rates and why and how trans women became so uniquely "killable." Instead of locating the origins of such violence in the mindsets of transphobic and misogynistic individuals, she offers an alternative genealogy of trans misogyny that locates its roots in colonialism, capitalism, and patriarchy.

The first chapter, "The Global Trans Panic," traces the origins of the trans panic defense to colonial India of the nineteenth century, where British colonial powers enacted a statewide campaign of disrupting the livelihood and criminalizing the societal functions of and ways of living of hijras, as their perceived femininity presented a political threat to British colonial sovereignty. Concurrently in the United States, American settlers had begun to target gender-nonconforming Indigenous people (who nowadays often use the term "two-spirit") for their misalignment with Eurocentric gender standards. In both cases, the fact that there were people who did

WSQ: Women's Studies Quarterly 53: 3 & 4 (Fall/Winter 2025) © 2025 by Lava Schadde. All rights reserved.

not conform to colonial gender norms and values but lived embedded in their respective societies was sufficient to set into motion state-sanctioned campaigns to destroy their forms of life and eradicate them. Tracing the varied histories of the trans panic defense, Gill-Peterson argues, is crucial if we are to understand trans misogyny as not just a modern phenomenon but one with a complex and varied history entwined with capitalism and colonialism.

Such a history of the longue durée of the specific form of violence that is trans misogyny has been outstanding and is methodologically faced with an array of challenges. One such challenge is whether, and how, to unite the many subjects that Gill-Peterson claims have faced trans misogyny across the globe in the last couple of centuries. She stresses that projecting the identity of "trans woman" onto historical subjects before the 1970s is anachronistic, as gender and sexuality only became conceptually distinguished at that time. Yet Gill-Peterson does aim to draw a line of connection between the violence such individuals faced and the violence faced by trans women today, by highlighting the intertwinements between gay culture, homosexuality, and gendered self-expression and self-understandings.

To do so, Gill-Peterson suggests working with the term *trans-feminization*, which should denote the feminization and dehumanization of certain populations deemed too feminine or emasculate by oppressive powers in the interest of maintaining their sovereignty. "Trans-feminization" should illuminate how systems of trans misogyny have historically targeted individuals who may not have identified—then or now—as transgender women. Thus, she claims that "trans misogyny, as a pattern of violence, exceeds trans womanhood in its scope. In the global trans panic, the target of trans-feminization was not trans women narrowly, but people who appeared to the state as feminine but were classified as male" (56). Trans-femininization, then, is a helpful tool through which to understand the workings of trans misogyny, for, as trans people nowadays know all too well, hatred and bigotry are not concerned with the self-understanding of the subjects they are directed towards. It is the *perceived* femininity of these populations by those in power that subjects them to punishment. In this sense, such trans-feminizing violence was prior to the identificatory marker of trans womanhood: "Everyone in this book may have been *trans-feminized*, and all may have been brought into the orbit of *trans-femininity*, but only some considered themselves to be *trans women* in response" (18).

The second chapter, "Sex and the Antebellum City," follows Mary Jones, a free Black sex worker in New York City, who was prosecuted not for her trans-femininity but because she stole from white men clients. Gill-Peterson argues that Jones's criminalization must be understood as primarily racially motivated, having less to do with her cross-dressing than with her status as a Black free person. By highlighting the absence of trans panics and trans misogyny in Jones's prosecution, Gill-Peterson first brings out how trans misogyny is a historically contingent phenomenon, and second, how Jones's trans-feminization was driven more by economic need than by her inner felt identity. In the third chapter, "Queens of the Gay World," Gill-Peterson turns her gaze inwards to the movements for gay liberation of the '60s and '70s, sharply criticizing the abandonment and disavowal of the street queens in favor of the possibilities of assimilation to mainstream capitalist society. Gill-Peterson traces how the distancing of gay cis men from the poor queens of color, who were considered trashy for not restricting their performance to the stage, as other drag queens did, was thereby racially and economically motivated, preserving hegemonic categories of white male masculinity by trading on those who were most vulnerable to it.

Trans misogyny, then, should describe the violence people have historically faced by being trans-feminized. Importantly, the violence of trans misogyny is not merely a product of a certain set of beliefs about trans women, as our usage of the term today would have us believe. Through the lens of trans-feminization, Gill-Peterson successfully broadens our view of trans misogyny as functioning in two further crucial ways. First, she claims that trans misogyny historically acted and continually operates as a handlanger of colonial-patriarchal violence, punishing those subjects that did not conform to prescribed standards of white femininity. In this logic, its expression in the individual minds of people, who then proceed to act it out, must be understood as a broader symptom of the underlying cause of colonial patriarchy, whose practicing of trans misogyny was one of a myriad of ways to secure sovereignty. Second, trans misogyny should not merely be understood as violence directed at a predefined group of trans women subjects. Instead, trans misogyny is the violence that aids, to a certain extent, in determining and constituting such a group of subjects in the first place.

This reconceptualization of the origins and force of trans misogyny is novel and important, showing us ways of tracing the dialectics that have given rise to trans-femininity and trans misogyny, whereby one is not understood prior to the other. Yet, Gill-Peterson's analysis loses some of its power when it comes to thinking through what this might mean for the conception of trans misogyny today. Following Kate Manne (2018), Gill-Peterson understands the primary function of misogyny as the systematic punishment and policing of those women who step out of line and transgress patriarchal social structures, and her analysis of trans misogyny often restricts itself to thinking in terms of misogyny as the discipline and punishment of women, cis or trans. Given her commitment to rejecting a clear-cut distinction between gender identity and sexuality in her selection of the subjects of her inquiry, and her focus on racialization and economic precarity as leading forces in the subjection of some to trans misogyny, such a theoretical framework seems from the onset quite limiting for cross-historical and cross-cultural application. It further leads her to neglect thinking about the patriarchal impetus to police gender-nonconforming men and masculinities (e.g., some gay men, effeminate men, etc.). To take seriously the idea that not just trans and cis women are the target of trans misogyny, but variously gendered and sexualized people who are subjected to trans-feminization, would mean thinking about how gender-nonconforming masculinities pose an active threat to the coherence of masculinity and patriarchal legitimacy. Acknowledging that those who were trans-feminized were punished not merely for their femininity but for their failed masculinity (even when their gender failure was something imposed by those perpetuating violence against them) might allow for tracing further histories that think through trans misogynist violence in relation to the policing of masculinities, racialization, and histories of colonialism.

  Looking forward, Gill-Peterson suggests building a new trans feminism that follows the lead of travesti communities of Latin America, who she claims organize around material needs instead of an assimilationist drive for state-sponsored recognition. Gill-Peterson paints a picture of a trans feminism that promises to solve many of the problems we have ridden ourselves into, yet by doing so, she runs perilously close to perpetuating the same kind of idealization that she criticizes as having been projected on specifically Black trans women, whereby such subjects are idealized as "a tragic figure who endures the worst of multiple oppression, and yet a revolutionary actor whose every breath signals freedom, she is the one in whose name justice will arrive" (124–25). I take it we should be wary of such a totalizing vision that is prone to erasing the complexities and contradictions inherent in any broader feminist movements, including that of the travestis. Nevertheless, Gill-Peterson's rallying cry to decenter questions of ontology and identity—and to focus instead on how to act in the face of the historically layered, material violence that is trans misogyny—provides us with a crucial reorientation from which our values and actions for the fight against trans misogyny can begin to take shape.

Lava Schadde (they/them) is a PhD student in philosophy and a fellow at the Center for Global Ethics and Politics at the Graduate Center, CUNY. They have interests in social and political philosophy and feminist and trans philosophy, and will dabble in critical phenomenology and ordinary language philosophy. They especially like to mull over the interrelations between embodiment, ontology, and language. They can be reached at lschadde@gradcenter.cuny.edu.

Work Cited

Manne, Kate. 2017. *Down Girl: The Logic of Misogyny*. Oxford University Press.

Review of *How the Earth Feels: Geological Fantasy in the Nineteenth-Century United States*

jah elyse sayers

Dana Luciano's *How the Earth Feels: Geological Fantasy in the Nineteenth-Century United States*, Durham: Duke University Press, 2024

If this issue's call for papers begins with Leah Lakshmi Piepzna-Samarasinha's question "Where does the future live in your body?," then Dana Luciano brings readers into this question by figuring our bodies as in relationship to the stories we tell about the earth in a multidirectional present capacious enough to hold the deep futures and deep histories of geologic time. Luciano extends the fact of the body into the fact of matter, reminding readers that the earth, too, is a physical body and a body in relation. Luciano ascertains these relations through the stories people—differently situated across disciplining fields, racializations, and genderings—tell about geology and its subject matter.

How the Earth Feels is a thoroughly researched and clearly laid-out text with a remarkably textured and multidirectional yet still cohesive building of interrogations of geology as biopower in the nineteenth-century American settler-colonial context. As part of the ANIMA Critical Race Studies Otherwise series, *How the Earth Feels* refutes geology's apparent concern with the inanimate and instead investigates its demarcation of the lively and the inert. Luciano argues that in geology's articulation with white settler-colonial regimes, its dominant demarcations build fantasies of colonized peoples as inert, or bound to be buried, in stratigraphic records while naturalizing white male settlers' futures on and over the land.

Perhaps most centrally, *How the Earth Feels* is about geological fantasy's role in developing and sustaining the overrepresentation of Man—a construction of the universal human as white Euro/American male of Western Enlightenment rationality and progressively linear futurity—as put forth by Sylvia Wynter. Luciano demonstrates geological fantasy's role through close readings of geological narratives across an impressive assemblage of

WSQ: Women's Studies Quarterly 53: 3 & 4 (Fall/Winter 2025) © 2025 by jah elyse sayers. All rights reserved.

genres—travelogues, poetry, fiction, political address, prophesy, church hymn, law, newspaper articles, spiritualist writings, and theory, inter alia, some of these from trained geologists and others gaining their knowledge of the earth's composition otherwise. Luciano keeps the reasonings and conclusions of source texts at arm's length and focuses instead on their rein-forcements, instabilities, discontinuities, and challenges to converging and diverging genealogies of knowledge about racial and gender hierarchies. With impressive distance and depth of description, Luciano asks how feel-ing toward the inhuman might sever or reinforce the orders of Man. These multigenre texts, as assembled and analyzed by Luciano, variously shore up and jostle geology as a field and thus work on colonial racial logics toward different ends, piece by piece drawing out otherwise representations of life, the earth, and possible relations.

Chapter 1 most centrally works toward a concept of *manifest geology*, or nationalized and racialized geochronology—perhaps otherwise described as telling time with the earth into a future of white supremacist settler-colonial domination of the land and racialized others. Luciano historicizes how geology came to animate and be animated by poetic imaginations through alignments with life and death and how Foucault underwrites the concept of biopower with Cuvier's geological catastrophism and insistence on human-species extinction as inevitable. These cross-genre maneuvers of taking up geology and geologic time broaden a sense of what texts might count as geologic, while simultaneously ushering readers into the time-scope of geology's freshness as a scientific discipline. This freshness, per Luciano's arguably political-economic framing of the coherence of a scien-tific discipline and its attendant disciplinary capacities, is alive with not only the death-dealing speculative possibilities of "manifest destiny" but also with frictionfully ambivalent contestations.

Having established both geology's imbrications with biopower and its itinerant and surrounding narratives' capacities for destabilizing scientific claims to objectivity and colonial inevitability, Luciano then uses chapters 2 and 3 to lay out events in two different time-scopes in order to materi-ally work out contested processes of geology's and the U.S. settler regime's entangled becoming.

Luciano deftly situates chapter 2 in the time-space of the decade follow-ing the 1803 Louisiana Purchase, through which the United States acquired the Mississippi River Valley from the French First Republic. A series of spectacular earthquakes shook the valley shortly after. Luciano takes up

Klein's disaster capitalism, in this context as disaster settler colonialism, to describe the ways that the settler state sought to cohere itself amid white settler Christian interpretations of the earthquakes as realizations of End Times prophecies and punishments for settlers' sins. Contrary to the narrative, told here by way of a geologist's travelogues, of the earthquakes burying the traditions of still-living Cherokee, Shawnee, and Delaware communities into the post-animate space of a linear stratigraphic record, Luciano dynamically takes up the meanings of these same earthquakes within pan-Indigenous political movement. Luciano focuses on brothers Tenskwatana and Tecumseh's (Shawnee) syncretic treatment of Indigenous place-thought and its challenges to both settler-colonial futures and traditional tribal governance and demands for a pan-Indigenous movement responsive to the earthquakes' reorientation of the land. Luciano historicizes the U.S. governmental implementation of a major relief act to enact settler prophecies of displacing Indigenous peoples. Luciano deals masterfully in reading affective assertions of the character of the ground and the futures that might spring from it, while also insisting on their conflicts and outcomes as political, historical, and as material as the earth beneath our feet.

Having illustrated lively and responsive contestations of settler power alongside geologically told damnation of Indigenous life to the fossil record in chapter 2, it is in chapter 3 that Luciano most directly takes up the Indigenous extinction trope and its circulation in U.S. political and poetic discourse following the Indian Removal Act (1830). Chapter 3 charts the 1835 discovery of fossilized footprints ("trace fossils") of creatures of long-extinct species in the Connecticut River Valley, and the subsequent establishment of the field of ichnology, or the study of fossilized traces, into the early 1840s.[1] Anxieties and prophecies of chapter 2 give way to wonder as Luciano walks readers through a geologist's turn to poetry and a poet's turn to geology. Luciano shows how, in these geological poetics, trace fossils registered movement made matter and were figured, then, to make the human matter morally in the vast scope of geologic time and the threat of species oblivion. Luciano demonstrates, however, that the poetics of trace were applied unevenly toward displacing Indigenous life to the absented presence of future trace fossils and offering white settlers the promise of time-transcendence through (human) action fossilized. Even in communicating the disparate race-making of these geological interpretations, Luciano insists on the potential enlivened by geological poetics to conceive of race other than through dominant biological conceptions.

Luciano thus firmly denaturalizes the natural sciences and politicizes their enacted uses for and against the uncertain futures of people, nation, and land before turning in chapters 4 and 5 to what she calls "minor geology," or geologies that interrupt fantasies of white masculine earthly domination.

Chapter 4 centers the use of geology by white femmes to destabilize gender and repronormative frames, again working against prevailing biologics. By introducing the concerns 1800s physiology discourse had about white women's allegedly superior "impressibility," Luciano argues that geological instruction was put to use toward racialization of white women by centering rational facts and discouraging the sense of wonder presenced in chapter 3 (115). This chapter's central texts rework the supposed impressibility of the female body toward decidedly queer relations with rocks, through both the 1865–1874 spiritualist psychometric experiments of Elizabeth Denton and Annie Denton Cridge and erotic investments in amber embodied by the character Yone in Harriet Prescott's 1863 fictional story "The Amber Gods." Luciano explores geophilic intimacies beyond the human and suggests that geology might open antiracist forms of belonging but ultimately underscores both cases' "retreat into whiteness and the raced hierarchies that uphold it" upon encounter with racialized human others (135). Luciano insists on the importance of understanding both gendered and racialized constructions of the human when engaging in attempts to transcend its limits. Luciano's exploration of these texts is both fascinating and compelling, but the texts' material "outside" remains subterranean despite their snug situation in a period of less than ten years. What structuring events and movements of the 1860s might shape the simultaneous gendered transgressions and racialized reinforcements of white femmes at this time? Despite insisting on material and temporal groundedness elsewhere, Luciano retreats here into a sense of timelessness of white femininity.

In chapter 5, Luciano situates a minor geology of Black men's speculative geologies of the 1840s and into the 1860s—the decades leading into the U.S. Civil War. Luciano continues to demonstrate geologic instruction's historically contingent use as a form of moral instruction, first in the forms of both violent eruptions and subterranean potentials of volcanoes and then in James McCune Smith's bending of ideas of impressibility and geology toward geologic theories of racial malleability. Luciano first works through figurations of the volcano in the Black press. Whereas earthquakes stood in for reorientations to land in chapter 2, here volcanoes function as threat indexing a potentially inevitable eruption of antislavery sentiment in the form of revolution. Luciano's close readings of speeches and articles are, as her close readings elsewhere in *How the Earth Feels*, remarkably careful and detailed. Luciano demonstrates a cadre of writers' geological fantasies *and* the apparent enthusiasm and demand with which they were met, while still illuminating frictional figurations of Black affect across authors and publications and their resultant fidelities to or departures from possibilities of Black agency and self-possession.

As *How the Earth Feels* is organized by case studies framed on the basis of racialized and gender identities, it is worth noting that Black women and women of color, though not represented in case studies other than as the bounds of white women's senses in chapter 4 or through their absence in Black uplift texts of chapter 5, contribute heavily to Luciano's theorization. Luciano builds with the careful scholarship of Black women and women of color, some cited in this sentence, as she centralizes "dehumanization as foundational to the United States" (Goffe, in discussion of guano in chapter 1) and imagines how a renewed "poetics of landscape" (McKittrick, in discussion of McCune Smith's speculative geologies in chapter 5) both "onshore and offshore" (King, also in chapter 5) can ground new stories that work against the overrepresentation of Man (and thus heed Wynter's calls). Luciano gathers and critically presences otherwise representations of earth, human life, and nonhuman life at the edges of geology's history toward its potential reworking. This work is especially crucial as geology, locked in debates about the naming of geological epochs even in a context of climate change and building planetary crisis, risks taking on the inertness we might, prior to reading *How the Earth Feels*, assign to rocks. Instead, Luciano's careful study of multiple frames of speculative geology illustrates the impressibility of the hard sciences and the impactful force of poetics and social narratives.

The text leaves scholars with questions of how geology can help us scale up, not in terms of distance away from life but toward making room for the "work or remaking and maintaining relation" in necessarily politically situated research that must face our collective vulnerability to extinction (176–77). By insisting on deep time and the ways differently positioned authors and speakers grapple with it, Luciano challenges a potentially alienating and disempowering reading of geological time. She calls for "transformative intimacies and responsible, responsive relations" bringing together the scales of the body and geological time (178). Reflecting on Luciano's drawing out of processes of mattering, it is clear that it matters not only *how* but *from where* we build our understandings of collective vulnerability. One might consider, then, reading *How the Earth Feels* alongside Malcom Ferdinand's *Decolonial Ecology: Thinking from the Caribbean World* and other texts that unsettle colonial land claims and move *from* rather than *to* the epistemologies that Luciano situates as minor geologies altering or interrupting the fantasies that sustain Man. Thinking and feeling from the many apocalypses experienced within the frames of specifically Black and Indigenous lifeworlds, it is colonial fantasy that alters and interrupts.

jah elyse sayers (they/them) directs their creative energy toward liberatory placemaking through research, writing, artmaking, and teaching. jah is a PhD candidate in Earth and Environmental Sciences at the CUNY Graduate Center. Their research focuses on embodied, enacted, and relational placemaking in tension with urban and environmental planning and policy in the context of changing landscapes. They argue against methods that conscript particular people to particular places, instead tending to embodied relationalities and mobilities as people make place. They can be reached at jsayers@gradcenter.cuny.edu.

Note

1. Other footprints left by long-extinct species had, of course, been observed in their fossil forms before, but they arrived now as legible to the discipline of geology, which displaced other explanations (Luciano 2024, 88).

Review of *The Way You Make Me Feel: Love in Black and Brown*

Asma A. Neblett

Nina Sharma's *The Way You Make Me Feel: Love in Black and Brown*, New York: Penguin Press, 2024

The Way You Make Me Feel: Love in Black and Brown, by writer and educator Nina Sharma, is a timely memoir with community at its heart. The first few pages foreshadow this. Followed by gratitude to Sharma's husband and parents is an understated dedication to her audience, who she recognizes as people "at the edge of a feeling," or an awareness.

Among the author's reflections about her youth, her addictive behaviors, her triumphs, and her enduring love story is her pursuit of solidarity, a topic that may resonate with her identified readers, and all readers at a time of shock and awe. Proving that her encompassing message is not at the expense of her memoir, Sharma first revisits scenes of her childhood and adolescence to locate and frame the makings of her point.

Case in point are key inflection moments in essays like "Kissable" that cut into Sharma's coming of age, which was significantly shaped by class and the erotic. Poignant in this essay are the moments that underscore Sharma's lack of community in her then upper-middle-class society. Counter to this current are the outlets that she finds in tandem in music and visual material. Those are the occasions for criticality, wonder, self-discovery, and, importantly, connection.

"Don't Even Tell Him" is a stand-out essay that offers a deeper dive into the author's identity as an Asian American. She addresses the pressure to assimilate as a "model minority"—a controlling image[1] or stereotype specific, though not limited, to Asian-Americans—and its significant impact on her experience. Sharma brings the reader into the twilight zone of her teens through the allegory of Albert Hitchcock's 1960 film *Psycho*, revealing the psychological harm, stigma, and erasure that tropes such as model minority status can introduce. Sharma finds community among other South

***WSQ: Women's Studies Quarterly* 53: 3 & 4 (Fall/Winter 2025)**

Asians who similarly struggle with the racialized demands of the status quo, and in some instances despite the rules of caste in her culture that might have made community difficult or rare across her intracommunal groups.

Sharma's grasp of social order is not limited to her background. The author peels the complex nature of model minority status in her exploration of Asian American identity to also understand its impact in American society. The latter is supported by key citations that lend to the specificity of her message, like the foregrounding questions in W. E. B. Du Bois's *Souls of Black Folk* ("How does it feel to be a problem?") and Vijay Prashad's *Karma of Brown Folk* ("How does it feel to be a solution?"). When aligned by Sharma, they illustrate different sides of a shared struggle and system that highlights an intertwined relationship among Black and Brown people.

Perhaps solidarity is also, if not preemptively, shaped by feelings like belonging, interest, and regard that emerge in periods of transition and change, be they private, societal, or a bit of both. If such is the case, then Sharma's memoir makes the argument for it in ways that emphasize the adages about the "personal as political," and if not, then she at minimum points to a political education (for solidarity) that is not predicated on or limited to the political expediency or rigid alignments that noticeably define the early 2020s.

On the topic, scholars and activists Mariame Kaba and Kelly Hayes suggest something similar in their 2023 article for the *Boston Review* (Kaba and Hayes 2023). The "task-focused" tend to dismiss opportunities to explore feelings such as discomfort that significantly foreground the route to meaningful solidarity. Kaba and Hayes are keen to primarily highlight these pitfalls as common for organizers who emerge from like-minded political homes, affinity groups, and close-knit circles that share the same values and points of view. In recent years, "anti-woke" rhetoric and legislation, and specific pockets of media, also exemplify this narrowing practice through their (mis)understandings of history, diversity, equity, and inclusion. Kaba and Hayes encourage organizers, and, by extension, lay people who are interested in organizing, to embrace a "stretch zone," a place through which communities prioritize feelings and process the discomfort that Sharma explores, and that solidarity demands, through practices such as listening.

"Birthmark" is another key hindsight that is focused on the role of caste in Sharma's upbringing. In a confession-like manner, Sharma explores the impact of her insecurities in lines that grapple with questions about beauty as a sign or measure of value: "I like to think I grew up to be someone who is not very preoccupied with coloring or appearance overall" (4). What begins as observations about the author's early take on the topic of complexion in Indian culture (gauri, or white, as good, and kali as dark or not favored) turns into a reckoning about the origins of such views in her background and Western culture, and the unlearnings they prompt as she encounters them in her core relationships as a teen and adult.

Her reckonings are especially apparent throughout stories about her marriage to Quincy Scott Jones, a Black writer, poet, and educator based in the Northeast. Essays such as "Animal Strip Club" and "Sacrifice" harken back to the overlapping obstacles that are connected to Sharma's earlier reflections about stereotypes, social order, and systemic violence. The flattening views that are initially held by Sharma's family in response to her marriage are unfortunately anticipated.

Beyond her message, Sharma's self-disclosure is the best quality of *The Way You Make Me Feel*. Amid her message and its call to action are diaristic moments between her stories that reveal who Sharma believes she is as she looks back at the moments that shaped her: She's a melophile and a scholar of her culture. Her experiences in clinics (one for wellness, the other for fertility) highlight her will. Her earliest memories with Quincy and her friends Justine and Aisha are abundant and filled with adventure and comedic relief. Most of all, Sharma, like many of us, has a self-admitted and lasting desire to belong and for this aspect to be taken seriously.

"We Can Neither Confirm nor Deny that Kamala Harris Is Our Time-Traveling Daughter," the last of sixteen essays (and one that could stand on its own without a title) is sobering. The historical impact of the former vice president, Kamala Harris—a woman of Jamaican and South Asian descent—on Sharma's message is undeniable in hindsight. Through her heritage, Harris is emblematic of solidarity to the author, particularly between Black and Brown people. Her representation clarifies a key aspect about the memoir's message and will inspire curiosity among readers about the future that Sharma seems to envision through the vice president. *The Way You Make Me Feel: Love in Black and Brown* does not resist imagining a way forward—together—and encourages readers to do similar through what it contends with, revisits, and reconsiders.

Asma (ahhs-ma) Neblett (neb-LET) is a writer and educator from Brooklyn, New York. She currently serves as an editorial committee member for CUNY's *Journal of Interactive Technology and Pedagogy*. She can be reached at asmaneblett@outlook.com.

Notes

1. I reference the concept of the "controlling image" from Patricia Hill Collins, "Mammies, Matriarchs, and Other Controlling Images," in *Black Feminist Thought: Consciousness and the Politics of Empowerment* (New York: Routledge, 1990).

Works Cited

Kaba, Mariame, and Kelly Hayes. 2023. "How Much Discomfort Is the Whole World Worth?" *The Boston Review*, September 6, https://www .bostonreview.net/articles/how-much-discomfort-is-the-whole -world-worth.

SECTION V. PROSE

Damages

Gina Alexandra Srmabekian

Please answer to the best of your ability. If not applicable, please leave blank.

1. If memory permits, what is your name?
The Japanese substitute the space between the shards of broken vases with gold. You must be priceless to be broken. Hebrew was a dying language until 1945 when a father locked his son in a room and taught him each letter. He saved a people's secrets. The universities in Iran have mats on the floors for women who wish to sit there. Sometimes I know my face has been corroded by acid. Then I run to the mirror and I am a man holding an empty chalice. As quickly as I am, they vanish. If you inject a pregnant woman's urine into a frog, an autopsy will show that they lay two hundred to three hundred eggs. In India, ultrasounds are illegal because there are too many abortions of little pink-bowed fetuses. This is a good way to know you are pregnant and to kill frogs. A Hawaiʻian bobtail squid hunts for food primarily through the phosphorescence of the parasites in its stomach. When all the parasites align inside all of the squids, the sea floor becomes illuminated. These are my memories and none are my own.

2. If memory permits, what is your age?
She is adjusting herself in the mirror with one eye closed and the other slightly open because when she looks with both, she sees all the faces that have come before her. She speaks to herself. She calls herself we.

WSQ: Women's Studies Quarterly 53: 3 & 4 (Fall/Winter 2025) © 2025 by Gina Alexandra Srmabekian.
All rights reserved.

3. To the best of your memory, was there a time when you had forgotten and then remembered again?

It is only when the door clicks closed in the foyer downstairs that she realizes she must be a figment of someone else's imagination. This, in some part, causes her great relief and regret: It is one thing to be imagined for mending by someone else; it is another to have imagined yourself only to be mended.

The someone else shuffles around in the kitchen for a long while. He has replaced his work shoes at the door with his house slippers. The scuff of wooled feet is abrasive on the cords in her neck. It extends a long, heartbeat-less moment in the juncture between the stairs and the front door. The shuffler is tired.

Then the pitter-patter resumes in closer quarters, the footsteps inclining, the steps creaking solid groans of obligation. She places the box of claims back underneath her mattress. He enters holding a large pot filled with corrosive acids.

He asks her to lie down and spread her legs.

4. To the best of your memory, what triggers these ruptures?

And then he takes her from me.

Before I can mourn what is mine, I have forgotten to whom it belongs. Except for the outline of some empty space in the crook of my arms, there is only the shutting of the door, the shuffling of footsteps, a pink-rimmed spatula on the nightstand like a tuning fork for the ears of ghosts.

My quiet is mine alone.

Empty space is frightening to some. If you look at a light in your room, lying this way on your back, away from the door that only lets in and never lets out, if you look at this light then close your eyes very hard you will see in the darkness the bright neon ring.

This is you behind your eyes.

And so what if you cannot remember your name?

5. If memory permits, do you fear what will return with your memories?

The shuffler has stopped holding a stethoscope to her chest, but he still frequently remembers to ask the robot to breathe in and out, though she no longer has the need. It is a small kindness, one he practices humbly, just as he still washes her car; even now, it sits dilapidated and crystalline in the front yard though the robot has forgotten she was once the woman who loved it. If he could, he'd remember the day it was purchased. The length of her coming down the staircase, her eyes puffy orbs of discontentment until, turning to the window, she saw a small freedom; everyone knows you are owned by the things you hurt, almost as much as they own you.

He'd tricked her with this future at the expense of the others.

You see, he said, I *am* a kind man.

And he had been for a while, for a longer while than he could bear it. She'd returned to him tussled with the knowledge of a world he could not fence in. Over time, he'd had to take even that. The day he'd purchased the car had been a good day but the days surrounding it had made him bury it.

This is the danger of eradicating memories; there are too few selfless, every memory is shared.

6. To the best of your memory, what benefits have you acquired in the erasure?

Before she began to malfunction, the robot was allowed to drive to the grocery and hardware store—the places where she was most necessary and welcome. He would let the robot drive it. Neither would think too long of her intimate knowledge of stick shift.

Neither would question why she knew the back window would stick if opened.

At the grocery store, she picks up the butcher's memories of his wife, dead a decade (and he, still expecting to find his socks tucked, one in the other), so she could pick up the apples, the arugula, the Swiss cheese, the mangoes—if they were in season.

She picks up the memories of customers who let her pass to the front of the line, as well; the time one got lost in the ocean, away from her floundering father, her instinct of survival a pariah that let the ocean drain him.

At the hardware store she stands in aisles, a hesitant mechanic. She checks the list twice, three times, and places her finger on the cords in boxes. She likes to think she is complacent in our consumption. She feels out the ones that will replace her collapsing veins.

7. Do you sometimes wake up because you think someone has called your name?

It is like sleep every time he is away. I stand outside of myself in a large silver disk and comb the cold want out of my hair. I try to be good for his eyes. I try to be good. He is oftentimes sulking now; he asks me less for my breath on the nape of his neck.

He says I smell like fish blood, metallic and sweet. But he still calls me by a name.

Before the change, he used to interpret my dreams. He'd walk into the room and the shutters over my eyes would project them onto the wide expanse of his torso. A tarantula would climb over his shoulder; a humming-bird would nestle into the hair of some woman in Costa Rica.

The dreams sulked inside my head, a thousand points of light.

In my sleep, the word *pain* was replaced by *parasite*, and so I could not tell him it pained me when he asked. He told me the tarantula meant good omens in dreams; the hummingbird in the hair, good health. He told me all these fates were mine. I told him they give me parasites. He brought break-fast in bed, shining metal eggs. He combed the electricity out of my spindle hair with a tuning fork. It wailed a clean C. He reminded me my name.

8. If memory permits, when was the first time you answered in someone else's voice?

But later when she returns to dinner, the shuffler becomes weary. She speaks Spanish. She laughs at anecdotes about her family in Kentucky; she has never left this city. Suddenly the memories are her own; at the grocery store, she begins to accost lost lovers and diagnose diseases. The memories were supposed to redirect her attention from me; now they glow inside of her like some broken marquee. The shuffler realizes he has made a mistake and stands over her bed that night. He locks her in the bedroom for safekeeping but the next morning at breakfast she is no better.

"What happened to my father?" she asks while they eat, a screw sticking out from the corner of her perforated lips. "Did he make it across shore?" she asks, the end of a cable cord sucking in.

9. Do you sometimes wake up because you have called your own name in your dreams?

He is not here to tell me. But I know other things of ourselves. For one, I'm female. This is evident by this thing between my legs. I have no use for it. I am not the one using it. I do not understand why others who come to see me are so apt to show me theirs. Some are mangled bits of torsos; others are coifed, endless slits.

I do not know why so many of their memories are attached to it.

When they are inside me, I try to kiss the parts of their flesh that align with my face. When they are inside me, I try to make them feel as if they are not giving themselves away. I do not know why I cannot use my own.

I cry over my alien body.

I cry over how claustrophobic she is inside of herself.

I sometimes wish I could look out to the ocean and not hear crying, but a Serbian woman came to see me and she misses the Black Sea. I sometimes wish my skin was the same color on the inside, grey and shining, like on the outside, like water flitting off of amphibian eggs. I wish I was soft in the place that makes the shuffler leave me, longer and longer, but one day the insulation just split apart like seaside cliffs. One day the parts that felt were shucked off like corrosive oyster shells. One day he fit his entire hand in.

He asked me how many fingers I loved him.

10. If memory permits, what have you gained by giving your memories away?

And then he takes it from me.

The heaving between us, to and fro and asunder, the wet rags of blood and oil; it makes no difference, his hushed whispers of comfort, his awe at my creation.

After the man with no family came, I made an entire birch tree out of fiber. After the woman with no hearing came, I made a cello, low and sober. She keeps the parasites in. They flood her wires. They become little specks of light, confused glorious synapses that glow like hunger. They dispose themselves inside of me. I die for them, the memories. I give them eggs for a new life.

This quiet labor is mine alone.

I name them by my name.

11. To the best of your memory, what are the risks of returning to yourself?

The shuffler has made three great mistakes in his life. One he no longer remembers. The second, he wishes to forget, so much so that the time in which he does not think on me takes up the better half of the day. The third stirs in front of him in some mimic of sleep as he stands over her bed every night, wishing he knew how to undo me. He takes up the couch in the den. He pulls up a claims form for lost memories and fills out her information as best he can, but before he presses send, he notices the subtitled section of risks and benefits.

It started out small. For an entire month after seeing a club promoter who had caused an electrical fire that killed four, the robot would hold a match underneath the fire alarm. When a woman who had driven her fiancé into a light post, then herself to a rehab clinic, came to see her, she began sneaking around the liquor cabinets, mourning something she'd never lost. The shuffler followed her around with a fire extinguisher, waiting helplessly for her to implode. This had not been an anticipated risk.

He began to lock her in the bedroom for longer and longer.

But, in the bedroom there was no external quantifier. They would fill me up, the people who wanted to leave their voices there. Less and less, she took him in. When he'd visit her she'd mirror the stories of the clients who had just descended the stairs, their outlines like golden rings in the doorway as they went back out into the sunlit world of ignorance.

She spoke without discrimination, without attention to the languages he did not understand; it didn't seem important what he had to say in return.

After every client there was a longer delay in returning to herself, to the space between her legs, becoming the absence of her. He gave her the memory claim forms that he gave to clients who wanted refunds.

He told her to write herself, perpetually.

The next day she placed his hand on her stomach and said, "Feel here."

12. If memory permits, what is the thing you most wish returned?

The shuffler comes into the room where the blinds have collapsed under dust. She has stopped even the pretense of an outside world: For who, knowing the insides of humans, would want to return?

From somewhere inside the null, he feels the smoothing of hair like stringing a violin. We are waiting for him, again. We are wailing a sharp C.

But it has been months since he has felt himself inside of her cold-fisted attention. He sees her outline sidle across the room like a bitch in heat. He watches her outlines change from soft to silver. How beautiful she used to be in her longing to be human; now she only hums like a refrigerator with molded oranges.

She wishes she could be the same color on the outside as in.

She wishes he'd fill her with gold, to dwindle the endless weight of me.

But he no longer does. He closes the door behind him, his woolen feet dragging hardwood floor through the particles of all the men and women who she has become in his absence. The shuffler is tired. He has failed to pull the root of want from her, though he has burned through countless metal gloves and throngs.

He has failed to pull the root of want from her.

Though he has pulled the squid perpetually from inside her, she glows like dusk.

13. If impossible to return, what is the best replacement for the memories you could not keep?

And me, this thing between her legs, I am humming the tune of a future that astounds her. The shuffler, this man that I have owned in my destruction, that I have told our stories so that when, we, sitting silent, in the repose of a night when the kingdom has fallen out of his hands, will feel magnificent in our departure.

This is the problem with eradicating memories: no one is separate, all memories are shared, and I am humming a tune of a future without us in it. We sit silent in the repose of a night when the world has given birth to itself.

I am the tourniquet of a million voices. I am the one they inject their refuse in. I give birth to squids and I give birth to acid. I give birth to words of pink-bowed tongues. I am a dying language but inside of me all the parasites are neon suns. And in ourselves, a murmuration of starlings; and in ourselves, we echo the word *human*. Come in to see me: Come in, I'll listen. Come in and I will entomb you into ourselves. We are a fused thing; we are a bible written in logos. We are the word of a god who has looked down on ourselves. Come in to see me, come in, I'll kiss them, the places that I can reach as you are losing yourself.

At my autopsy, they will find two hundred amphibian eggs. They will hatch into a destruction of wildcats. My autopsy will find me all of these fates.

My autopsy will give all daughters fangs.

Gina Alexandra Srmabekian is a writer whose work grapples with transgenerational trauma, memory, and identity. She writes toward her own freedom and toward the freedom of all displaced peoples from Artsakh to Palestine and beyond. She writes about grief and in times of grief, because it is the most powerful articulation of love. Her upcoming or published works can be found in *Ninth Letter*, *Mizna*, *DIAGRAM*, and more. She is a lecturer at California State University, Northridge, and lives in Los Angeles with her dog Bailey. She can be reached at gina.srmabekian@csun.edu.

The Rotten Department

María Mínguez Arias

Preface

The following text is an exploration through memory and language of institutional (in this case, university) violence toward women's bodies in my native country. By mirroring academic language and formatting, it confronts the very institution on its own turf. And yet the blank page becomes the negative space or the void that refuses to share the space or to put the spotlight on that same institutionalized violence. "The Rotten Department" is an excerpt from the forthcoming hybrid memoir and essay collection *Naming the Body: A Queer Woman's Restorative Mapping of the Self* (Mouthfeel Press, 2026), translated from Spanish by Robin Myers.

WSQ: Women's Studies Quarterly 53: 3 & 4 (Fall/Winter 2025) © 2025 by María Mínguez Arias.

THE ROTTEN DEPARTMENT

1. It's not the first time that the professor has opted to teach in Latin.
2. Although the author (then a twenty-one-year-old student) can't prove it, she could swear that the professor's intent by delivering an incomprehensible speech in the Roman language was twofold: first, to demonstrate the limitations of his students' intellect; second, to mentally masturbate in public (the author recalls a look of pleasure on his face).
3. The student has been able to ignore the professor's twisted shenanigans until this date.
4. The incident in question as recalled by the author (henceforth referred to as "the incident") lasted only a few minutes, but it marks a before and after in her patriarchal imaginary.
   LINGUISTIC CLARIFICATION: The term *patriarchal* won't be incorporated into the author's vocabulary for over two decades, which means that on the day of the incident, the student lacks the language necessary to discuss and explain the true significance of what transpired.
5. Intuition (*Merriam-Webster*): "The ability to understand something immediately, without the need for conscious reasoning."
6. Intuition (the student's own definition): *There are lines that shouldn't be crossed under any circumstances.*

7. Most of the students enrolled in the class where the incident occurred are young people who identify as women. This statistical data point is relevant in any evaluation of the incident and its consequences.

8. Textual citation from the student's journal on Friday, April 5, 1991 (approximately one year before the incident): "This college business gets darker and darker. . . . I'm tired of this shit."

9. The student begins the 1991–1992 academic year, her fourth, after an attempt to drop out. Her mother has prevented this from happening, with the now epic line "The only thing your father and I can offer you is an education. We have nothing else to give." Had this conversation taken place in the present time, the author would have told her mother that "an authentic education, the real kind, is what you're already giving me at home, and the academic kind can't touch that with a ten-foot pole." But that day, she says nothing and retreats to her bedroom to cry.

10. The student's long silence (which precedes the moment when she feels like yelling and shaking her fellow students) results from trying to determine whether what she has just heard the professor say aloud is, in fact, what the professor has said or just a figment of her imagination. The silence is long because the professor has spoken entirely in Latin until a few seconds prior. The change in register from Latin to Spanish causes confusion and hinders comprehension of the message.

11. During the first couple of years, the smell goes unnoticed, but by the third, the student starts to detect a certain rotten stench when she walks through the door of the School of Journalism each morning. The stench is accompanied by the peculiar sensation of inhabiting a body that has no presence within the walls of the institution.

12. The fourth year is the year of the revelation, otherwise defined as the year when the student determines the source of the stench: Both among the professors and the student body of the institution, the student discerns (1) the Spain whose Franco- and post-Franco-era privileges have adapted to and even benefited from a decade of socialist government; this Spain feels and behaves as if it were formidably superior; (2) the Spain that started from the ground up two decades prior; that is, the Spain of the descendants of those who lost the war; (3) the Spain that views everything in terms of plunder; and (4) the Spain devoted, body and soul, to the democratic experiment. The professor may personify the subcategory of misogyny under one or several of the four abovementioned Spains. The author can't prove it, because she has no further contact with the professor after the incident.

　　LINGUISTIC CLARIFICATION: The terms *privilege* and *privileged* won't be incorporated into the student's vocabulary for over two decades, which means that in her fourth year of college, she lacks the language to discuss and explain the true significance of the rot.

　　SEMANTIC CLARIFICATION: Although she doesn't know how to name it, the student has a well-formed mental image of privilege as a concept in her country, and of its surrounding artifice. Her understanding of privilege will evolve over time.

13. During the same spring as the incident, war has broken out in Yugoslavia, and both the professor and the student body are familiar with the testimonies of ethnic cleansing and the mass rapes of Bosnian Muslim women.

14. In *Frances* (1982), a film based on the life of actress Frances Farmer, the protago-
    nist, of untamable body and mind, is ultimately subjected to a lobotomy following
    various psychiatric institutionalizations. In *Thelma and Louise* (1991), the protago-
    nists, of undisciplined bodies and minds, are subject to a chase and end up throwing
    themselves off a cliff. Even though these are two of the student's favorite movies,
    she has never watched them again. The author believes that the student's refusal to
    rewatch the films is associated with the use of misogynist and institutional violence
    toward the subjection of the untamable and undisciplined woman's body.

15. Direct quote from the student's journal, dated Tuesday, December 17, 1991 (several
    months before the incident): "I'm exhausted and ready. I think I can handle any-
    thing, or almost anything."

16. The student is familiar with the work of the Madres de la Plaza de Mayo in Argenti-
    na, who march in white every Thursday to uphold the memory of their loved ones
    forcibly disappeared during the dictatorship. She doesn't know, however, that during
    that same spring, in Belgrade, Yugoslavian women of all ethnicities, also known as
    Women in Black, march silently every Wednesday to protest war, militarization,
    nationalism, ethnic cleansing, sexism, and rape.

17. The incident comprises (a) three gestures: the professor speaking in Latin and fixing his eyes on the girls seated in the front rows, the professor smiling, and the professor addressing the boys, and (b) sixteen words: "Look at them, sitting there, not a word, not moving a muscle, like raped Bosnian Muslims."

18. As the professor continues with his lecture, now in Spanish, the student debates between telling him off or shaking her female classmates to jostle them out of their self-absorption (the student has attempted both strategies in different contexts, albeit with poor results). The student listens, the student hesitates, the student argues with herself, the student gathers her things and walks out of the class, never to return.

19. There's a philosophical question that wonders *If a tree falls in a forest and no one hears it, does it make a sound?* Unwittingly, and by leaving the class, the student is saying: (a) "Here there was a shameless asshole who opened his mouth to suppress a group of women and relish the suppression of others" and (b) "I heard it."

20. The student emigrates to the United States, with one incomplete on her transcript, on April 9, 1996.
21. The student receives her university diploma on March 20, 2012, through a resolution issued by the college's credit panel, the Junta de Compensación de la Facultad.
22. During the war—according to the verdict issued by the International Criminal Tribunal for the former Yugoslavia, created one year after the incident and dissolved in 2017—Serbian forces practice mass rapes on the Muslim women of Bosnia. The court estimates that the victims may number between 20,000 and 40,000 women.

María Mínguez Arias is the author of *Nombrar el cuerpo* (2022), named among the Best Queer Lit of the Year in Spain, and of the International Latino Book Award–winning novel *Patricia sigue aquí* (2018). Her writing appears in anthologies and journals in the U.S., Spain, and Mexico. She is coeditor of *#NiLocasNiSolas: Narrativa escrita por mujeres en Estados Unidos* (2023), and an active member of the #NewLatinoBoom, a movement of contemporary writing in Spanish out of the United States. She aims to widen the space where literature exists, because it has been way too narrow for way too long. She can be reached at maria.m.minguez@gmail.com.

The Facts of Comportment

Melissa Chadburn

The '80s was Pop Rocks and soda—sparking a constellation in my mouth. The '80s was Slip 'N Slide at lola's in the summertime and collecting oily stickers. The '80s was Jo Polniaczek. Jo was the tomboy character on the NBC hit show *The Facts of Life*. I was hooked from the beginning. At the time, I spent summers with my lola, checking out books and records from the library across the street and watching TV in her bedroom. The show was set in the fictional Eastland School.

My life and the girls who went to Eastland couldn't be more different. Eastland was an all-girls boarding school in upstate New York. The girls who went there usually lived in The City—penthouse apartments with doormen. While these girls had parents who could send them to a college preparatory school, and wore braces and uniforms, I was a latchkey kid whose mom was still in college and worked days as a secretary. We got food stamps back when they were actually a book of stamps, and our bills constantly swapped out for shrewder shades of pink when the utilities were getting close to being shut off. Ma liked to go out dancing, and during the school year, I was mostly left to fend for myself.

The day Jo arrives in Eastland, the girls—the youngest, Tootie Ramsey, usually on roller skates; and her best friend, Natalie, the jokester; and blonde heiress Blair—are all gathered around Mrs. Garrett. Mrs. Garrett, a spunky redhead, gives cool-aunt vibes, loving with a sense of humor and a bit of a rasp to her voice, like she was once a supermodel who smoked Virginia Slims, but only at parties. You hear a loud clangy motorcycle; Mrs. Garrett runs to the window and says, "Sounds like a wild bunch." Then, in all denim and a motorcycle helmet, a heavily New Jersey–accented person saunters

WSQ: Women's Studies Quarterly 53: 3 & 4 (Fall/Winter 2025) © 2025 by Melissa Chadburn. All rights reserved.

in and asks, "Uh, is this where I'm supposed to be?" Blair, who would later become this newcomer's nemesis and then, even later, her best friend, replies, "Uh, delivery boys usually use the rear entrance." The newcomer removes her helmet, exposing two French braids; Blair exclaims, "I don't believe this." Nearby, Natalie says, "You don't! I was gonna ask him to the fall dance." I was delighted by the gender reveal of it all. A tomboy. Who rides motorcycles. At Eastland. Jo raises her arm to smack Natalie. Mrs. Garrett inserts herself between the two girls.

That was it. Life was never the same. Jo Polniaczek. Jo was tall and had thick, long brown hair that was always back in a braid or ponytail. She moved with ease. Jo was at Eastland on a scholarship. Like I'd been dreaming of, she made her way out of her working-class life.

The Facts of Life ran from 1979 to 1988, and I tuned in at every moment I could to study Jo and her tomboyhood. To me, what made Jo a tomboy was, yes, her masculine interests, motorcycles, fixing things, and the way she dressed, but it seemed that, unlike the other girls at Eastland, Jo's attention was inward. She did not concern herself with the mirror; she was not pandering to boys. Her attention rested on her internal life. She was smart. She got to Eastland on a scholarship, scored highest in her entrance exam, and eventually graduated valedictorian. There was something of her tomboyishness—this was not a stop on the transit to queerness; it was the destination. She liked specific things, and she knew what they were; she liked motorcycles, and she liked boys, and she liked dressing like those boys. Or perhaps she liked *the freedom* and the power that came with a more masculine aesthetic. It seemed to me Jo found a way to reject the domesticity that was foisted upon femininity, that was being foisted upon me especially hard at the time the show was airing.

According to the *Oxford English Dictionary*, in 1533, the words *tom* and *boy* together meant "rude boy." Then, in the 1570s, a tomboy was construed as a bold or immodest woman. By the early 1600s, the word took on its current meaning: "a girl who behaves like a spirited or boisterous boy, a wild romping girl." I find it kind of a neat trick that by now the word *tomboy* is intended for a girl even though "girl" is found nowhere in the word. I picture this wild romping girl bopping her way through the dictionary. In the Philippines, the word *tomboy* takes on a different meaning, more of what we refer to as "butch" here in the States: a masculine-presenting woman who has relations with feminine women. In the Philippines, women like myself, femmes who have relationships with other women, are still considered heterosexual.

By the 1800s, French writer and political scholar Alexis de Tocqueville had written *Democracy in America*, where he unpacked the concept of separate spheres. That is, women and men were to operate in different realms, public and private. Of these, women were relegated to the domestic/ private sphere. Tocqueville wrote: "In no country has such constant care been taken as in America to trace two clearly distinct lines of action for the two sexes and to make them keep pace one with the other, but in two pathways that are always different" (Tocqueville 2004, 222).

Domesticity was regarded as one of the greater virtues, as the home was considered a woman's proper sphere. As a first-generation Filipina American, I felt these stations tugging at me, my lola dressing me in patent leather shoes for church every Sunday. Rushing one early Christmas to unwrap a giant present under the tree only to discover it was a bag of rice; I, the eldest female grandchild, was responsible for everyone's sustenance. I was encouraged from a young age to find a mate, preferably a man ten years older than me, in uniform. Both lola and my mom insisted I curtsy when I met people. Ma warned against such vices as deodorant or shaving my legs, as these were the marks of a promiscuous girl, so I was to somehow lure a man but not by way of my body. Perhaps through cooking or being polite.

It was in my grandmother's house that I wrestled between these two spheres of public and private. My same-aged cousin Tyrone also spent summers with her, and I saw how different the expectations were for us. I always got called in from playing outside, careful not to ruin my Shirley Temple curls or dirty my Sunday best. My uncle, who was home from the Navy, would sneak in snakes and dogs, and I always made it my business to be their handler. Taking after his mother, Tyrone was scared of most animals. My favorite afternoons were when my uncle took us with him, shooting and traipsing through the woods with his crossbow. Still, when things seemed to get too too, too late, too dirty, too somehow masculine, my grandmother would call me in. I made my disappointment well known—stomping off to her room to watch TV while it seemed everyone else, every boy on the block, got to play well into the dark, the bioluminescence tickling the shores of Sand City.

Not having a father may have had something to do with the way I felt about more masculine girls. Tomboys seemed to know something I didn't. How to have a father, for instance, how to navigate the world, from tree branch to tree branch. How to like what you like, regardless of all the frilly things thrust upon you on holidays and birthday parties. I know this is an overgeneralization, but looking back now, I can see how masculinity was a deep mystery to me. My mother was man crazy. She'd go to watch the Chippendales dancers perform and give her friends cards that said things like "beef cake." I was scared of the prospect of a man having the same powers over me that I felt they had over her.

I developed young, and I found all my feminine bits a curse, the thicker flesh around my tummy and thighs, the pimples, the boobs, the pubic hair. I felt self-conscious changing in front of other girls. In this way, I was in league with the tomboys, who hunched their shoulders to hide their breasts. I craved a sports bra rather than the white floral thing with the tiny blue bow my mom came home with one afternoon.

But what I took the greatest interest in at the time was a tomboy's freedom, ease of movement, and rootedness in her body. I still find myself tracking them today, watching a tomboy stand at a counter, one foot tucked on tiptoe. Walking, hitting, throwing with her whole self. As someone who eventually landed in foster care, I became interested in movement. My biological mother was clumsy, tripped and fell a lot. She was a terrible driver. I feared inheriting all these traits, which I found to be stereotypically feminine. Meanwhile, my foster mother was tall. She walked upright, shoulders back, hips forward; it seemed she walked with her spine rather than her waist swirling around like a peppermill.

I've come to learn that what I was studying back then when I was trying to emulate the walks of confident women was comportment. When I say "comportment," I don't just mean our conduct but our physical positioning. Comportment as a facet of phenomenology. Phenomenology is, as I understand it, the philosophical study of our experience with one another and with objects. An even greater expansion of that fifth sense of proprioception, our body's sense of the spatial relationship between ourselves and other objects.

Feminist scholar Gayle Salamon writes of comportment in *The Life and Death of Latisha King: A Critical Phenomenology of Transphobia*; in the text, Salamon performs a close reading of the court trial of fourteen-year-old

Brandon McInerney, who was on trial in 2008 for the shooting of fifteen-year-old Latisha King. The trial referred to Latisha, assigned male at birth, as Larry. Salamon unpacks the consequences of representing the victim as Larry, a gay boy, instead of Latisha, a trans girl. In building on the concepts of comportment, Salamon considers how gender functions in the social world. Salamon notes how some in the trial intimated that King was "throwing" her gender at others, as if gender expression can be experienced as an aggression. In one scene, a teacher was asked to describe and imitate King's walk.

> Walking is an act that we perform with our habit-body. We build up this habit-body over time, slowly, starting with our first few toddling steps. The style that any walk will eventually develop is unavoidably inflected with gendered meanings, as well as racial and class markers, which strengthen and deepen and become more pronounced in adolescence, developing like other characteristics of gender. (Salamon 2018, 32)

Feminist scholar Iris Marion Young has also explored the concepts of comportment and phenomenology in her seminal essay "Throwing Like a Girl: A Phenomenology of Feminine Body Comportment, Motility, and Spatiality." In this essay, Young points toward German American phenomenologist and neurologist Erwin Straus's insistence that a girl throws a ball differently than a man because of "a feminine attitude" in relation to the world and to space. The difference for him is biologically based, but he denies that it is anatomical.

Whereas for Simone de Beauvoir, a woman is "defined not by her body but by her situation," and Beauvoir tends to treat a woman's body as a burden. In the essay, Young asserts that Beauvoir creates the impression that somehow biology determines a women's "unfree status" (Young 1980, 139).

In reading this and reflecting on my intense fascination with Jo, I wonder: Was, is, my body or my *situation* the burden? My body had developed faster than I was prepared for; my body had interpellated me, thrust me into a place of feminine womanhood, faster than my mind or spirit could follow. I was a child. A child who had breasts, a child who had been raped. I know that breasts do not cause a rape, that rapists rape. I know that children are not aggressively throwing their gender around town. I was not thrusting my breasts under predators' noses. But I can't help but think of them as a bullet in the gun. Or perhaps a bull's-eye on an eight-year-old.

However, my *situation* was also very much a burden. I'm very fond of the word *situation* here. In foster care, I was expected to tell the story of my *situation* over and over. To cops. To social workers. It wasn't the story of how I was gifted or what I wanted to be when I grew up. It was the story of how my mother punished, how she yelled at me and locked me in closets, of how she left me home alone. Later, I would repeat my story in the rooms of twelve-step recovery. The more I told it—the more it'd shift, slip away from me, become its own thing. No longer an imprint on my soul.

Just a void—the thin valley of ache I've filled with American Spirits menthols and Trader Joe's Two Buck Chuck—little did I know it's more of a *feeling*, an agitated, never-sated feeling my people have beaming at the core of us, the impulse to do damage and singe the edges. Throughout my childhood, I felt strongly that both my body and situation had failed me, particularly our money situation.

That void, that imprint, will be the source of the urge that sent me to the streets at night. I was desperately running from the only other stain I knew I had, the stain of poverty and an apartment with too many roaches, one I vowed none of the other kids would ever see, they were wealthy kids, children of celebrities, this was Los Angeles in the '90s and poor kids and rich kids were the ones without rules, our parents away working, and we'd all converge in Westwood Village, the only place the bus lines of the west side all catered to with ease. Until that one year my mom organized a surprise party for me and I was mortified. All these rich friends of mine sitting there in my dirty apartment—the one with the popcorn ceilings and the thick ugly carpeting where you can smell the neighbors frying chicken.

One episode of *The Facts of Life* brings up this issue of class and how money situations can lead to objectification. Blair's family friend from home comes to visit, and Blair shares that their families hoped they'd one day join their great bloodlines. Jo quips, "What are you, racehorses?" Blair replies, "At least we're not jackasses."

Blair brags about her guy friend's Porsche, and after some back-and-forth banter about the mechanics of the Porsche, Jo challenges him to a race. He eventually leaves, but only after finding out where Jo will be after dinner. Blair is convinced he has come to town to ask her to a cotillion, but it turns out he finds Jo at the arcade and won't leave her alone until she agrees to go to the dance with him. Jo has a Cinderella-esque transition back at Eastland, where she changes into a pretty dress; Mrs. Garrett, Natalie, and Tootie gush at her while Blair sulks in the corner.

Jo returns disheveled. Instead of taking her to the dance, the guy took her to the golf course and tried to rape her. Jo goes directly to Mrs. Garrett's room to tell her what happened, and she confesses that she harbored a fantasy of going to the dance and everyone who saw her there wondering, "Who's that classy girl?"

The guy shows up at Eastland later with Jo's shoe and tells Blair, in his defense, "There are the kinds of girls you marry and the kinds of girls you don't." Jo was the kind you didn't. Jo translates for Blair, "When you're from the wrong side of the tracks, guys think you're easy."

In rewatching this episode to write this, I appreciated that they tackled the subject of sexual assault. Date rape had just entered American parlance around the 1980s, after social scientists administered a series of surveys about sexual victimization on college campuses. Marital rape hadn't yet become a crime in all fifty states—and wouldn't until July 5, 1993. I appreciated that this wasn't the presentation we were often given, of a woman we had come to know as risqué being objectified. Still, it brought another idea into my consciousness: Nothing keeps us safe. However, according to that guy, Blair's class kept *her* safe. She was the type of woman one would marry and not sexually assault.

It was our money *situation* that may have placed my vulnerable female body in unsupervised *situation*s. Young writes that masculine movement is characterized by ease and naturalness, and yet that is also man's relation to his world. Feminine movement is hampered and constrained, and therefore, her relationship with the world can be, too.

Notice the use of the word "feminine": This is not all women; this does not account for how tomboys, butches, or trans people move through the world. Although I lacked the words, it felt to me then that Jo was able to enjoy that same ease of movement of other masculine people. That Jo could move and throw with her *whole* body.

Women have learned that to move freely, she not only risks but *invites* objectification. In her essay, Young writes, "To open her body in free, active, open extension and bold outward-directedness is for a woman to invite objectification" (Young 1980, 154). Therefore, we build enclosures around ourselves. The domestic sphere, an enclosure that men built around women, that women have been acculturated into reinscribing for their daughters and granddaughters. These enclosures seem also to have been built into our own bodies, into feminine movement.

Much of the premise of the show was that after Jo arrived, she convinced the girls to steal the school van and use fake IDs to go to the Chugalug Bar to get some beer. They ended up wrecking the van and getting caught by local police, and so as punishment they were forced to work in the Eastland cafeteria to pay off the debt they owed, and therefore they had to live in a room that adjoined with house mother Mrs. Garrett's quarters.

Their movements constrained, every action under Mrs. Garrett's watchful eye. The opening montage shows all four girls trying to get ready in the bathroom together, with Blair outstretched, blow-drying her all-over-the-place hair. Now, decades later, I'm left with no way to ditch the feelings that linger from all the traps I've set. My feelings stuffed, like the small space the girls were forced to share at Eastland.

As a teenager, when I looked for myself in each of my foster families, I'd see my image moving from my birth mother to foster mother to foster mother, a restless mocking spirit. I was the self-made woman, a woman who folded laundry by the TV, ran an ad agency, and walked back straight, shoulders back, hips forward. I was the woman who slept with strange, unsafe men. I was the woman who taught herself English in high school and made all my clothes. I was the woman who went back to school in her forties and raised three daughters. I was the girl who rode in cars down Topanga Canyon, while her brother drove, nodding out at the wheel. I was the child, afraid, shoved in the back corner of a closet. This may be when I first developed the gift and desire of Elsewhere. Elsewhere is not just another place, but another time.

There is the time of Before, the time of After, and the time of Elsewhere. The time Before rape, which was very little time, the time before foster care, the time before I longed for a biological echo. And yet still, every instance I saw my mother, it only served to puncture the balloon of the original wound, free-floating in my soul.

For a brief period in the '80s, Jo Polniaczek was the salve to that wound. Jo seemed to be untethered to other people, her own person. That this character existed. I did not want to be her. I wanted to feel what it was like inside her skin. I wanted to move like her. I wanted a world to exist where she was possible, and that world did; it was called Eastland, and it was one that I could escape into summers on my lola's bed, with its frilly comforter, stamped with roses, an ornate wooden headboard, matching dresser, all of that there around me, poised to hail me into place. While I sat folded into myself, bounced back and forth, on my knees, rocking, moving, resisting, "You take the good, you take the bad, you take them both, and there you have . . . The Facts of Life."

Melissa Chadburn's debut novel, *A Tiny Upward Shove*, was published with Farrar, Straus, & Giroux in April 2022 and was longlisted for the PEN/Hemingway Debut Novel Award. She's done extensive reporting on the child welfare system and appears in the Netflix docuseries *The Trials of Gabriel Fernandez*. She was just awarded her PhD from USC's Creative Writing Program. Melissa is a worker-lover, and through her own work and literary citizenship strives to upend economic violence. Her mother taught her how to sharpen a pencil with a knife and she's basically been doing that ever since. She can be reached at fictiongrrrl@gmail.com.

Works Cited

Salamon, Gayle. 2018. *The Life and Death of Latisha King: A Critical Phenomenology of Transphobia*. New York: New York University Press.

Tocqueville, Alexis de. 2004. *Democracy in America*. Translated by Arthur Goldhammer. New York: Library of America.

Young, Iris Marion. 1980. "Throwing Like a Girl: A Phenomenology of Feminine Body Comportment, Motility, and Spatiality." *Human Studies* 3 (2): 137–56.

It's My Body and I'll Hack at It If I Want To

Lohitha Kethu

Collecting experiences across past generations or past lives, I think we become archivists of the body by having bodies. Blood, like water, carries memory. Cells keep time and record macro phenomena, data. Cells talk to us, too; it is an unflinchingly loving and violent dictation that may help free us if we listen. Particularly in the disabled and gender-variant body-mind, we hold this love and violence in all their undulations. Every cell that makes up every function and dysfunction is a horror of material pain and an ecstasy of one's truth. Too often, I cannot tell where the ecstasy ends and horror begins.

When inhabiting a body that is of little to no use to normative social functions of marriage, reproduction, and tireless productivity, there can be joy in celebrating its "invalidity." As I have gotten sicker, housebound due to illnesses and a climate of multi-pandemic denialism, as I have grown more restless to alter my body to mirror "boy" to me, accepting the body as a surreal, multidimensional patchwork of horrors renders me whole and underscores my aliveness. Body horror is a well-loved genre of fiction and a visual aesthetic that uses biological, technological, or psychological mutilation and the exaggerated grotesque, often to explore ideas of transformation, loss of control, and othered identity (Leatham 2024). As an artistic practice and framework for personal exploration of gender, sexuality, pain, isolation, and disability, body horror has always been precious to me.

According to Jean Baudrillard's *The Ecstasy of Communication*, consumer society is a society of alienation, where alienation and othering beget spectacle (2012). By making the invisible starkly visible, we step out of alienation and hidden spectacle "into the ecstasy of the obscene," where it then becomes communication. The body is the most basic unit of theater, where

WSQ: Women's Studies Quarterly 53: 3 & 4 (Fall/Winter 2025) © 2025 by Lohitha Kethu. All rights reserved.

our collective shadows, fears, and anxieties are personified as monsters and aliens, realized as autoimmunity or epigenetics, to produce a transformative picture of what it means to be human or beyond human. Body horror narratives are often produced from pain, othering, or an inability to exist in normative society, but pain does not have to be the greatest motivator of body horror. After all, we can know deep love by confronting our most shameful, most monstrous shadows. Perhaps there is freedom from oppressive systems in celebrating one's desires, joy, and love through an imagined vocabulary of bodily hyperbole. In a spiritual context, body horror may be a way to integrate or transmute fear, isolation, separation of self and other, and the shadow into new possibilities for love, acceptance, and future-building.

If those of us with divergent bodyminds already exist in alternate structures, timelines, and margins, shouldn't our imagination and definition of horror function the same?

When I am in immense pain and unable to move from bed, I uncover my horror-body. A large gash stretches open from sternum to navel. It is a portal into the bottomless freefall of desire that I trace with my index finger. I no longer struggle to breathe. Slashes open in areas of my body that constantly radiate pain. Half-moon gashes at either hip joint. Sharp, arrow-shaped cuts down thighs and another half-moon across the lower belly, across areolas. A giant gash down the spine exposes vertebrae, stacked and vibrating like a zipper caught on wool. These gashes are illuminated in soft and bright light, vermillion from dimensions above. Auric messages from the past and future so warm that I can forgive the pain. Each swollen joint expands into bubbles that buoy me as I float in the ocean in my bed, dressed in blue for this reason. The open, pleading basket made by two clasped pelvic bones dissolves in the ocean, like I have always wanted. Skin and nerve endings burn and spark and fizz—this is how they talk to me. With every cut I make, every dissected layer and loosened fiber, I become more and more the gestalt. I have made pain my companion and I hack and slash out of duty to witness, to take obscene inventory of all that was *before* me, *is* me, and *will* be. At last, I wash the cuts with a hot cyan light. Another last flash and release.

It's my body, and I'll hack at it if I want to.

In addition to reflecting social and cultural anxieties, I believe body horror has been and continues to emerge as a way of grounding in a collective consciousness and spirit. In Theravada Buddhism, the Maranasati meditation technique calls on the practitioner to visualize the nine stages of body decomposition. One contemplates the body as blue, bloated, and pecked by maggots and dogs, then tendons and bones with flesh, then with-out flesh, until bone has become dust (Rosenberg 1993). The function of confronting the grotesque is to accept death and the interconnected nature of one's decomposition, how it is unremarkably the same as that of every other body. Meditating on this decay may allow the practitioner to detach from self and enter a nondualist space where humans are plants are bodies, are paper and plastic and computers too; where the body's constant decay is superimposed with its constant processes and proliferation.

Similarly, it is through the visualization and integration of an alien symbology of pain, a metaphysical autopsy, that I feel I can connect with my humanity, divinity, and a collective consciousness. If I can witness and be present for my pain, I may be able to for another's. My pain is not just my pain: it is of generations before me and from social and cultural phenomena beyond me and absorbed from my peers and the food I eat and the health of the planet. Perhaps we are due for an expansion of our collective imagi-nation's semiotics or visual vocabulary of horror. Moreover, maybe we only perceive an experience or symbol as horror because society defines normal and because similar horrors really exist, often invisiblized and normalized against marginalized peoples.

I do not think we can engage with body horror outside of the context of real-time violence after collectively witnessing ongoing horror, blood-shed, sexual violence, mutilation, and murder during genocides in occupied Palestine, the Congo, Sudan, in occupied Kashmir, caste-based violence, state-sponsored eugenics, and systemic violence within the United States. With the internet at our fingertips, we have seen actual, unimaginable but painfully real horrors of the body. We have seen people and children mutilated into oblivion. What does it mean to have a body horror creative practice in the context of real violence and horror becoming the true, visi-ble "obscene" due to the ubiquity of social media?

How do I, a disabled person living in the U.S. with health insurance and sick days, responsibly embody an artistic practice of body horror when comparable mutilations are being enacted and have been enacted against peoples of the global majority? I often see disabled people online post info-graphics such as "fibromyalgia is like being hit by a bus" or "long COVID is like being buried alive." I empathize with the hyperbole in a society that does not believe or treat such kinds of pain, but I also think fibromyalgia is like fibromyalgia, a mirror funhouse of shapeshifting pains. I do not know what it is like to be buried alive or to be hit by a bus. I do know that real people are subjected to such brutalities and I also know that our individual pains are real and connected, unforgettably outlined by James Baldwin in *The Price of the Ticket* (1985). In holding real horror with imagined horror or horror simile, a need for specificity, radical imagination, and intention feels even more urgent.

Mikhail Bakhtin's discussion of the carnival and the grotesque body suggests the potential for a joyous hyperbole of the body that celebrates life and death, that frees us from the constraints and structures of normative culture and late-stage capitalism (Leite 2023). A liberatory direction for body horror may use the absurd theater of the body to offer a spiritual reimagining that connects our collective pain and thus, our freedom. Perhaps an integral part of this reimagining may be to move away from hyperrealistic depictions of gore, exaggerated features, psychiatric illness-related personification, physical disabilities, and bodily mutilation to symbols, fantasy, and aesthetics that exist outside of this knowable reality. Pain cannot always be compared but maybe it can be translated. While there are many video games and visual media that achieve this effect, beloved monster, alien, technological beings, and other fantastical archetypes are translations of pain and could even be celebrations of transformation and life. In a nondualist sense, pain and joy are indistinguishable parts of the whole. Pain becomes joy becomes pain in a cycle that spins faster and faster due to the speed and availability of information; body horror art that can hold both at once and honor the archives embedded within the body may be a remedy for the times.

Lohitha Kethu (they/them) is a queer, caste-privileged Telugu and multiply disabled medical and visual artist and writer. They've illustrated patient education and health literacy books, created award-winning art for publication and exhibition, and had work featured in *Tilt*, *Womanly Mag*, and more. Their creative practice aims to explore the body beyond the visceral, as a multidimensional collection of fluid desires, offerings, and connections, through body horror mythologies and narratives. Lohitha's work can be found at lohithakethu.com. They can be reached at lohitha.kethu@gmail.com.

Works Cited

Baldwin, James. 1985. *The Price of the Ticket: Collected Nonfiction, 1948–1985.* New York: St. Martin's/Marek.

Baudrillard, Jean. 2012. *The Ecstasy of Communication.* Los Angeles: Semiotext(e).

Leatham, Tom. 2024. "What Is 'Body Horror'?" *Far Out Magazine*, May 25. https://faroutmagazine.co.uk/what-is-body-horror.

Leite, Francisco Benedito. 2023. "Grotesque Realism and Grotesque Body in Bakhtin." *Bakhtiniana: Revista de estudos do discurso* 18 (4). https://doi.org /10.1590/2176-4573e62064.

Rosenberg, Larry. 1993. "Shining the Light of Death on Life: Maranasati Meditation (Part I)." *Buddhist Inquiry*, November 20. https://www .buddhistinquiry.org/article/shining-the-light-of-death-on-life-maranasati -meditation-part-i.

SECTION VI. **POETRY**

Transformation

Damien Kritzer

A scream tears out of his mouth,
echoing and *wet.*

As if you can hear the foaming spit
at the corners of his lips,
leaking down his chin.

Slime that coats his neck,
and brings a sickening sheen.

It's hard to tell where the spit stops and the tears begin.
Birth is always painful as they say
but this is different.

His shoulder blades cracking,
the plates of ivory shooting out of the skin of his back—
    a mockery of angel's wings.
The skin stretched to its breaking point, curling in on itself.
Peeling duo tones of flesh and red.
One could call them petals . . .

He calls them transformation.

They call him wrong.
Wrong like the lines in his chest
or the growth on his crotch—
Unnatural.

But hasn't he always been?
Nothing has ever felt right,
never natural.
Not to him.

He stares up at the sneers and the scowls with a smile,
too many teeth shining back at them.
Curling lips that make valleys on the smooth canvas of his cheeks . . .
Pure now tainted.

He was bound to be tainted one way or another.
At least this taint was of his own making.

Why is it so wrong to play god when he gave us the tools to do so?

To be human is to create.
Just as we were made in the creator's image,
let us create a new form of being.
Sculpt our forms into something new.

Let us all be monsters.

Damien Kritzer is a master's student in women's, gender, and sexuality studies at the University at Albany. He specializes in research on topics related to sexuality and trans identity. His current research project looks into the connections between the transgender experience and horror. He can be reached at DamienKritzer@gmail.com.

Salon

Vanessa Chica Ferreira

8

year-old me sits on the salon chair listening while the women speak loudly about their unwanted body parts, their flabby arms, the rolls on their backs, bumps on their thighs, their slightly hanging bellies.

9

year-old me already feels her body is too big for the chair. Confining chairs—because beauty has never been for the weak. There is a certain strength to those who will sit uncomfortably for such a stretch of time. There is a certain strength to those who are willing to be subjected to sitting squished in a narrow chair, seeing all their parts conform into something more and one would think that the transformation to be seen is the hairdo, but you'd be wrong, at least half wrong, right? Surely there is a message here.

10

year-old me sits on the salon chair listening to the women talk about the diets they are on, how much weight they have lost, and how much better they feel. They tug at their pants to show how loose they have become and boast how good men say their asses look.

I am 11

Eleven-year-old me sits on the salon chair watching the latest infomercials. The meal replacement powders, the water pills, the tightest Colombian fajas, I watch as the women furiously write down the information to purchase so that they can keep or steal husbands.

12

year-old me sits on the salon chair, looks in the mirror and does not like what I see.

WSQ: Women's Studies Quarterly 53: 3 & 4 (Fall/Winter 2025) © 2025 by Vanessa Chica Ferreira.

Vanessa Chica Ferreira (she/her) is a New York City–based educator, poet, playwright, and fat activist. She creates works that challenge societal norms and invite deep vulnerability. Her cowritten play *Live Big Girl*, focused on body positivity and fat activism, was performed to sold-out audiences at the National Black Theatre, The Tank, and BAAD. In 2024, her second poetic play, *Live Big Girl: A Chair That Fits*, premiered at Lehman College. Her work has been featured in publications like *Snapdragon* and *The Acentos Review*. Learn more at www.VanessaChica.com. She can be reached at vchicaferreira@gmail.com.

A Poem in Which Gloria Guides Me Inwards, and I Thank Her with Ink

Avery C. Castillo

—for jo

Her body, a crossroads, a fragile bridge,
cannot support the tons of cargo passing through it.
—Gloria Anzaldúa

I begin   at the mouth
tunnel wide
open and dry

Enter insects, incense, intelligence
through the gaps of jagged teeth
like forgotten trap doors

Footprints step over ulcer kinks
bringing hidden gum-lined scars to
the surface: an archival act of remembering

Flushed, rushed out,
trapped, choked &
struck down

I begin   at the mouth
lips unclosing and projecting
whole as ocean waves hum in caves

Cuing curses or serenity for silent
speech that echoes off fleshy cave cheeks,
Do not go quiet, now.

WSQ: Women's Studies Quarterly 53: 3 & 4 (Fall/Winter 2025) © 2025 by Avery C. Castillo. All rights reserved.

Am I at the edge
of this throatcave
ready to jump?

Cleansed by swallowed thick blood
drowning me heavy to the tongue,
I am no longer the fragile bridge.

This mouth pulsed before
words ever graced the tongue
before the body was birthed to

Bleed and bleed and bleed
before   —   after

The jaw broke at the hand of man
hammered and drilled back
together again, metals replacing form

Now, only the spleen remembers
the hurt so deep, she still
mourns in hiccups

          Begin at the mouth: trace lip,
run fingertip over hanging incisors
cemented in the shadow of voice & tongue—

Bloomed joy with teeth and all and still
not quite over the injury, she will reopen
the wound to bleed

Open wider: show teeth
and how they will rip open
the wound in a fist-full bite
                         releasing
to the surface la caminante
nude with memory
as she remembers

the land   as it was

the body   as it is

as she   becomes   an open wound

                                        mouth

                                            a resurrection

                                                of dreams

Avery C. Castillo (she/her) is a Mexican American poet, artist, and editor from South Texas. She received her BA from Texas Tech University and is pursuing an MFA in creative writing at the University of Texas, Rio Grande Valley. Her work is published in various anthologies and literary journals. She has also contributed poetry for the 2024 Texas State Poet Laureate's Praisesong for the People. She is currently working to publish her debut poetry collection on chronic illness, invisible pain, and womanhood. For more, visit writingsbyavery.com. She can be reached at hello@writingsbyavery.com.

The Secret of Marination

Megha Sood

The sizzling juicy blobs of skewered meat marinated long enough
for the grief to steep in slowly but surely long enough for the flavors to set in.

Just enough for the colors of resentment to take hold.
My eyes burn with the harsh realities as I deep fry

my thickly-coated resentment but that is how everyone likes it.
Just enough crunch to give you that extra bite.

But I never let them know the secret ingredient that I hide inside
the thin parchment of my skin. A secret that I dearly hold.

A secret that could bring down this house of cards
with one quaint blow. A secret sauce that makes everything edible,

so that they can even gulp down a swear
said out loud in a room meant for praying.

Nobody wants a show and everyone wants to keep the family
tightly tinned for generations. Deeply shut for any one of us to breathe

easily behind this secret veil. The history of marination stays put
when everyone in the family takes a bite juicy

enough to keep their slobbering soul satiated.

WSQ: Women's Studies Quarterly 53: 3 & 4 (Fall/Winter 2025) © 2025 by Megha Sood. All rights reserved.

Megha Sood is an award-winning Asian American author, poet, editor, and literary activist from New Jersey. A literary partner with Life in Quarantine at Stanford University, her four poetry collections include the award-winning *My Body Lives Like a Threat* (FlowerSong Press, 2022). She has received support from VONA, Pen Women, Dodge Foundation, Kundiman, and Martha's Vineyard Writing Institute. Her more than nine hundred works have been featured in Poetry Society of New York, *Ms.* magazine, New York Public Library, Pen Magazine, PBS, and WNYC Studio. Her work "The Medusa Project" has been selected to be sent to the moon in 2025 in collaboration with NASA and SpaceX. See https://linktr.ee/meghasood.She can be reached at megharani1409@gmail.com.

Anagram No. 4: Middle-Aged Woman

Jia-Rui Cook

Am I a madam now

a dawn dimmed   a goad
a lag   a midge   a dammed

maw   a wan mom   a domed
lid on glee?   I am wide.

I do waddle.   I low.
And   I am eagle-gilded wind

and I am a mile-long ledge   and I am
done-a-damned-deed-and-am-glad-I-did.

I wade in now.   I angle.
I dig.   I limn in gold.

Jia-Rui Cook is a writer, editor, and producer in Los Angeles. Previously a staff writer at the *L.A. Times* and the news events and projects manager at NASA's Jet Propulsion Laboratory, she is a senior communications officer at the California Wellness Foundation. Jia-Rui's poetry has appeared in *Air/Light*, *Alta Journal*, *Hunger Mountain Review*, *Only Poems*, *Puerto del Sol*, and *Zócalo Public Square*. She is working on her first book of poems. She can be reached at @funjiable.

***WSQ: Women's Studies Quarterly* 53: 3 & 4 (Fall/Winter 2025)** © 2025 by Jia-Rui Cook. All rights reserved.

SECTION VII. ALERTS AND PROVOCATIONS

On Palestinian Embodied Futurities

Dana M. Olwan

On February 8, 2025, Israeli army forces opened fire on Sondos Jamal Muhammad Shalabi, a twenty-three-year-old Palestinian woman who was eight months pregnant when she was shot and killed in Nur Al Shams refugee camp in the West Bank. The targeting of a Palestinian would-be mother and her fetus occurred within a context of escalating Israeli attacks against Palestinians in the West Bank that have so far left more than nine hundred people dead. To understand the significance of the death of Shalabi and her unborn, would-be child, we must place it alongside the murdered bodies of over 61,709 Palestinian men, women, and children whose lives were extinguished in Israel's genocidal attack on Gaza between October 2023 and the time of the writing of this piece. As Palestinians have insisted, the macabre and brutal violence to which Palestinians in Gaza have been subjected is not an aberration or interruption in settler-colonial violence but is part and parcel of a larger, planned, and systematized campaign of Indigenous elimination that begins with the Palestinian Nakba, or the Catastrophe of 1948 (Barakat 2018). For feminists who have witnessed over fifteen months of brutal, daily, and televised attacks on Palestinians that have decimated Palestinian bodies, homes, environments, and domiciles, shattering collective lives and livelihoods, what might theorizations of the body—as both a material site of violence and a tool of resistance—reveal about the possibilities and limits of feminist thinking about the body today? What might a theory of the body, one that does not center Palestinians as abject or inevitable targets of colonial violence, offer us by way of imagining the materialities of Indigenous bodies and their livable futurities?

Feminist scholars have long argued that bodies are crucial nodes in the making and unmaking of hierarchies of life and death. As Gala Rexer notes

WSQ: Women's Studies Quarterly 53: 3 & 4 (Fall/Winter 2025) © 2025 by Dana M. Olwan. All rights reserved.

in their work on bodily mattering in Palestine, "bodies are integral to the workings of biopolitics and necropolitics, and different bodily materialities are made disposable or productive at the various intersections of race, class, gender, and sexuality" (2023, 4–5). The racial logics of capitalism are thus predicated upon an asymmetric arithmetic of bodies, a crude calculus used to determine and produce the conditions of (un)livability (Puar 2017). In other words, bodies come to matter in and through the routines and practices of making them matter or not matter (Butler 2011). Like Black and Native feminist scholars have taught us, the act of making things matter is of course neither innocent nor coincidental, as mattering is a material act, imbricated in the very practices of life: in the crafting of language, in the writing of histories, the designing of ideas, and the implementation of policies (Hartman 1997; Goeman 2016). Within this context, the calibration of bodies, the making of hierarchies of the living and the dead, resuscitates anew ideas about who can be worthy of life and who is a target of dying and death (Spade 2016). While feminist theory continues to write against such hierarchized ways of marking bodies, what does feminist silence about the mounting number of Palestinian dead and the deliberate targeting of Palestinian bodies suggest about systems of value that determine the worth of bodies within the vicissitudes of feminist theory and feminist praxis? How might we remember the mounting dead beyond reciting the inordinate number of bodies injured, maimed, and broken (Puar 2017)? And how might feminist theory reckon with attacks on the Palestinian body that target Palestinian people's right to living futurities?

In a statement written shortly after the beginning of the Israeli genocide against Gaza, the Palestinian Feminist Collective (PFC) called upon feminists committed to reproductive justice to center Palestinian liberation, and to advocate for the right of Palestinians to live free from attacks on their bodies, livelihoods, and environments, in their work. The statement defines reproductive genocide as the "policies, discourses, and practices that delimit, restrict, target, or diminish the life-giving capacities, choices, access, short-term health, long-term health, and life chances of communities made vulnerable by systemic military violence and occupation, besiegement, settler colonialism, and/or imperial warfare" (2023). By naming the attacks on the bodies of Palestinian men, women, and children as part and parcel of the "annihilation of environments and life-sustaining agriculture," the statement carefully maps an understanding of reproductive justice that refuses to unmoor the Palestinian body from its homeland. The PFC's vision for reproductive justice thus employs a notion of the body that situates it within and in relation to the environmental contexts and conditions which make livability possible. Reproductive genocide, on the other hand, is the mass enforcement of conditions of unlivability on both the living and the dead, on human and nonhuman elements whose existence and interactions make bodies come to matter.

Key to the PFC's statement and its work in the diaspora is this insistence on a notion of the Palestinian body that is always already whole, a body that it insists has the right to live, despite settler-colonial efforts to diminish these capacities and to extinguish their possibilities. Through its mandate and mission, the PFC centers a Palestinian body that refuses to understand itself in the singular, a body that manifests its power to stitch a collective Palestinian future. In its imaginary and its practice, the PFC employs a notion of the Palestinian body that brings together narratives of struggle, survival, and resistance across generational, geographic, and social divides that center Palestinian livability, that insist on the mattering of the Palestinian body. In materializing such a body, the PFC makes possible what Sarah Ihmoud names the "praxis of Palestinian decolonial feminism," a praxis that invites feminists "to think with the Palestinian feminist imaginary [and] thus to imagine a new world beyond settler-colonialism, exclusionary nationalism, nation-states, and the isolation of social movements" (2022, 295). Put differently, the PFC's vision is crucially inspired by the politics of a present, grounded in an understanding of the past as living and the future as not dead.

What bodies and bodily practices might such visions open? And how might we politically, strategically, and ethically reckon with the bodies they center and make matter in the new worlds imagined by Palestinian feminists and their beyond? In a call issued by transnational and women of color feminists to end the genocidal war on Gaza, feminists remind us of the importance of the practice of bearing witness and breaking silence. In this call, the group of feminist scholars and activists write that "A feminist practice of bearing witness means understanding that violence and power work as deeply in the mind and the soul as they do on the body and the land. And to shield the mind and soul—to protect it from this violence— requires a militant and tenacious dedication to affirming truth" (Qutami et al. 2023, 532). Within this context, silence in the face of what is well known becomes an act of complicity, an outright lie against mounting and undeniable truth. The call to break this silence thus enumerates a feminist praxis that insists on the capacity of truth to extinguish fear and to refuse the disposability of Palestinian life—and Palestinian bodies—as just. In this feminist version of the body, Palestinians are configured beyond their metaphorization or inevitable demise. A serious engagement with this call would insist on an alternative conception of the Palestinian body—not as a site of suffering that is assured but as a portal to an alternative future freed from the threat of war and the ravages of colonialism: a body whose truth will not be inscribed by violence that is normed or normalized.

Since reading about Shalabi's story, I have been thinking about her body not at the site or moment of its death but as a being with dreams and aspirations for a different—but still possible—type of living future. I do not know, nor can I presume, what Shalabi dreamed of or what she desired for herself, her unborn child, or her family. I cannot speak her unwritten story, nor can I surmise what her life may have looked like in a decolonial present or future. But I can imagine that she would not have wanted her story to begin and end at her death by Israeli soldiers, who left her body and the body of her unborn child to die by preventing them from reaching medical assistance, like the bodies of many Palestinians before them. I can also imagine that she would not have wanted to see her husband, twenty-four-year-old Yazan Shula, critically shot and left unconscious. I can hope that she may have dreamed of a future in which she, her unborn child, and her husband would be alive today.

As her mother, Muna, would tell journalists, her daughter "was calm and kind and loved her husband very much" (qtd. in Shalash 2025). Shalabi was excited about the quickly approaching birth of her first child and, in preparation, her mother—the unborn child's would-be grandmother—had set up a crib, a resting place for the hope that Palestinian children embody. In an alternate story, in which Palestinian death is neither norm nor normalized, and where Palestinian bodies matter beyond their demise, I imagine that Shalabi reaches the lifesaving medical care she needs or, more hopefully yet, she isn't shot and is not in need of medical assistance. In this version of the story, Shalabi's husband, a Palestinian would-be father, is alive, excitedly awaiting the birth of his child. Muna, Shalabi's mother, would be welcoming a grandchild born to loving parents, and her daughter would be caring for her child in a free Palestine. The infant's crib would not be empty and the over twelve thousand Palestinian children killed in Gaza would also not be dead. In this story, Shalabi, her husband, and their future unborn child are all safe and whole—freed from the threat of violence and bodily unmattering. In this version of the story, they embody the living hope for futures otherwise that Palestinians collectively inscribe against the flames of colonial violence, imperial ruin, and capitalist collapse.

Dana M. Olwan is a Palestinian scholar who writes on gendered and sexual violence and transnational feminist solidarity. She is associate professor of women's and gender studies and affiliate faculty in the Native American and Indigenous Studies Program at Syracuse University. She can be reached at dmolwan@syr.edu.

Works Cited

Barakat, Rana. 2018. "Writing/Righting Palestine Studies: Settler Colonialism, Indigenous Sovereignty and Tesisting the Ghost(s) of History." *Settler Colonial Studies* 8 (3): 349–63.

Butler, Judith. 2011. *Bodies That Matter: On the Discursive Limits of Sex*. New York: Routledge.

Goeman, Mishuana. 2016. "Indigenous Interventions and Feminist Methods." In *Sources and Methods in Indigenous Studies*, edited by Chris Anderson and Jean M. O'Brien, 185–94. New York: Routledge.

Hartman, Saidiya. 1997. *Scenes of Subjection: Terror, Slavery, and Self-Making in Nineteenth-Century America*. New York: Oxford University Press.

Ihmoud, Sarah. 2022. "Palestinian Feminism: Analytics, Praxes and Decolonial Futures." *Feminist Anthropology* 3 (2): 284–98.

Palestinian Feminist Collective (PFC). 2023. "The Palestinian Feminist Collective Condemns Reproductive Genocide in Gaza." https://palestinianfeministcollective.org/the-pfc-condemns-reproductive-genocide-in-gaza/.

Puar, Jasbir K. 2017. *The Right to Maim: Debility, Capacity, Disability*. Durham: Duke University Press.

Qutami, Loubna, Inderpal Grewal, Caren Kaplan, et al. 2023. "A Feminist Practice of Bearing Witness to Genocide." *Feminist Studies* 49 (2): 531–33.

Rexer, Gala. 2023. "The Materiality of Power and Bodily Matter(ing): Embodied Resistance in Palestine." *Body and Society* 29 (4): 3–28.

Shalash, Fayha. 2025. "Family Describes Israel's 'Cold-Blooded Murder' of Pregnant Daughter in West Bank's Nur Shams." *New Arab,* February 14. https://www.newarab.com/news/family-describes-israels-murder-pregnant-daughter-wb.

Spade, Dean. 2016. "Their Laws Will Never Make Us Safer." In *Everyday Women's and Gender Studies*, edited by Ann Braithwaite and Catherine Orr, 156–61. New York: Routledge.